Many Happy
of Enjoyment

Love
Uma

TRY ANYTHING ONCE

BY THE SAME AUTHOR
Channel Packet

RAYMOND MORTIMER

Try Anything Once

HAMISH HAMILTON

LONDON

First published in Great Britain 1976
by Hamish Hamilton Ltd
90 Great Russell Street, London WC1B 3PT

Copyright © 1976 by Raymond Mortimer

SBN 241 89463 8

Printed in Great Britain by
Elliott Bros. & Yeoman Ltd., Liverpool L24 9JL

To my cherished old friends
George Rylands and Monroe Wheeler, who in a garden beside the Loire
persuaded me to prepare this hotch-potch

CONTENTS

AUTOBIOGRAPHICAL PREFACE

The author, born in 1895, has retained many characteristics of the Victorian professional class to which his family belonged. Though much indulged as an only child, he has never entirely recovered from early training in such old bourgeois habits as self-control, industry and politeness. What's more, he remains a shameless élitist, convinced that the well-being of the nation depends upon the brains of a small minority, and that liberty is more important than equality, with which it is incompatible.

None of his relations could possibly have been called an intellectual or an aesthete. Yet in his home he relished pleasant old pictures, furniture and, above all, quite a lot of books, mostly Victorian and Edwardian novels, often in the convenient Tauchnitz editions now alas extinct. He learnt to read, as was common at the time, when only three or just four. Children's books then being happily few, Conan Doyle, Thackeray, Scott and, less successfully, Dickens were offered to him at what would now be thought too early an age, and not long afterwards Macaulay's essays and Tennyson together with Hall Caine, W. J. Locke and a quantity of other rubbish.

Having never heard a voice at home raised in anger, he acquired a confidence in life that has kept him cheerful; nor has he suffered from the manic-depressive tendencies so common in writers. At nine, however, he was sent away to an over-large, harsh preparatory school at Eastbourne, which employed two cricket professionals, and five years later to one of the most philistine and brutal public schools of the period, where unhappiness dulled his ability to learn. He made one or two close friends in each of those penitentiaries; and the misfortunes they brought him were largely his own fault. A prig as well as a muff and a swot,

A*

he had not the wit to conceal unpopular opinions; and he accepted his lot fatalistically, not confiding it till afterwards to his kind-hearted family. Bliss in the holidays deepened his misery in term-time, which left him distrustful of authority and accepted ideas.

A narrowly classical education has helped him to write more correctly in English; but after translating hundreds of passages into Latin and Greek prose and verse he now can read neither language without a dictionary, to his deep regret and shame. His schools taught him hardly anything about English literature, apart from a few Shakespeare plays; nor was there a single lesson in chemistry, biology or any science except elementary mathematics. Both his headmasters were moustachioed, Low Church clergymen, who perhaps believed that the theory of evolution, like sex, should never lift its ugly head. Only much later did he acquire a keen, if ill-informed, interest in hominids and pre-history. The chief lessons retained from schooling were that one must not expect life to be just, and (despite sermons exalting the team spirit) that if one didn't look after oneself, nobody else would.

Until he went to school, he was in the care not of a traditional English 'nanny', but of two better-educated girls successively, who were Swiss. They taught him French, though piano lessons proved hopeless. He was also taken to France repeatedly from the age of six, spending his summer holidays there twice; and before going up to Balliol as a commoner, he spent six months with a family in Paris, not only attending lectures at the Sorbonne but revelling in museums, operas and plays. At Oxford, though delight in general reading and making friends led to a neglect of studies, his tutor in history, 'Sligger' Urquhart, gave him friendship as well as wise instruction. Then in 1915 he went to work at a hospital for wounded French soldiers in the south of France. Medical boards repeatedly rejected him for active service, and after the last of these in 1918 he became a temporary member of the Foreign Office. After the armistice he did not go back to Oxford and take his finals, but was given a war B.A. None of his employers was ever to ask if he had a degree.

Next he continued to educate himself agreeably by frequent travel on the Continent, and soon began writing for the *London Mercury*, the *Nation*, *Vogue*, and the *New Statesman*, of which he was to become literary editor—a job he hugely enjoyed for some fifteen years. During the last war he worked for a year as head of the French section in the Ministry of Information, chiefly concerned with the BBC broadcasts to France. Finally the *Sunday Times* took him on as a regular reviewer. He has never kept a diary, and his memory, never good, has become a broken sieve. This outline of his life will therefore never be expanded into an autobiography, portraying the many remarkable figures, French and English, whom he has met. He remembers the old Greek maxim: 'Never call a man happy until he dies; at best he is merely fortunate.' Yes, but knowing that self-pity dilapidates us and bores our friends, he seldom recalls anything that has gone wrong in his life, and is thankful for his exceptional good luck.

Like everyone who worked for the *New Statesman and Nation*, he was grossly underpaid. (Though his friends Kingsley Martin, its editor, and Maynard Keynes, its chairman, were at loggerheads on most points, they agreed in their stinginess even when the paper was paying excess profits tax.) He was thus often worried about money. Unlike most people, however, he has never had to face lack of a home or of a meal as an immediate prospect. Had he written his memoirs, they might therefore have been called 'A Sheltered Life'. That may sound out of keeping with the title chosen for this book 'Try Anything Once'. Well, he has not tried *everything:* who could? But he has tried most of the things he could expect to enjoy, including a trip on mescalin, which produced despair. Wide curiosity he believes to be his happiest endowment.

The temptation to commit murder, rape or arson, though the burning of many buildings in London and a few in Venice would be a public benefit, has been resisted. Gambling has never tempted him, though he is addicted to bridge, nor have many other pleasures, such as mountaineering, playing a musical instrument, hunting, counselling the poor, standing for Parliament, sailing a boat and teaching in a school. His reading in English and French has been wide, though he is no scholar; and he has made his way through a number of books in Italian and a few in Spanish. He particularly regrets that he is not a better linguist. Appetite for travel has taken him to most countries in Europe and in Asia, to North and East Africa, to the United States four times (chiefly as a pilgrim to museums), to Mexico, the West Indies and Brazil.

The Fine Arts have proved no less exciting than books. In 1913 he discovered for himself the fascination of the still little-known Post-Impressionists; and the first article he ever published was in praise of Baroque architecture: his taste extends to most styles of building, and to ruins. Though not naturally musical, he has loved opera from the age of fourteen, and throughout his adult life has been much exposed to music by expert friends, notably Edward Sackville-West and Desmond Shawe-Taylor. French composers of the last hundred years are his favourites. In the holidays from school he became an enthusiastic playgoer. Later, Diaghilev ballets made an indelible impression.

Metaphysics are beyond his grasp, and his imagination is as limited as his intellect. To originality he makes no claim, and had he written a book, it would have been of no more permanent value, he believes, than the journalism reprinted in this selection and in its predecessor, *Channel Packet*. Yet he does not affect humility. His interest in the craft of writing has been acute. Careful revision has made his work, he hopes, lucid, concise and sometimes entertaining. His efforts to brief himself before producing a review have been conscientious.

This selection from his journalism fails to display a number of his enjoyments, hardly mentioning for instance his favourite poets, painters and buildings. The essays on *The Victorian Philistines* (which is based on a Clark Lecture he had the honour to give at Cambridge) and on *Ideal Ward* have not been previously printed. His interest in the will to believe has given him a taste for ecclesiastical history that is now rare among general reviewers. The other papers were first published in the *New Statesman and Nation*, *Vogue*, *The Listener*, *The Times Literary Supplement*, *Horizon*, and (most usually) in *The Sunday Times*. To the editors who accepted and often improved them he remains grateful. He is deeply indebted also to Mr. George Rylands and Mr. Raleigh Trevelyan for help in making this selection from a formidable heap of yellowing newsprint. Some repetitious passages have not been removed; and the dates of the reviews have been given only when this seemed necessary. This is a shapeless, scrappy book, seeking to entertain rather than to instruct. The reader is invited to take it in small doses.

Artist, Critic, Public

'From most contemporary painting I can get no pleasure; often I can't make out even what the painter is trying to do; and you critics, when you praise one picture and damn another, seem to use no criterion except your personal taste. I can see the difference of course between a Munnings and a Matisse, but none between the "modern" painters you admire and those you despise. You critics give me no help about this, for you don't agree even among yourselves. Why is there now this discordance among experts, and this gulf between the artist and the public?'

Such objections as these trouble a great many persons who are thoughtful, well-read, fond of music and widely travelled. (To the uncultivated, of whatever class, modern painting is merely a joke.) The problems raised are alarmingly important, unless you fancy that humanity has outgrown its need for art; they are alarmingly complicated. Theorists always run to simplification; they tend to explain a phenomenon by one cause when it has several; and this weakness seems particularly tempting to those of us who theorise about art. I am anxious now to avoid it, even at the risk of appearing intricate or evasive.

First a counter-attack upon those who offer such objections. 'How many hours a year do you devote to the study of painting? Do you go to the National Gallery as often as once a month? If you did not listen to music twelve times a year what would you expect to get out of Beethoven, to say nothing of Bartok?' Here, I suggest, we find a vicious circle: people don't learn to enjoy pictures because they seldom look at them; and they seldom look at pictures, because they have not learnt to enjoy them. The public that does look and does enjoy is much larger than it was fifty years ago, yet I doubt whether for every fifty persons who have

I

made the effort required for the appreciation of Gibbon or Bach, there is one who has similarly trained himself to delight in Raphael.

This brings me to the critics, among whom I include not only professional writers but museum-directors and collectors. Among these (who all have devoted much time to looking at pictures) the agreement is very much wider, I believe, than my 'objector' supposes. If I found myself, for instance, with the art-critics of *The Times*, and the *Sunday Times*, the editor of the *Burlington Magazine*, the Directors of the National Gallery, the Tate, and the Victoria and Albert, we should be unanimous, I suspect, in our general estimate of ninety-nine painters in every hundred. Each one of us might greatly admire, no doubt, a few contemporary artists whom some of the others found merely respectable or not even that. Differences of temperament would show also in our several valuations of some Old Masters. But there would be found a consensus as general as any that exists among persons similarly occupied with the arts of fiction or music. 'What about the Chantrey Bequest?' some one may ask. 'There is, after all, a controversy.' Yes, but the six experts I have instanced would, I am confident, think about this much as I do; and, of the people who don't, precious few, I suspect, have spent much time looking at Old Masters.

Now for the suggestion that critics judge by their individual sensibility rather than by any objective criterion. This is true; it has indeed, I think, always been true. The 'rules' that critics once pretended to apply were mostly used merely to rationalise their intuitions; and if we have now ceased to apply such rules, it is because they have been proved invalid. In the past critics used to complain, for instance, that a figure was not anatomically correct; and, if the painter was aiming at such anatomical correctness, the censure may have been justified. But if you apply this criterion to the frescoes of Giotto (or the sculpture at Chartres), these supreme masterpieces would be condemned: it cannot, therefore, be universally applicable. To a trained eye some pictures are no more like works of art than Hansard is like verse, but the laws of pictorial composition cannot be reduced to a rule of thumb as can the laws of the sonnet. Every criterion in which critics have sought to generalise their experience has been exploded. Modern critics are not more arbitrary than their predecessors: they are merely more candid in their dependence upon a trained sensibility. These points made, I must admit that painting today is enormously more difficult to approach than ever before. What are the causes of this disaster?

Just over a hundred years ago Western Europe suffered a sharp decline in visual taste, a decline even more conspicuous in architecture than in sculpture and painting. Whether this was chiefly due to the increased power of the bourgeoisie, or rather—as I suspect—to the spread of machinery, it opened between the painter and the public a chasm which has continued to widen. Good artists learnt that their innovations were unwelcome; and poor artists, instead of imitating their betters, as had been their practice, found it profitable to satisfy and to debase further the public taste. First Courbet, then Manet, then the Impressionists, mystified—and therefore disgusted—even those who thought themselves to be cultivated. It must have seemed at the end of the century that the gulf between the painter and the public could not become any larger.

Alas, it has; and for the following reason. Good painters have always sought something beside the exact representation of appearances; and since the early years of the twentieth century they have become less and less concerned as a rule with representation of any sort. Some of them have been no more concerned with imitating anything in nature than are composers of music: these concentrate upon constructing objects that delight by the formal relationships they contain. Most painters, however, do still represent a subject, more or less recognisably, but the subject is seldom either so chosen or so treated as to please in its own right. You are not encouraged, indeed you are hardly allowed, to enjoy the charms of a nude, for instance, *qua* nude. Another school of artists, the surrealists, are often exact in representation, but use this only in order to disquiet. Their painting is more puzzling than Frith's or Marcus Stone's, but it is equally 'literary' in the bad sense of the word. The cubists and surrealists stand at the extremes of two contrary currents in painting. The only thing common to them is that they alike fail to communicate successfully to the public.

Now communication is the purpose of all art. Though a man may paint or write merely from a desire for self-expression, the result does not function as a work of art until somebody receives a communication from it. Often there may be a time-lag in such communication, due to the variety of styles or idioms now in use, and to the rapidity with which these have changed. Until the 1930s Van Gogh's pictures bewildered a majority even of experts, and excited in the general public howls of derision. Today, in reproduction, they have gained the popularity once enjoyed by *The Monarch of the Glen*. On this analogy can we expect that the cubist works of Picasso or the abstractions of Mr. Ben Nicholson will delight the next generation of Suburban Man? I am doubtful. When Van Gogh failed to communicate, it was because of novelties in his technique (drawing, handling and colour) rather than of any great deviation from the traditional subject-matter of the painter: he was passionately interested in representation. His *Sunflowers* are popular just because they suggest so vividly the sunniness of the sun and the floweriness of the flowers. No suggestion of this sort comes from cubist or abstract painting; and the emotion they seek to communicate by purely formal or plastic means reaches only a most limited public.

At the heart of what may be called the problem of non-communication we find the question: is it poetry or music that painting ought to resemble? The answer may well be that it can rightly approximate to either, as the artist prefers. But if he opts for a self-contained world like that of the string-quartet, if he sacrifices the pleasures made available in poetry by what men find noble or seductive in actuality or in imagination, if—in fact—he is unconcerned with subject, then he deprives himself of what has hitherto given inspiration to the greatest painters as well as delight to their public.

Until the middle of the nineteenth century artists were usually happy to treat the subjects required by their patrons. The resulting works represented aspects of real or imaginary life that were edifying, informative or sensuously pleasurable—as in a Fra Angelico Madonna, a Botticelli Venus, a Raphael portrait, a Rubens battle-piece, a scriptural scene by Rembrandt, a Fragonard *fête* or a Corot landscape. To enjoy such works as these there was no need to be a serious devotee of painting; and usually, one may suspect, what patron and public enjoyed was the subject of the picture rather than its specifically aesthetic qualities. Interest in the subject, however, could eventually lead anyone with an eye for painting so to train it that he learnt to make the full and discriminating aesthetic response. Today many such potential enjoyers of painting are never tempted into the habit of looking at pictures. The painter plumes himself upon an independence such

4

as was never dreamt of by Piero della Francesca or Titian or Watteau. To paint the subjects that people relish is, he thinks, below his dignity. In fact it is above his capacity—not because he lacks the accomplishment, but because he lacks the impulse.

If painters are now so seldom concerned with subjects which are intrinsically significant or attractive, this may be partly because the reaction against the popular painting of the nineteenth century has not yet exhausted itself, partly because the photographer has taken over some of the artist's old functions. The chief reason is more profound: it is the decline alike of Christianity and Humanism, the rarity of faith in the glories of either Heaven or Earth. But what about Communism? This is a religion vital enough to inspire both martyrs and inquisitors. It might be expected to inspire painters; but who can pretend that Soviet painting is not feebler even than anything our dear old Royal Academy can produce? Is this because it has to be propagandist? I fancy not. Didacticism is far less of a burden to the painter than to the novelist, because subject is so much less important in painting than in fiction. Many of the greatest painters can indeed be considered propagandists, whether for the Church, or for a city such as Venice, or for some monarch. The trouble with Communism is rather that it requires the painter to please the untrained eyes of bureaucrats and the populace. Happily it has not yet conquered any European people with a great pictorial tradition.

The art of painting has, I believe, been everywhere declining since 1914; and the decline has been to some extent concealed only because artists who were at work before 1914 long remained active. The simultaneous diminution in concern with subject is only a symptom of this decline. Its cause is the spiritual and material distress that has descended upon the world. The flight from representation is a turning away from the world into oneself: it reflects, however unconsciously, a distaste for the environment, not to say an aversion from life. The regeneration cannot come from a return to subject. This would probably be one of its results, but the only cause for it would be one of two highly improbable occurrences: either a revival of religion, or a renewed sense of the splendour and tragedy that can dignify the fate of man.

The Fine Art of Reading

A Daniel come to judgment—or, some will say, a traitor within the gates. Here is David Cecil, a Professor of Eng. Lit., declaring *ex cathedra*: 'The primary object of a student of literature is to be delighted.' I have for years been sticking up for this old-fashioned belief, against critics, far more learned than myself, who pretend that literature exists not to be enjoyed but to be evaluated.

Their novel doctrine has not yet captured Oxford (home of lost causes and impossible loyalties); and even in Cambridge, its birthplace, this critical puritanism still finds bold opponents. In most of our other universities it is imposed, I gather, upon the docile students of Eng. Lit.; and after graduation these spread the glum gospel through our secondary schools. All over the kingdom, it seems, boys and girls are being taught to look down their noses at Milton and Dickens. If this silliness is as widespread as some of my correspondents suggest (which I find hard to believe), there can be no better antidote than the lecture from which Lord David Cecil's new book takes its title.

Our professor insists that reading is both a pleasure and an art in which we need to train ourselves. (I should compare it with playing the piano, skating and dancing.) Let me try to summarise his thesis in a series of extracts. He begins with the university teaching of English:

'The academic approach and method was devised for other subjects: for philosophy, for instance, for mathematics, for history; intellectual ascetic studies, concerned with facts and ideas and whose aim is the discovery of impersonal objective truth. When they turn to the fine arts, academic persons tend to treat them in the same way. With literature this is easy. For

6

literature is not a pure art like music. It also deals with facts and ideas and can be studied with an intent to discovering objective truth.'

To read literature for information, however, is not to read it for the purpose intended by its authors:

'Art is not like mathematics or philosophy. It is a subjective, sensual and highly personal activity in which facts and ideas are the servants of fancy and feeling; and the artist's first aim is not truth but delight. Even when, like Spenser, he wishes to instruct he seeks to do so by delighting. It follows that the primary object of a student of literature is to be delighted. His duty is to enjoy himself: his efforts should be directed to developing his faculty of appreciation.'

Pater, he explains, made this point almost a century ago, but it needs repeating. For today 'some academic teachers seem to take perverse pride in possessing a taste so queasy as hardly to be able to stomach any books at all.' I believe that they are the victims of native puritanism. Our professor, on the contrary suspects moral deficiencies:

'To enjoy literature as it should be enjoyed is a task of immense difficulty; requiring, in addition to common sense and uncommon sensibility, faith, hope, charity, humility, patience and most of the other Christian virtues. It also involves a long and unhurried process of self-training.'

We shall never enjoy all the books that are worth enjoying (he continues) unless we learn to subdue our moral and aesthetic idiosyncrasies:

'Hopkins and Bridges, Bunyan and Gibbon, Kipling and Sterne, are all in their different manners and degree genuine artists. He who aspires to be a man of taste should suffer from a sense of failure if he does not enjoy them all. To do so, however, may mean subjecting himself to a stern course of self-discipline and self-effacement.'

This is admittedly a counsel of perfection, and the general reader cannot be blamed if he falls short of such a standard. I cannot enjoy *The Pilgrim's Progress* or (but this does not produce the same feelings of guilt) *The Testament of Beauty*. Our professor himself cannot enjoy Meredith's novels, he tells us, as much as they deserve. Yet we can, he insists, broaden our sympathies far more than we expect, when we start to try; and he denounces the critics who refuse to make the necessary effort:

> 'They take their first raw instinctive reactions as axiomatic: and instead of trying to widen their sympathies and correct their taste, spend their energies in constructing a philosophy of aesthetics to justify their first reactions.'

Here I think he is too charitable. Most of the critics he has in mind, so far from indulging the quirks of their own temperaments, have merely adopted, I believe, the personal prejudices of some fasionable pontiff. Poets (and painters and musicians) often cannot see the merit of their great predecessor or rivals because their vision is limited by their own aims and methods. The blindness of critics has no such excuse, especially when they put on borrowed blinkers. If T. S. Eliot had not declared his dislike for Milton and Shelley, would these poets ever have incurred the censure of the teacher-critics?

Fowler's Modern English Usage

Writers 'look it up in Fowler' whenever uncertain about a point in English grammar, the meaning or respectability of a word, or even its pronunciation: that thick little dark blue volume has sold over 600,000 copies. It was first published almost 40 years ago; and the Oxford University Press has decided to prepare a revised edition, because usage is always changing. The work was entrusted to Sir Ernest Gowers. To invite a man born in 1880 to bring anything up to date may sound strange, but in my view the choice could not have been bettered: to revise Fowler's book it was essential to find an expert who shared his point of view. Sir Ernest has given eight years to his task, and the result is longer, more concise and less podgy than the original. Certainly I shall seldom, except by accident, neglect any of his advice about grammar.

A revolutionary in his time, Fowler demolished some absurd old rules dear to Victorian schoolmasters but disregarded by most of our good writers. (Today, only very simple folk still think it wrong to begin a sentence with 'but', to end one with a preposition, or to split an infinitive.) He was, however, a 'prescriptive' grammarian—that is he believed English to be subject, like Latin and classical Greek, to grammatical rules. Some experts now think that a grammarian should be concerned only with what is said and written—by the uneducated as well as by the scholarly. Well, language is a convention needed to communicate facts, thoughts and feelings. Some measure of agreement about it is essential (if we talked *Finnegans Wake* lingo we could not even order a meal); and the authors who have used English most effectively are the surest guides to grammar and idiom.

Most of our younger writers, however gifted, disdain the

niceties discussed by Fowler and Sir Ernest. Their language therefore is often not neat, or even lucid. Possibly English is now changing very much as Latin did on its way to become Italian, French and Spanish. That distresses the old, for it is usual to prefer the linguistic habits in which one was brought up. And when we come to pronunciation, class rears its ugly head. What Sir Ernest calls the 'received pronunciation' has been denounced, he tells us, by a Cambridge lecturer in English as 'the dialect of an effete social clique.' Yet the stronger a man's dislike of class-distinctions, the more he should wish for an accepted pronunciation that would conceal them; and the most acceptable seems to be the one recommended by Sir Ernest, which is that not of a clique but of the original B.B.C. announcers and of such actors as Sir John Gielgud. The egalitarian may hope (as I cannot) for the disappearance of local accents from Yorkshire, for instance, and Dorset.

Many readers, as I know from letters I receive, enjoy arguing about grammar and words; but it would take many pages to summarise the changes made by Sir Ernest. Like Fowler, he takes almost all his examples of bad usage from the newspapers, and pitches especially into reviewers for using out-of-the-way words. For my part I enjoy coming across such words in my reading, and venture to use one occasionally. But I doubt if we reviewers deserve Sir Ernest's censure any more than biographers and novelists—whom he never pillories. He would have no patience, I presume, with poor Henry James's wail, 'I have sweated blood to give an amusing surface to my style.'

Sir Ernest is slightly more indulgent than Fowler. He permits, for instance, some forms of the fused participle. 'We must account for nothing having happened' is not grammar, but 'We must account for nothing's having happened' is not idiom (I agree) and therefore worse.

His chief business is with novelties that have become popular since Fowler's time. Most of them have come from the United States, and were unusual even there, I believe, in the nineteenth century. Many modern American writers did not start with English as their mother-tongue, and therefore lack an ear for idiom. 'They suggested that he go away' (instead of 'should go away') is now becoming common even over here. Other examples are 'enjoy to do' instead of 'doing,' 'aim to do' instead of 'at doing' (again now quite common over here), 'prefer *than*' instead of '*to*', 'did it just

enough *that'* instead of '*to'*, and a swarm of phrasal verbs 'to miss
out on,' 'to visit *with,'* 'to match *up with,'* in each of which the words
italicised merely clutter up the sentence. The word 'whom' seems
to be vanishing, and so do other accusatives: one now often reads
such phrases as 'We are not thinking of he who habitually travels,'
and 'It gives great pleasure to my parents and I.'

Sir Ernest points out that 'underprivileged' is an illogical
substitute for 'unprivileged'. (It is another American invention,
used as a euphemism for 'poor'.) He omits two recent borrowings
from France that are always used in a sense unknown to the
French, 'rapportage' and 'expertise'; nor does he give warning
against 'they exit' and 'a strata'. He does mention a number of
what I call 'red flag' words, because they bring the careless writer
into danger, 'decimate', 'literally', 'oblivious', 'proposition',
'sensational', 'undue', 'unique' and 'viable'.

Pronunciation has also been changing fast. The growth of
popular education, Sir Ernest points out, has produced a 'speak
as you spell' movement. Fifty years ago clergymen often spoke in
that way; and nobody else, I believe, would then have given three
syllables to 'regiment', 'medicine' or 'venison'. The sounding of
the 't' in 'often', on the other hand, was a purely proletarian habit.
Today it has become general among persons under fifty, and is
therefore accepted by Sir Ernest.

There is also a tendency to shift the stress, usually backwards
but sometimes forwards, as in 'for*mid*able', 're*mon*strate', 'Cap*ri*'
and 'Sev*i*lle'. A novelty not mentioned here is the long 'o' frequent
on the wireless in such words as 'involve' and 'revolve'. Sir
Ernest deplores the use of the 'modern' Latin pronunciation for
words that have long been naturalised, like 'a priori' and 'prima
facie', (I expect soon to hear 'arliarse' and 'alibee'), and the similar
absurdity of 'Don Hooan' and 'Don Keehotay'; but he does not
refer to the worse use of French pronunciation for names we
spell differently in English, like Lyons, Rheims and Marseilles.
(I have even heard 'Munich' pronounced as if it were a German
word with an *Umlaut*, though its German name is München.)
Disregard of tradition seems peculiarly tiresome when due to a
mixture of ignorance and pedantry.

Many of the points discussed in Fowler-Gowers may seem
absurdly trivial; and our pronunciation matters only to ourselves,
unless we are actors or public speakers. But misuse of words in
writing can easily alter the sense of a phrase. Sir Ernest explains

the distinction, for instance, between 'economic' and 'economical,' 'disinterested' and 'uninterested,' 'historic' and 'historical,' 'masterful' and 'masterly'. He quotes C. S. Lewis: 'The language which can with the greatest ease make the finest and most numerous distinctions of meaning is the best.' That strikes me as unanswerable. Let me beg readers as well as writers to keep the revised Fowler at their elbows. It brims with useful information.

Desmond MacCarthy

As a journalist-critic Desmond MacCarthy wrote weekly about
plays or books from 1903 until his death in 1952. Was his influence
upon taste and opinion trivial, or even pernicious (as some
teachers of Eng. Lit. would now assert)? Or was it robust,
although difficult to define, because his character and experience
made him an empiricist, uncommitted to any doctrine? That is the
question now to be considered; but before attempting an answer
I must 'declare an interest'. First he gave me as an apprentice
reviewer patient tutorials; and, having later succeeded him as
literary editor of the *New Statesman and Nation*, I now occupy his
post as reviewer for the *Sunday Times*. Despite differences in
temperament and, alas, in talent, I write here as his disciple,
prepossessed by affection and gratitude. It is not irrelevant to
insist upon his kindness, charm and humour, for he was extremely
sociable, and the character revealed in his talk made a great
impact upon all who knew him, and also upon listeners to his
broadcasts.

His articles and reviews have been anthologized in eight
volumes (which regrettably overlap); but none of them is in print or
has yet appeared as a paperback. Probably few of the young are
familiar even with his name. Although they would surely relish
his writing, especially the book entitled *Portraits*, they could
not share all his enthusiasms. He was a great champion, for
instance, of Samuel Butler and George Moore, whose reputations
are now in what he called 'the trough of the wave'. D. H. Lawrence and T. S. Eliot, still riding its crest, may well traverse in
their turn a period of neglect: every generation revolts against
the idols of its predecessor.

Changes in taste interested MacCarthy all the more because he was less swayed by them than most critics. Almost alone among his contemporaries he applauded, for instance, the writings of Ruskin and Carlyle. Nor did his relish for the youthful Eliot and the aging Yeats ever weaken his love for Tennyson or, of course, Milton. His tolerance, however, had its limits: he attacked what he thought humbug in the first Lord Cave, silliness in Gertrude Stein, hardness of heart in Dean Inge and also in two authors he admired, Shaw and Proust.

His direct influence was strongest upon actors (who valued the detailed suggestions he offered in their dressing-rooms or in his notices) and upon the reviewers who profited by his advice, for instance, G. W. Stonier, Edward Sackville-West, Cyril Connolly and T. C. Worsley. But most of the good literary journalism of the 1920s and 1930s owed something to his example: the temptation to moralize or lay down the law was more often resisted; and the tone became more conversational. His easy-seeming style was the fruit of exceptional care. Though he always set to work at the last moment, he wrote slowly, struggling to find the exact word and to give every sentence the proper shape. Had he been engaged upon a book, not an ephemeral review, he could hardly have taken more trouble to make his language limpid, euphonious and telling.

Like Hazlitt, Macaulay, Bagehot and all good critics writing primarily for journals, he knew he must catch, and retain, the interest of the inattentive, who would be reading him for pleasure, not out of duty. But he assumed that they were cultivated, and wrote as if he were talking to his friends—who included such disparate figures as Lord Oxford, Scawen Blunt, the philosopher G. E. Moore, Hilaire Belloc, George Moore and Roger Fry. The range of his sympathies induced a various public to welcome his guidance. A Liberal himself, he made Conservatives read the *New Statesman* and Socialists the *Sunday Times*.

When still at Cambridge he made friends with future members of the Bloomsbury group, now sometimes wildly described as aesthetes with little concern for morality or conduct. As a critic, MacCarthy—like Virginia Woolf, Lytton Strachey and Mr. E. M. Forster—was fascinated by character, seeking its manifestations everywhere, in history, politics, religion, painting. The best criticism, in his view, had always been largely 'discourse upon human nature'. He had hoped to become a novelist or biographer, and although fascinated by the handling of words, remained always intent upon relating literature to life.

When writing about a play or a book he knew that the reader's first question would be 'Shall I enjoy it?', and sought to provide an answer. 'The first step to culture is always to learn to enjoy, not to know what is best.' This outlook increased his influence upon the general reader—and of course got him into hot water with some academic puritans. His respect for scholarship, however, was profound. He always told young reviewers to join the London Library and to keep on their shelves the authoritative histories of English literature. 'Professors did not write for their pupils: they wrote to keep people like you and me straight.' Today more and more teacher-critics write only for their pupils and colleagues, while fewer and fewer journalist-critics depend upon the London Library. This deepening gulf would have horrified MacCarthy, with his continual concern for the general reader who seeks criticism that is neither pedantically dull nor ignorantly bright. To obtain an influence as wide as his, we reviewers need to improve our knowledge, and some dons their style.

Red Flag Words

After years of editing there are a number of words which I can't come on without seeing, constantly above them, fluttering red flags, of the sort that announce not the Marxist's faith or the golfer's hope, but danger from a minefield or at least a steam-roller. The red flag words are those which are either commonly misused or mis-shaped or otherwise nasty. The word-lover needs to be on guard also against indiscriminate distaste for novelty. English is not a dead language; additions to it are desirable; our vocabulary cannot be too rich. Imports from abroad, if made in due form, should be welcomed; and history proves that slang also can devise acceptable bequests. But to impose a different or a looser sense upon a word already established is usually to blunt a tool: by doing this the lazy writer adds to the difficulties of conscientious craftsmen. Even the best writers, I must add, sometimes fall into traps. Imprecision in language is growing more and more common—partly, I suspect, because of the decline in classical studies, which, whatever their defects, do at least enforce, through 'construes,' an attention to the meanings of English terms. Here are some notes on words that always give me pause. References to *The Oxford Dictionary* (O.E.D.), to Fowler's *Modern English Usage* (F.) and to Mr. Eric Partridge's *Usage and Abusage* (P.) reveal only a part of my indebtedness to these authorities.

Avocation means an occupation that is not one's principal business, Mr. Gladstone's Homeric studies, for instance. O.E.D. quotes Thomas Fuller: 'Heaven is his vocation, and therefore he counts earthly employments avocations.' The use of the word as the synonym instead of the antonym of *vocation* can be found as far back as the seventeenth century in Boyle (oh! these scientists!);

16

it defaces the Despatches of Wellington, and even the Essays of Macaulay. The added syllable makes *avocation* sound more imposing to the ignorant, but the mistake deprives the writer of a useful distinction.

Instinctively: neither F. nor P. comments upon the slipshod use of *instinctively* instead of *automatically* to denote mere absence of forethought or conscious intention. The actions we perform instinctively are extremely few. There seems little likelihood that we inherit (though we may acquire from our parents) an attitude to Milton, rock-gardens, cricket or baroque architecture, though one finds writers declaring that they love or hate these instinctively.

Literally is used more often than not as what grammarians call an intensive—merely, that is to say, to add emphasis, like the word *positively*. The results are usually comical since its true meaning is the opposite to *figuratively*. A pretty instance of misuse is 'I was literally beside myself with agitation'.

Mutual, as in *Our Mutual Friend*, where no reciprocity is possible, is called by F. a well-known trap. Many writers continue to fall into it. Friendship can be mutual, but not a friend. The trouble is that the correct word can be misunderstood. Who likes to say 'our common friend'?

Phenomenal means perceptible to the senses. In the sense of 'extraordinary' or 'prodigious' it seems to have been launched by Rossetti. Junius and the Duke of Wellington had already used *phenomenon* to mean a prodigy, and Dickens was probably drawing on current raree-show language when he talked of 'the infant phenomenon.' P. says that to divert *phenomenal* thus from its proper use to a job for which it is not needed is a sin against the English language. F. says that it should not be debased to equivalence with *unusual*, but may be used as a synonym for *prodigious*. He gives no reason for this strange indulgence.

Protagonist meant originally the chief personage in a drama, and its use can properly be extended to denote the chief personage in a story or a factual event. F. says 'To talk of *several protagonists*, or of a *chief protagonist*, is an absurdity as great, to anyone who knows Greek, as to call a man the *protagonist* of a cause or of a person.' The notion that it means a champion attracts those who know the meaning of *pro* and *anti*, who do not know that *protagonist* comes from the Greek *protos* (meaning first) and who therefore fancy that a protagonist is the opposite of an antagonist. An analogous confusion intrudes a hyphen into *homosexual*, which comes from the Greek word *homos*, meaning *the same*. The error of deriving it from the Latin *homo* is doubly absurd for this means 'a human being,' not 'a man as distinct from a woman,' which is *vir*.

Quietus means a discharge or acquittance given on payment of sums due, a receipt (cf. German *Quittung*); also a discharge from office or duty. Hamlet's correct use of the word has been misunderstood, and its suggestion of the calm that comes with death led to its use in the sense of *coup de grâce* among sportsmen and careless writers. Thackeray went so far as to describe a nurse giving its accustomed quietus to a screaming infant, by which he meant not that she paid it or even killed it, but that she calmed it. There seems no excuse for the pretentious misuse of this word.

Sadism, a word derived from the pornographic daydreams of the Marquis de Sade, means cruelty that is used to excite sexual desire. It is now used to mean any cruelty that seems to be enjoyed by those who inflict it, and even any cruelty, however little pleasure it gives. This needless innovation seems due to the popularity of Freud rather than of the divine Marquis.

Singular is often misused, though neither F. nor P. takes account of this. It can be applied exactly only to what is unparalleled, and therefore it is careless to say 'An eleven of singularly good cricketers'; though one can properly talk of 'a singularly good eleven,' if it has proved such. It is worse than careless to speak of a person being *very singular* or *most singular*, a habit popularised by Lytton Strachey, who liked using the word to denote oddity. This is almost as reckless as writing 'very unique' or 'most unique.'

Professor used as a title in front of a name began as a horrid German neologism. Who was ever heard to talk of 'Professor Pusey'? But the great Bentley did use the word in this way, and the usage seems to have been common in Scottish universities in the eighteenth century. It has been spreading in England (I do it myself). I gather from a Cambridge Professor, who shares my distaste for it, that at Cambridge the style is smiled upon, at Oxford smiled at; and Gilbert Murray, I understand, never allowed himself to be addressed as 'Professor Murray.'

Face up to.—English is suffering from a mysterious rash of otiose prepositions pimpling upon transitive verbs. This is a common specimen. It can be justifiable when used to emphasise a bold acceptance of danger or indeed of anything unpleasant.

18

Now for two words which it has become useless to attack, though the nice writer is unlikely to sully his pen with them. *Conscript* as a verb originated in the U.S.A., and the first reputable writer to use it was the genial, ill-educated Whitman. The correct word, to *conscribe*, has been in good usage for over four hundred years. The misuse is now established beyond all hope of banishment, and one must hope only that it will not bring fellow ruffians with it. Or we shall read: 'My finances are so circumscripted that I cannot subscript to the fund for inscripting a stone with a passage descripting the remedy prescripted for snake-bite.'

Evacuate means to empty. A city or a building can be evacuated, a person only by a purge, an emetic or a Caesarean. The current use of the word to denote the removing of groups occurs as early as 1639, but so far as I know very seldom defiled the pen of a respectable writer before the First World War. This solecism is unlikely to disappear, since it describes an activity characteristic of our civilisation.

Next, some supposedly French words. *Chichi* is a slang expression that originally meant a piece of false hair. It has come to be used in France to denote undue formality, affectation or even effeminacy. In English it is commonly made an adjective denoting over-elaboration in style. The particular error I wish to denounce is the intrusion of a hyphen, making *chi-chi*, which is Anglo-Indian for *Eurasian*.

Bon viveur. The expression *un bon vivant* suggests a man addicted to the pleasures of the table rather than of the alcove. A *viveur* is a rake, and though one may hold that rakes can be good, the expression *bon viveur* is not French, and represents in English a pointless distortion of a useful Gallicism.

Exposé means an orderly setting out or *précis* of a body of facts or beliefs. It is a convenient importation, but I wish that the native form, exposition, had been retained. The common use of *exposé* to mean the unmasking of some scandal reveals ignorance of French, and quite gratuitously, since *exposure* carries just this sense.

Rapportage. The French took over the English word *reporter* a century or so ago. Later it became customary for *les reporters* to write *de grands reportages*, the word being applied, for instance, to descriptions of trials and of journeys by special correspondents. Between the wars this French offspring of an English word became popular among English journalists, who kept the foreign pronunciation of its final syllable, as in garage. Reporting took on a new dignity, it seems, from this whiff of Paris. Recently a further and grotesque evolution has occurred here, the spelling rapport-age. This French word denotes the activity of a retriever—also a report by the secretary of a committee. Its only merit, when used in English to describe a certain form of journalism, is that it is thought to look even more exotic and dignified than *reportage*. We need a word meaning 'a piece of reporting'; and reportage, despite its origin, is a respectable formation from the verb *to report*. Portage, which has been good usage for five hundred years, provides a precedent. *Reportage* itself occurs in Webster's *White Devil* in the sense of reputation. I think that this word should therefore be accepted in the French sense, on condition that it be pronounced, and spelt, as an English word. *Rapportage* must be dismissed to an even lower limbo than *serviette* and *lingerie*.

Onto seems first to have been used as one word by Keats, and so illiterate did this seem to his editors that in 1876 they substituted for it *upon*. Following F., I think it odd to prefer *onto* to *on* or *upon*. He advises those who like the preposition to own up and write it in one word, *onto*. I disagree, preferring the hypocrisy that is a homage to virtue.

Only and *even* are red-flag words only because they are sometimes misplaced by even the most punctilious of writers. F. is indulgent to the misplacing of *only* except where it may lead to ambiguity, less indulgent to the misplacing of *even*. P., usually not so rigorous as F., trounces the misplacing of *only* and does not mention *even*. 'Aspasia even feared that Socrates was in love with her' (not only suspected but positively feared), 'A. feared that even S. was in love with her' (not only Athens but Socrates himself), 'A. feared that S. was even in love with her' (not only liked but was in love with): each of these statements differs according to the placing of *even*. Even where no ambiguity results, it is better to attach *only* and *even* to the words they qualify, except in the rare cases where euphony forbids.

Irridescent and Idiosyncracy.—These are the two mistakes to which, I have found, good spellers most often succumb.
P.S.

Two silly newcomers have become usual even in *The Times*. *Cohort* is the English translation of a Latin word that means a body of at least four hundred infantry. Now we read that a politician has mounted a platform accompanied by several cohorts (who would leave little space for an audience). The use of the word to signify *supporter* or *companion* is pointless.

Furore in Italian can mean *fury*, but the Victorians took over the word in its other Italian sense to signify *popular enthusiasm*, such as greets the performance of a singer. That valuable addition to our vocabulary is now being destroyed by those who use it as a mere synonym of *fury* or *excitement*.

B

Reviewing

A couple in my train were chatting about a new biography. 'There was a bad review of it,' the chap said, 'in the *Sunday Times*.' 'No,' the sharp girl replied, 'that was in the *Observer*; Mortimer wrote the good one.' Overhearing a kind word about oneself is a jolly surprise, but this gave me no pleasure: she meant merely that I had praised the book, and that is what most people mean by 'a good review.' Dare I suggest that a review, like a story or a poem, may in its humbler way be a good job or a bad one.

Whatever I may know about reviewing, or indeed about any other sort of writing, I owe chiefly to Desmond MacCarthy who, as literary editor of the *New Statesman*, tried me out as a critic of novels. He would give me a tutorial on every piece I brought him, showing me how to rewrite my sentences. In ten years of old-fashioned education in two schools and a university, I had been taught to write verse as well as prose in Latin and Greek, but hardly anything about the handling of English.

MacCarthy proved the ideal mentor, being not only a penetrating critic of both books and the drama, with wide knowledge of the world and a rare understanding of human nature, but also as masterly in his style as anyone then alive. The wittiest and most imaginative of his pupils was Cyril Connolly.

Few readers realise how hugely we reviewers depend upon our literary editors. They allot the books to us, often at our own request, scrutinise our work before it appears, and will suggest cuts, additions, or improvements in our language. Some of them are said to press upon us books advertised in their papers, an experience unknown to me. How lucky I have been in my bosses, MacCarthy, Leonard Woolf, David Garnett, Leonard Russell and now J. W. Lambert!

Let me summarise what kind MacCarthy used to tell me. Academic critics have a ready-made audience in their pupils and colleagues. Reviewers by contrast have to capture and to retain the readers' attention. Good judgment and bright ideas are not enough. You must also give an edge to your words, making them pleasing to the ear, lucid, neat and succinct. Few of us can achieve an easy-seeming style free from clichés, without hard work and patient revision.

Tone is also important. Some editors like reviews to be either black or white. I don't. That is a cheap path to popularity. Begin by absorbing the point of view taken by the author you have to discuss! Instead of acting as counsel for the defence or the prosecution, try to produce a judicious summing-up, including the good points in a feeble book and the feeble points in a good one! Don't lay down the law! Don't be censorious! Self-righteousness is the worst of English faults. Irony works better than straight invective.

You must brief yourself, if you are dealing with an English classic, by consulting great academic critics such as Grierson and W. P. Ker, or if it is a modern book by reading previous works of the same author or on the same subject. Admit your lack of expert knowledge! Don't assume that readers remember dates or know about an obscure author you happen to have read; but offer information—without assuming that they don't possess it! Let yourself go, don't play for safety, and don't show off either!

Such was the advice that I have at least tried to follow. Some brilliant reviewers have worked on different lines. Even so there are traps that we all ought to avoid. A review, for instance, of John Betjeman's new poems gave us a relevant account of his subjects and feelings without a single sentence about his versification. Another recent review called not for additions but for cuts. Mr. John Wain's delightful life of Dr. Johnson was discussed by an expert upon the subject. He gave half his space to airing his irrational and total contempt for Boswell, because that supreme biographer had been a drunkard and a debauchee.

The savage review is a too easy form of fun, usually better left, I believe, to the young. Far too many worthless books are published every year: why pick out one for attack, unless it is likely to win more respect than it deserves? Most readers want to be told about what they might enjoy. I now seldom tackle any sort of book that I can't recommend, with one exception: priggish studies of Eng. Lit. that may discourage students from wide reading.

How far do reviews affect sales? Precious little, according to many publishers, who are anxious, however, to obtain them, if only to gratify the authors on their list. A book, I agree, may excite the enthusiasm of the best critics, and fail with the public. Success depends, as a rule, on what its first few hundred readers say about it to their friends. On the other hand, if it gets no notices, who can be expected to buy it, unless it is a romantic novel or a book on such subjects as cookery, gardening and astrology, which somehow find their own market? Wise publishers therefore often launch unknown authors in January or August, when these don't have to compete for reviews with established favourites.

All reviews (except brief notices) ought in my view to be signed. By adopting that practice, belatedly, *The Times Literary Supplement* has become far more valuable. Most of us get to know which critics share our tastes, or (when they don't) can hold our interest. Some of them I should read on any subject, others on none. Besides, anonymity is unfair on young reviewers, giving them no chance to earn a reputation.

The signing of reviews, I admit, brings two disadvantages. First, it makes one dislike discussing books by one's friends. The praise they usually take for granted; and they are mortified by any mild reservation that strangers would take in their stride. Secondly, anyone whose name crops up regularly in the Press risks becoming vain, the mere reviewer as well as the *prima donna*, the footballer and the pop star.

Critics may be written off as parasites, though some are themselves also novelists, poets or historians. In any case we can all help to make more important authors better-known. The blessed word 'symbiosis' is used by scientists to denote the mutual dependence of two species of animal or plant, usually differing in size. Let us then struggle every day in every way to become more and more symbiotic!

Literature made Difficult

Two series of *Casebooks* published by Macmillan deal respectively with groups of particular authors and books. Each of them ends with a list of dismal questions such as may confront students of Eng. Lit. at their exams. 'What would *Hamlet* lose if it were not a poetic play?' 'Do you think that *The Tempest* appeals simultaneously to sophisticated and naive tastes?' 'In what sense, or senses, is *Emma* a comedy?' 'Examine Yeats's use, or misuse, of history in *Last Poems.*' The *Modern Judgements* series (general editor P. N. Furbank), though not disfigured by such questions, seems also aimed primarily at examinees.

That is what alarms me. I trust that no student will read right through the seven that have appeared, much less through the thirty-one that are to follow (which include a volume entirely devoted to *Look Back in Anger*). If the young mug up all this erudite argle-bargle, they may easily lose all freshness of response to the books discussed, lack the time to read nearly as much creative writing as they should, and even suppose that poems and novels are meant to excite not enjoyment but evaluation.

They also may not realise that a first reading of most novels (though not of most poetry) should be not intensive but rapid: the author wants us to lose ourselves in the story and not to interrupt the flow in order to make elaborate notes. Students will be warned by their instructors, I hope, against all these dangers.

Older people can be advised to look at any of these books that discuss an author or a work they already know quite well and particularly enjoy. The two general editors have entrusted each of these anthologies to a patient scholar, who has selected from huge dust-heaps of criticism the papers he reprints.

All but two of the contributors are university teachers of Eng.

Lit., a group who for some reason is more prone to moralise than other academics. Experts on Greek and Latin, for instance, seldom waste their time, and our own, by complaints about the bawdiness or the bisexuality of classical authors, or their respect for class distinctions. The difference between the Ancient World and ours is taken for granted. And besides, these teachers of Eng. Lit. can hardly ever allow themselves any lightness of tone, or employ the irony that they often applaud. More surprisingly, they almost always concentrate upon the ideas of a poet or novelist, neglecting the style. For instance, the bizarre Leavis judgment that Milton's verse lacks variety and delicacy is mentioned, but not discussed. Whereas we general readers chiefly enjoy the poetic expression in *The Tempest* and Milton, the criticisms here concentrate upon the notions expressed.

These learned critics devote much of their energy to contradicting one another; and nobody can want to read Mortimer's view of David Lodge's view of Hough's view of Leavis's view of *Emma*. But let me note a few of the many points that struck me in these anthologies.

Hamlet. Ideal subject for one of the anthologies: no play has excited wider differences of opinion, although it has been admired by almost every critic except Voltaire and Eliot. D. G. James says here that 'the plain issue' confronting the hero was 'Does God exist or not?' Did Shakespeare, I wonder, feel much interest in this problem? Hamlet wavered characteristically between belief in the after-life and doubts, which must have seemed shocking. One may notice also that, when the many characters in Shakespeare die on the stage, nobody ever thinks of summoning a priest to comfort and absolve them.

All the essays on this tragedy are thoughtful, and I specially enjoyed Professor Helen Gardner's. Eliot rebuked Hamlet for making 'a considerable mess of things' and 'dying fairly well pleased with himself.' As she points out, however, the audience at the end of the tragedy forgets everything odious that he has done or said, and accepts wholeheartedly the praise heaped on him by Horatio and Fortinbras.

Emma. Excellent pieces by David Lodge, Graham Hough and Edgar Shannon. But, again, no discussion of the author's style; and the novel brings out a sad priggery in most of the contributors. They treat it as a tract, not a comedy. Trilling, usually so perceptive, finds it more 'difficult' than anything by Proust or

Joyce. In my naive view the characters are all crystal-clear, and so is the author's view of them. Moreover they, and the situations they found themselves in, might well have existed here within living memory. Emma gossiped idly and once made a cruel remark (which she instantly regretted). If there are any critics who have never done the same, they are to be envied. What I admire in Emma is that, profiting from experience, she not only repented of her defects, but amended them at the age of only twenty-one.

Marvin Mudrick decides that she was a latent lesbian, and refuses to believe that her marriage proved happy, despite the straightforward statement in the novel. Though Arnold Kettle ends by sharing our delight in the book, Jane Austen shocks him to death by not questioning 'the right of the minority to live at the expense of the majority'. No, she never thought in such terms. Neither did any of our finest playwrights and novelists from Shakespeare until the end of the nineteenth century. We therefore automatically read them in their historical context. Mr. Kettle, however, says that to do this is insulting. What a funny fellow! Does he blame Homer and Horace for not anticipating the teaching of the Gospels?

Dickens. Not an author, I think, whom the critics can often help us to enjoy, though a paper on his astonishing use of language would be welcome. We are given nothing of the sort. The critics in this anthology, however, are not overweighted with moral considerations. *Hard Times*, for instance, is here admitted to be a failure (I believe Dickens made it so short because the subject proved so uninspiring). Trilling is particularly good in praise of *Little Dorrit*. He suspects that Blandois was derived from Balzac's Vautrin (whom he oddly describes as 'wholesome'). I have suggested the same source for Magwitch. We know that Dickens read Balzac, because he expressed envy of his freedom to write frankly about sex.

Henry James. Tony Tanner is excellent in his paper as well as in his introduction. The other contributors all teach in the North American universities. They say little about James's humour, or about the wit that dazzles me, for instance, in *The Awkward Age*. But let me applaud the 'explication' of his syntax by Ian Watt, and Walter Wright's account of Maggie Verver. How I agree with Leavis that we cannot share James's entire approval of her or of her father!

Tony Tanner fears that the critics and scholars may bury Henry

James under their pontifications, explanations, speculations. The other great authors treated in these anthologies are all in the same danger. Reading in one week seventy such learned critics has left me wiser, but sadder and in a daze. Will not the young find them even more discouraging?

Eng. Lit.

During the last fifty years, our schools and universities have given an increasingly prominent place to the teaching of English—and the standard of written English has no less conspicuously declined. Cause and effect? Let us not argue *post hoc ergo propter hoc*: various other changes have been blunting and enfeebling our language. *Sed quis custodiet ipsos custodes?* Do all University lecturers in English write as if they thought clarity important?

English Education is a collection of papers by teachers of Eng. Lit., most of them in schools. One of the co-editors, Mr. Denys Thompson, has written two books in collaboration with Dr. F. R. Leavis, whose influence is evident in several of the papers here, and whose name looms large in the bibliography. He has never shown a gift for invective or indeed for eloquence of any order; but when not over-excited he can bring close argument to support his judgment upon a writer. I am told, moreover, that in discussions with his pupils he displays a charm, lucidity and humour that he disdains in his writings.

The contributors to the book in any case make their points clearly; and some reveal the effectiveness of their own teaching by brilliant extracts from their pupils' writings. The general reader, however, who knows no more than I do about current schooling, may well be dismayed by the many charges here brought against the system on which English is being taught.

Out-of-date grammars and text-books, 'shorter versions' of English classics that rearrange sentences shaped by authors of genius, intelligence tests and ordinary examinations are submitted to devastating criticism. Here are a few phrases from Mr. Denys Thompson's article:

B*

'Examinations cannot test what the teacher of English is constantly trying to evoke—a response to literature ... The O-level language paper tells us nothing about a candidate's capacity for expression ... The universities through their examining boards have helped to deaden much of the teaching of English ... Enormous and stultifying.'

That very neatly sums up the impact of examinations upon the teaching of English—the text-books fence off children from the enjoyment of literature.

If English has indeed been made as tedious as Greek and Latin in the old days, it had better not be taught. Boys used to leave school determined never again to look at Euripides or Cicero. How much worse if their lessons now give them a similar distaste for Shakespeare and Dickens!

How absurd to require from boys and girls at school 'a full response' to an entire novel! If they give intensive reading to all the passages that reward close attention in our great novelists (and also in the other great prose-writers whom they are presumably encouraged to enjoy), they will leave school having read through almost as few English classics as I did Greek and Latin classics. Any potential relish for literature could only be discouraged by such a behest. Luckily boys and girls can be trusted, I believe, to disregard it: if bookish, they will still read voraciously; if unbookish, they will merely think their teacher daft. Wordsworth told Wilson that 'the appropriate calling of our youth' was 'not to analyse with scrupulous minuteness, but to accumulate in genial confidence: its instinct, its safety, its benefit, its glory is to love, to admire, to feel and to labour.'

Some of the contributors are obviously inspired teachers. Nor do I question the importance of English as a school subject. On the other hand I should never advise anyone to read English Literature at the university. If you choose Greats, History or Modern Languages, you will do a lot of English reading for pleasure, provided that you have any feeling for literature. Without this, what can be the use of struggling through the Learned Gower, the minor Jacobean dramatists or the weakest precursors of romanticism?

The Tympany of English Studies

The Rise of English Studies by D. J. Palmer is an account of English
as a university subject, which I can recommend as scholarly,
brief and often amusing. It explains, for instance, why students
of Eng. Lit. have to read the delicious *Beowulf* at Oxford and
London, but not at Cambridge or most of our universities. Just
how delicious *Beowulf* may be I don't know. Like most verse, it
does not delight me in translation: Racine and Mallarmé become
dreary in English. A distinguished poetess and novelist has
recently proclaimed the impossibility of understanding our
language without having read Anglo-Saxon poetry in the original.
But which of our great poets from Chaucer to Yeats could do this?
None, I believe, except Hopkins. If they did not understand the
language in which they wrote, their achievements are supernatural.

The history of English education reveals a comical conservatism. Nobody ignorant of Latin could be well-informed until the
end of the seventeenth century. After that, the use of modern
languages by philosophers, historians and scientists became first
widespread then universal: Latin and Greek lost their utilitarian
importance. The centuries rolled by; and fifty years ago it was
still impossible to matriculate at Oxford and Cambridge without a
smattering of both these languages. The university authorities
seem to have agreed with Dr. Arnold that Latin and Greek had
been given by Providence 'for the very purpose of forming the
human mind in youth.' No other subject, it seems, could foster
such refinement of taste—or even such exalted morality, which
strikes me as bizarre. Many classical authors are by Christian
standards deeply unedifying.

The first of our universities to teach English as a substitute for

31

Latin and Greek was London, in 1828. It had just been founded at the instance of Utilitarians, such as Bentham, and of Dissenters (whose schools had never been enslaved by the Classical curriculum). The old universities detested all reforms: Oxford waited almost sixty years before following suit, and Cambridge even longer.

Fearing that English might prove a soft option, London, and Oxford in its turn, emphasised the study of language at the expense of literature, and made Anglo-Saxon a compulsory subject. Fierce polemics raged about the educational value of philology. Critics justly pointed out that Latin and Greek had long been made repulsive to the young by a wretched system of word-mongering. 'For heaven's sake do not let us murder Shakespeare by treating him as we treat Aeschylus and Sophocles.' Thomas Huxley weighed in: 'The establishment of Chairs of philology under the name of literature may be a profit to science, but is really a fraud practised on letters.' He complained also that young Englishmen could leave the university without any knowledge of our noble literature—a defect that posterity, he thought, would find incredible. Such views eventually triumphed at Cambridge, where the Eng. Lit. School came close in its purpose to Greats: it required the study not of language, including Anglo-Saxon, but of 'Life, Literature and Thought.'

Oxford still requires an exact knowledge of Anglo-Saxon grammar, which may absurdly entail twice as many tutorials on *Beowulf* as on the whole nineteenth century. Students of our literature should ideally know German or Russian (which I don't) as well as French and either Latin or Italian. By contrast the literature in Anglo-Saxon is sparse. Knowledge of it is needed by experts on language; but German is far more valuable to those who seek merely to cultivate their minds. Since the Eng. Lit. School must cater for both these types of student, would it not be reasonable to let them choose between *Beowulf* and *Faust*?

The bookish will read for their own pleasure authors who are enjoyable (to study writers who are still alive for examination purposes seems to me premature): and unenjoyable authors are seldom worth reading, unless one intends to become an expert on literary history.

The handling of English by professional writers has long been growing more and more slipshod, partly perhaps because a smaller proportion of the young have learnt Latin and Greek. Badly and boringly as these languages used to be taught, they instilled attention to grammar and idiom. Even the writing of verse in the styles of Euripides and Virgil, which may seem futile, forced one to think of words as objects with a particular shape and sound, not as mere symbols for ideas. Until recently, no one could attain a scholarship, or Honours, in Latin and Greek without being able to write these languages with neatness and euphony.

So far as I can discover, examiners in English make no equivalent demand. 'Practical criticism' is taught at Cambridge; but does any university provide rigorous teaching in English composition, the art of shaping sentences and paragraphs? I am not denouncing Eng. Lit., which a number of my friends have read with profit, and which several of them have taught. My contention is that this subject should be used for training authors as well as scholars, and that it should always be accompanied by other studies (as it is at Cambridge). Mr. Palmer applauds the new universities for embracing wider areas of study within a single degree structure.

Specialisation at school remains the curse of our system. It is no longer permitted, I believe, in other countries; and most people agree that the old Classical education was grotesquely narrow. Yet university requirements now encourage in schools the same premature concentration upon a single subject. The great advantage of Eng. Lit. is that those who intend to read it are not obliged to specialise in it before matriculation. A knowledge of *Beowulf* does not yet, I fancy, help anyone to win a scholarship; and for this let us be truly thankful!

Dr. Leavis

This year, 1952, is unlikely to produce a more controversial book than *The Common Pursuit*, a collection of critical essays by Dr. F. R. Leavis. He lectures on English Literature at Cambridge, and is the most combative of scholars. Whether he writes of Shakespeare, Milton or Johnson, he finds reason to insult living writers who have incurred his disapproval. I always delight in the acrimony of the learned: it is so much out of keeping with their dignified, cloistered vocation. Dr. Leavis's wrath is the more comical because, unlike Bentley and Housman, he abstains from all levity or wit. His noble indignation escapes through pursed lips. Even at his most discourteous he never ceases to be prim.

It may be necessary to explain that, in several books, and in a magazine called *Scrutiny*, Dr. Leavis has expounded his theories of criticism, which he takes to be a science rather than an art. This, I believe, is a delusion, and not one from which we can expect life-enhancing results. Dr. Leavis treats literature as a cadaver in a post-mortem. But his mind, if narrow, is extremely acute; and he can be enlightening about the select authors whom he admires. His study of Swift as an ironist is excellent.

The title of his new book is taken from a passage in Mr. Eliot:

'The critic, one would suppose, if he is to justify his existence, should endeavour to discipline his personal prejudices and cranks—to which we are all subject—and compose his differences with as many of his fellows as possible in the common pursuit of true judgement.'

Dr. Leavis seems to achieve the exact contrary of this ideal. His book on the English novel could hardly have been more cranky; and now, so far from composing any old differences, he picks a number of new quarrels. Keynes, Bertrand Russell, G. M.

Trevelyan, Maurice Bowra and John Hayward are among the miscreants about whom he feels it his duty to be supercilious. Was it not Shakespeare who spoke of 'folly—doctor-like—controlling skill'?

Today the Doctor's displeasure extends even to Mr. Eliot. He wrote a book about him in 1932, acting—he seems to think—as the bold solitary champion of a neglected untouchable. In fact, Mr. Eliot had won rapid recognition many years earlier, in particular from the Bloomsbury group of whom Dr. Leavis is so contemptuous. Virginia Woolf, speaking in Cambridge in 1924, took it for granted that her audience was aware of Mr. Eliot's importance.

To discriminate is the first duty of the critic, even though he be accused of hedging; and Dr. Leavis is right to point out what he takes to be the weaknesses either in Mr. Eliot's later prose or in the poetry of past ages.

My complaint is that he suffers from a bias against enjoyment. He quotes, apparently without disapproval, a remark by Hopkins: 'I disapprove of damfooling people. I think it is wrong, narrows the mind, and, like "parvifying glass" makes us see things smaller than the natural size.' Yet this is his own regular practice. Milton, Shelley, Tennyson, Arnold, Thackeray and Dickens are among the authors he has sought to belittle. Living scholars and critics he seldom mentions without scorn. He might be speaking not sarcastically but in self-defence when he declares: 'It is pleasant to believe that an unusual capacity for egotistic animus means unusual distinction of intellect.'

All this can be relished as a whimsical eccentricity. Dr. Leavis, however, wields wide influence upon teachers in English schools and American universities. This vogue, which makes his sourness less comprehensible, seems to me alarming. Pharisaic rigour is dangerous to the young. They ought not to be discouraged from finding more pleasure than Dr. Leavis can in the diversity of our literature.

Aggressive characters usually are persuaded that they are the victims of persecution, and Dr. Leavis complains repeatedly of being misrepresented. If I have done this, let him blame my stupidity. I cannot pretend always to unravel his meaning. Let me quote one specimen of his style:

'It is the sense, perhaps it may be said, a perception of the need to cultivate which made Dr. I. A. Richards, in the book in which he speculates about a future in which we shall "have learned enough about our minds to do with them what we will" and "the question 'What sort of mind shall I choose to be?' would turn into an experimental matter" (*Practical Criticism*, p. 347), invent his "ritual for heightening sincerity" (*ibid*, p. 290) —that invention the crudities of which Mr. Eliot is, if not excessively, perhaps unnecessarily severe upon in *The Use of Poetry and the Use of Criticism*.'

Could such a sentence be published by a good critic, or indeed by anyone with a feeling for the English language?

Landscape

Very few if any of the most prominent artists anywhere, except in this blessed isle, now display any interest in landscape, or for that matter in portraiture or the nude. How regrettable, and how astonishing! All the supreme painters from Van Eyck and Piero della Francesca to Matisse and Bonnard have found inspiration in one of those subjects, and a great many in all three. The current neglect of portraiture and the nude hardly can be blamed on loss of interest in human personality or in love-making; and the neglect of landscape, we must hope, does not betray blindness to the beauty of Nature.

The word 'natural' (often misapplied) has two principal and contrasted meanings. In one sense everything in the universe is natural, Westminster Abbey no less than ant-hills, a performance of *Carmen* no less than bird-song. We need for our happiness to feel ourselves a part of Nature, as Wordsworth did, although few of us can share his belief that its workings are moral. We can trace moreover in Nature the origins of our own impulses and emotions. Flowers have bright petals, because these attract the insects on which their fertility depends; birds have bright plumage, because this attracts their mates; and palaeolithic Man presumably evolved the ability to paint, because he believed this to be a magic that would help him as a hunter.

Man, however, has placed himself in a different class from all other creatures on earth by his imagination, foresight, strength of reasoning and moral sense. We can thus usefully employ the word 'natural' to distinguish everything else from human artefacts. Until modern times even philosophers, I think, treated beauty as a quality to be found in objects belonging to both those categories. Now they usually declare that the pleasure of looking at art is absolutely distinct from the pleasure of looking at mountains, plants and animals. That seems to me dubious. Do not our notions of visible beauty originate in the horizontal symmetry and vertical asymmetry of our own bodies?

In any case we certainly find some of these natural objects more beautiful than others; and I cannot help believing that the spectacle of a peacock bay, an apple tree in blossom or an antelope gives us the same sort of delight as a painting of it. On the other hand beautiful paintings can be made even of a disgustingly mutilated corpse or of Oxford Street. When Constable declared that never in his life had he seen an ugly thing, I fancy that what he meant was not 'ugly' but 'unpaintable'—or did he detect beauty in the London slums?

Now for a glance at the history of landscape painting. Small children adore flowers and individual trees (which their eyes can identify), but seldom, I believe, take in distant scenery, until they are at least seven.

Interest in pure landscape developed similarly late in the history of art—among the Chinese of the tenth century A.D. The ancient Greeks and Romans seem to have depicted hills merely as backcloths; but from the fourteenth century onwards we find in the figure paintings of the Sienese, the Flemings and the Florentines delicious, lovingly-observed landscapes. These attained a further importance and beauty in Venice with Bellini, Giorgione and Titian. The seventeenth century brought the idealised landscapes of Poussin and Claude (never, I believe, without a figure, except in drawings); and almost simultaneously the pure landscape was invented in the Low Countries. The best account I know of all this is *Landscape into Art* by Kenneth Clark, whom I hardly dare mention: he is now in danger of being ostracised, like Aristides, because his countrymen are tired of hearing about his virtues.

Many of us love pictures in which we can go for a walk, past trees and cattle and perhaps a farm to the shores of a lake or the sea. It is chiefly painters, occasionally also poets, who have guided us to the enjoyment of scenery. This is proved by the word 'picturesque' which we took over from Italian early in the eighteenth century—at the time when part of a Wiltshire valley called Stourhead was shaped to imitate a Claude painting, with an artificial lake and temples above it in the classical style, a process widely followed later.

We must remember also that (apart from seas, moors, mountains and some downs) English landscapes owe their present appearance to rearrangement by Man, the woods, the Thames, the fields, the hedges (now alas vanishing) as well as the parks, gardens and buildings, few of these attractive, unless put up before 1850. The decadence of architecture and the hideousness of cities now intensify our love for the countryside and our longing for occasional solitude.

The Victorian Philistines (1945)

According to George Otto Trevelyan, the nephew and biographer of Macaulay, 'History and literature cannot be fully comprehended, still less fully enjoyed, except in connection with one another . . . those who read or expound literature should be soaked in history.' Let me add that the stronger the contrast between a man and his background, the more clearly we should be able to distinguish both his individual shape and the general character of his environment. Karl Marx, and independently of him Hippolyte Taine, have exaggerated, I believe, the extent to which art is a product of circumstances climatic, economic, and political. Writers, artists of any sort, are interesting chiefly in so far as they are different from, and superior to, their contemporaries. The essential fact about Giotto and Shakespeare is not that circumstances encouraged one to paint religious subjects rather than portraits, and the other to write plays rather than psychological novels; but that each brought to his labours extraordinary personal genius. Marx, Taine, and their followers do nothing, so far as I can discover, to explain what is the chief concern of the critic—the superiority of Giotto and Shakespeare to the other artists who were the product of the same environment.

To form an image of our mid-Eighteenth Century one must consider Gainsborough and Adam and Arne, reconcile the so various evidence of Bishop Butler and Hume, Horace Walpole and Dr. Johnson, Sterne and Smollett. How conjectural, unless we are great scholars, must be our conclusions! Yet we know—the oldest among us—something of the Victorian Age from direct experience. As early as the Eighties Victorianism was in decline, yet I come from a home that remained in many ways Victorian. Samuel Butler and Wilde had not penetrated to it, nor even Pater and Meredith. The authors held up to my infant admiration were

Macaulay and Dickens and Tennyson. On Sundays I was taken to Church by grown-ups wearing tall hats—this was in the country; and, not in my own home indeed, but in houses where I stayed, there were family prayers. I can still see the bottoms of kneeling housemaids in their caps, aprons and print dresses.

When we look back upon the Victorian Age it is outlined for us by the stature of competing statesmen and fecund authors. The policies and themes of these great personages, however, were not planned and constructed without some thought of accommodating the public. To understand them we need to know something of their audience. Large masses of the reading public were little influenced by some of the writers we think most eminent. John Bright's *Diaries*, for instance, an enormous volume, contain no reference to Rossetti, Ruskin, FitzGerald, Matthew Arnold or Pater: and Carlyle is mentioned only as having refused a baronetcy. I want to discuss here not the Victorian of genuis but the common Victorian, not Carlyle or Matthew Arnold but gigmanity and the Philistines. I shall emphasize, in fact, the dingier features of a dazzling Age.

We can immediately recognise a building or a picture as Victorian. Is it very much more difficult to recognise an action or a sentiment? Compare Mr. Gladstone with Chatham, Tennyson with Goldsmith, Macaulay with Gibbon, Dickens with Fielding, Herbert Spencer with Hume, Bishop Wilberforce with Archbishop Secker, Queen Victoria herself with her uncles: the distinctions are glaring.

What had intervened? Two events in particular, I suggest. A progress in science; and, separate from this, a change in feeling that had excited men—alarmingly in the form of the French Revolution, delightfully in the form of Romanticism. The progress of applied science which multiplied production and population enlarged the wealth and influence of the middle classes. I think that the year 1830 makes a convenient date for the establishment of Victorianism. In that year George IV ended his dandified and dissolute life; a bourgeois monarchy was established in France; and Lord Grey introduced the Reform Bill that was to transfer much of their power from the nobility to a section of the middle classes. (We may note too the publication in 1830 of Sir Charles Lyell's ominous *Principles of Geology*.) The Puritans, triumphant in 1647, defeated in 1660, and not restored in 1688, returned in triumph with the great Reform Bill.

Their predominance coincided with the development of theories that later sapped the foundations of their ethos. The science that had given them their factories and their trade proceeded to make their Protestantism untenable. But from 1830 for some fifty years the puritanism of the middle classes dominated England.

Convenient as it is to generalise about an Age and to define roughly its extent, one must never forget that at any given date several generations overlap, each with its prevailing tastes. Robert Bridges was an undergraduate while Landor was still alive; FitzGerald could have read the early writings of Bernard Shaw; Palmerston, the embodiment of pre-Victorian profligacy, outlived the Prince Consort. And if a population can be divided as it were horizontally into different generations, so it can be divided vertically into different classes, each again with characteristic tastes.

Victorian Puritanism sought to discipline the proletariat; it succeeded in imposing upon the Nobility the mask, and often the reality, of its own favourite virtues. It permeated the Church of England, and infiltrated the English provinces of the Church of Rome, turning a Cardinal into a missionary teetotaller. It tyrannised even over the champions of infidelity: a George Eliot and a Leslie Stephen were sternly intent upon showing that puritan ethics were valid quite independently of puritan faith. The vigour with which public opinion could impose accepted standards was beyond anything with which we are familiar. Significantly the most usual term of disapproval—the contrary of 'nice'—was the adjective 'peculiar'. And this was applied to the most innocent deviation from conventional behaviour or opinion.

The puritanism of the English middle classes goes back at least as far as the sixteenth century, I suspect farther. It is not an unworldly asceticism such as has distinguished saints since the Primitive Church. It is an asceticism that aims at satisfying Mammon as well as God. It perpetuates the belief, usual among backward peoples, that precision in religious observances brings mundane prosperity. This belief was dear to the early Hebrews; and Protestants seized on it with delight when the Reformation made the Old Testament available in the vernacular. 'I have been young, and now am old: and yet never saw I the righteous forsaken, nor his seed begging bread.' Dr. Tawney and Weber have illustrated the kinship between piety and capitalism among the seventeenth century Protestants, such as Dryden's Shimei who

> 'Did wisely from Expensive Sins abstain
> And never broke the Sabbath, but for Gain.'

John Wesley, the great religious reformer of the Eighteenth century, continued the tradition, giving it new life. Not only did he condemn 'innocent songs or talking in a gay diverting manner'; not only did he forbid recreation even to children—'He who plays as a boy will play when he is a man', but, when a playhouse was planned in Bristol, Wesley argued that a theatre was 'peculiarly hurtful to a trading city, giving a wrong turn to youth especially, gay, trifling and directly opposite to the spirit of close application'. This was the train of thought that dominated the Victorian middle class; and Hannah More provides one of several links between Wesley and Samuel Smiles.

Honesty, industry, thrift, chastity and sobriety—these qualities were pleasing to Jehovah; and also they made for affluence and power. This the Victorians believed from their own experience. They were not mistaken. Wine, gambling and loose women not only cost much money but divert much energy from the proper business of man, which is to make money. (The enjoyment of the arts, one may note, often entails the same disadvantages.) When the Victorians said a man was 'doing well', they meant that he was growing richer. Samuel Smiles was the chief lay missionary for these salutary truths. 'The man', as he says, 'who spends ninepence a day in liquor squanders in fifty years nearly £2,000'. Again, 'To be thriftless is . . . to deprive one of all manly spirit and value'. And here is a snatch from a popular song by one A. Boyle:

> Right men are wanted high stations to fill!
> Men of good manners, of wisdom and skill.
> Drunkards can never attain to the prize!
> We *will* be teetotal for we all want to rise.

Another lively instance of the Victorian nexus between religion and money is provided by a Mr. Potto Birn. He allotted, we are told, his subscriptions to different missionary societies in proportion to their achievements. His method was to divide the incurred expenses by the number of reported converts.

This puritanism, this money-minded or *arriviste* asceticism, was the core of what Matthew Arnold described as Philistinism. Carlyle and Ruskin were also continually attacking the vulgarity and materialism of these Philistines. And their Philistinism showed at its most fervent among the Dissenters.

To understand the Victorians, I believe, one must study Nonconformity. This is not a pleasing task. There are many admirably written books by and about the Tractarians, latitudinarians, Catholics, and agnostics of the Victorian Age; but it is difficult to find a good book by any devout Dissenter of the period except Mrs. Gaskell. This is the more odd, because many of them were highly cultivated. Ruskin and Browning came from Nonconformist homes. Nor are the Victorian Evangelicals of the Church of England much better represented. Their parents had enjoyed their time of just glory at Cambridge and Clapham; but in the generation after Simeon and William Wilberforce and Clarkson and Zachary Macaulay, the only Evangelical of great eminence was Lord Shaftesbury. Despite their poor showing of talent the Nonconformists and Evangelicals exercised immense influence. 'In the long run,' Palmerston remarked, 'English politics will follow the consciences of the Dissenters.' Their influence upon politics was usually good, I think; but upon taste it was deplorable.

One must make some rough distinction between the principal sects. The Unitarians (and some Congregationalists and Quakers) were intellectually and socially superior to the other Nonconformists. They were not Sabbatarians, and opposed the persecution of atheists. I fancy their Puritanism was very mild; and in Mrs. Gaskell they produced an admirable writer. The Wesleyans continued for a long while to think of themselves not as Dissenters but as peculiarly enlightened members of the Church of England. Their services, as Wesley had ordained, were timed not to clash with the Anglican services; and many of them retained their pews in Anglican churches, long after they had abandoned the high sacramental beliefs of their founder, beliefs that they did their utmost to conceal. (The inscription written by Wesley to commemorate his mother's life was removed because of the sacramental doctrines it affirmed.) Wesleyans were often prosperous, and until the death in 1858 of their great dictator, Jabez Bunting, apt to be Tories. In habits of mind they differed little from the other Puritan sects. The English Presbyterians were not very important: in the eighteenth century most of their

Evangelicals now are 44 usually prosperous (197

churches had become Unitarian. A squalid attempt in 1844 to take these churches from the Unitarians excited one of Macaulay's finest speeches. In it he talked of 'that prescriptive right of talking nonsense which gentlemen who stand on the platform of Exeter Hall are undoubtedly entitled to claim'. (Exeter Hall was the secular meeting-place of the Evangelicals.) The Baptists and some sorts of Methodist were the most intolerant and the most intolerable of the sects; but we must not forget the Plymouth Brethren, a sect distinguished by the extremity of its puritanism, by the mysterious charm it exercised upon persons of title, and by its unsurpassed genius for sub-dividing itself into even smaller subsects devoted to the pleasures of internecine warfare. A quotation from the autobiography of John Addington Symonds provides a vivid picture of Plymouth Brethren about 1850.

'And what company my grandmother kept! It was a motley crew of preachers and missionaries, tradesmen and cripples— the women attired in rusty bombazine and drab gingham— the men attired in greasy black suits, with dingy white neckties, all gifted with a sanctimonious sniffle, all blessed by nature with shiny foreheads and clammy hands, all avid for buttered toast and muffins, all fawning on the well-connected gentle- women, whose wealth, though moderate, possessed con- siderable attractions, and was freely drawn upon.'

The hatred of the Dissenters for the Establishment was second only to their hatred of what they called pleasure—that is to say the sorts of pleasure they had no mind to. Often, it is to be feared, they mistook their social envy for moral indignation. A trait that was always to characterize Puritanism appears already in the Primer of Edward VI: 'Lord,' one of its petitions goes, 'Lord, grant me to tell my neighbours their faults meekly, without dissimulation.' In the Victorian Age the meekness was not apparent, but in other respects the prayer did not go unanswered.

No other religion encourages self-complacency so much as Calvinism. A favourite text with the Calvinists, because it can be used to attack the Catholic belief in good works, is Isaiah's 'All our righteousness is filthy rags.' Yet while the Puritans held that their righteousness did nothing to save them, they none the less remained enviably certain that they were righteous. They knew that they were predestined to salvation, the elect of God. 'If I might ask one thing of God,' a great Baptist preacher declared, 'if it were not sinful to ask such a thing, methinks I would ask "Let me die now, that I may go and be without fault before Thy throne"': Spurgeon's self-satisfaction was not exceptional. The Dissenters looked with contempt upon the unregenerate. What would rank, what would education, count at the Judgment Seat? When Spurgeon as a very young man applied for the post of minister in a Baptist chapel in Cambridge, he confessed the defects of his education. 'If you came from college,' the deacons said to him, 'If you came from college, you would not have much savour or unction.' Such contempt for learning brings us again near the heart of that philistinism which Matthew Arnold never wearied of denouncing.

The Dissenters—make no mistake about it—found great pleasure in their way of life. The trouble was that they persistently sought to impose their own taboos upon their less favoured countrymen. Not only were the unregenerate doomed to Hell fire, but they must not be allowed to enjoy themselves in the meanwhile. On a Sunday afternoon there must be no band for them to listen to in a park, nor must any museum open its gates to them. Books no less than behaviour excited the vigilance of the Nonconformists; and as owners of bookstalls and circulating libraries two of them, W. H. Smith and Mudie, were well placed to exercise an officious censorship. Some novels were admitted by the less rigorous, but dancing was forbidden, and the theatre was a gateway to Hell. Cards were the devil's playthings, and billiards equally damnable, though bagatelle was harmless. And some of the rigid teetotallers—so a friend brought up in a Dissenting home assures me—upheld a conviction that port must not be accounted alcoholic.

Self-complacency is ineradicable, and probably essential to human happiness. Good breeding however demands that it should as far as possible be concealed. The Philistines were wonderfully ready to lay down the law on matters of which they knew little. On a visit to Rome in 1857 John Bright wrote:

'I am not able to feel the enthusiasm which some men feel, or affect to feel, for the 'crack' pieces of sculpture, if one may use a familiar or slang word. Our notions of beauty are associated with a draped form, and with a countenance full of benignant and intellectual expression, and, I suspect, if the

46

truth were acknowledged, a figure like the Modesty or the Minerva communicates generally more of what is pleasing to the mind than any of the more famous nude figures which are to be seen in the Italian Galleries.'

This eminent man, because he had not trained himself to appreciate the Fine Arts, presumed that those who had done so were affecting emotions they did not possess.

'Cant, pharisaism, snobbishness, love of money and the pride of stupidity'—these, in the opinions of an Oxford critic, York Powell, were the national sins of Victorian England. He might have added greed and idolatry of work. The puritans who sought to prevent others from even temperate drinking were apt to take pride in the lavishness of their own repasts. I do not think it is fanciful to see a connection between the strain thus put upon their livers and the bile with which they inveighed against other forms of self-indulgence. *I agree*

And then there is the constant worship of work for work's sake or for work as a prophylactic against pleasure. The ant and the busy bee were held up as examples to children, and schoolrooms resounded with the old hymn:

> 'For Satan finds some mischief still
> For idle hands to do.'

Even Leslie Stephen committed himself to the following pronouncement: 'To recommend contemplation in preference to action is like preferring sleeping to waking.'

If the Dissenters felt morally superior to supporters of the Establishment, these latter were no less conscious of their social superiority. It would be a mistake to suppose that class distinctions were more marked in the Victorian Age than in its predecessors; but snobbery was more noticeable, because the occasional rise of a newly rich man had developed into an ugly rush. On this matter Thackeray has said all, and more than all, that needs saying. Even in many Nonconformist chapels specially comfortable pews were reserved for the prosperous. Let me quote also an Anglican to show how snobbery was involved in religion:

'Depend upon it, association has a great power, and those passages in the Bible which bring children most clearly the image of their mother, are those which, in after life, are loved and valued most.

And surely those childish memories owe *something* of their charm to the recollection of the quiet, well-modulated reading, the clear, refined enunciation, the repose of the attitude in the sofa or chair, the white hand that held the book, with, it may be, the flashing of the diamond ring in the light, as the fingers turned the pages!'

These words, from Florence Montgomery's popular novel *Misunderstood* could not, I think, have been written in either the Eighteenth century or the Twentieth.

I agree

If we compare the great Victorian novelists either with their English predecessors or with their French contemporaries, we must be struck by their prudery. The public, and almost all the critics, had decided that every book must be suitable to the young person. The middle class moreover was evolving a new feminine ideal. In the eighteenth century women were trained in the upper class to be agreeable, in the middle class to be useful. Now not agreeableness or usefulness but a subservient and ostentatious innocence became the ideal. The first Victorian heroine, I think, made her bow as early as 1814, Fanny Price in Jane Austen's *Mansfield Park*, though she was at least fairly useful. Thackeray's Amelia, Dickens's Dora, took up the wondrous tale. Modesty became a fetish. As late as 1877 a gifted novelist urged the following advice.

Exposure of the face is one of the great tendencies of the time; and although it is not exactly indelicate in itself, yet the bold confronting of notice that is involved in going out with a totally unprotected countenance, thrown into prominence by the headdress, cannot be modest in itself; nor does a veil coming close over the nose materially alter the matter.

This admonition came from a woman (Charlotte M. Yonge). I suppose that today nothing in the Victorian Age is more mysterious than its prudery. The student finds it everywhere. A little girl, on a long train journey with her father, was we are told 'of course' unable to tell him of a natural need—and in consequence became seriously ill for months. In order to understand the so pervasive and irrational inhibitions about sex, we may examine the current attitude to differences of class. Many persons shy at any reference to these, prefer to pretend they do

48

unprivileged better word · see Page 11

not exist. The Americans have invented an elegant euphemism
for what used to be called the lower classes. They call them 'the
under-privileged'. But do not most of us feel impelled to use
similar evasions when we have to indicate that somebody is of a
higher or lower class than ourselves? The whole subject has
become too painful—we take refuge in references to educational
or economic differences because we are too embarrassed to
mention class differences. In just the same way the Victorians were
embarrassed by sex.

" 'Background' is usual now

Let it not be supposed that, because they were prudish, they
were also pure. Though the nobility became more careful of
decorum, high living and idleness produced their usual results.
Until 1857 divorce was a luxury open only to the very rich, and
persons of rank indulged in it often. A special Act of Parliament
was necessary, which cost at least £1,000. A Victorian told me a
story to show that even Mr. Gladstone was not so shockable as
might be supposed. At the time of the Parnell divorce case he is
said to have remarked: 'I have known thirteen Prime Ministers,
and all but three were adulterers.' Evidently some of these were
survivors from Regency times, Wellington, Melbourne, Grey,
Palmerston, Lord John Russell and Disraeli. But it must be
remembered that the great Lord Hartington, who was not born
till 1833, entertained for years an unconcealed liaison with the
wife of a Duke, and she seems to have been universally received.
The women of the middle class were much more particular. Yet
foreign visitors were amazed at the extent and openness of
prostitution. There were countless houses of ill fame, and no
respectable woman could venture on foot in the streets between
Piccadilly and the Strand. What is particularly horrible, there
was more juvenile prostitution in London than in any continental
city. This is the evidence of an official from Scotland Yard:
children 'without number', he said, aged 16, 15 and 14. That
prudery and prostitution should thus have flourished side by side
is not, I think, altogether an accident. Public opinion was supported by eminent medical authorities in the belief that the great
majority of women were entirely frigid. The severe virtue of the
Victorian girl and wife drove men to meretricious beds. I cannot
help finding, moreover, a sinister connection between the childlike
heroines beloved of the Victorian novel-reader and the unhappy
little girls who crowded the pavements of the Haymarket. The
Victorian male, it seems, was so attracted by the notion of

49

innocence that he preferred to purchase the embraces of the barely nubile.

The Victorian woman did not expect her menfolk to attain the standard they imposed on her. I think Lady Fawn in *The Eustace Diamonds* can be taken as fairly characteristic: 'Woman-like, she regarded the man as being so much more important than the woman.' She had 'a very bad opinion of men in particular' which 'sprang from the high idea she entertained of men in general.' 'A man,' she concluded, 'was so important that he could not be expected to act at all times with truth and sincerity.' The power of the paterfamilias was prodigious. Until the Married Woman's Property Act of 1882 he automatically controlled any fortune his wife might possess; and his children were expected to offer entire submission in return for the privilege of life that he had conferred upon them. The language used by Victorian fathers often suggests that begetting is a painful act. It was assumed by all, except a few cranks like John Stuart Mill and Mrs. Browning, that men and women should be as different from one another as possible. Let us listen to Aurora Leigh's aunt:

> She owned
> She liked a woman to be womanly,
> And English women, she thanked God and sighed,
> (Some people always sigh in thanking God,)
> Were models to the universe.

An appearance of helplessness was thought womanly, so were an absence of appetite and a disinclination for exercise. I do not think that it was only unskilled doctoring that made the 'confirmed invalid' so common a Victorian type. Elizabeth Barrett was a drug addict who for years never left her bedroom except for an occasional drive. Its windows were never opened, could not be—for ivy grew across them; and to survive she must have enjoyed an exceptionally robust constitution. Lady Tennyson spent most of her life on a sofa, diverting attention from the Laureate; and of course everyone else had to fetch and carry. An exquisite instance of maternal methods of tyranny occurs in the life of a pioneer doctor, Sophia Jex-Blake. 'You behaved,' her mother wrote to her, 'so ill that I doubt if I could have borne it another day without being laid on a bed of sickness, and I might never have recovered.' Again, when women first started to study medicine, the male students rioted against such unwomanly ambitions. Decency forbade the sexes to be mixed, when listening to lectures on anatomy; yet the men—such is the tyranny of custom—did not object to male doctors' treating their wives and daughters. *(The nurses in my school preferred a male doctor! 1925)*

No less conspicuous is the favour with which the Victorians regarded the epithet 'manly'. ('Wholesome' is another favourite Victorian word. They applied it to the most unappetizing books and pictures, very much as their nursemaids used to recommend bread-and-milk, or semolina pudding.) 'Manly' is always cropping up. Leslie Stephen's criterion of literary merit, for instance, was that a book should make us 'recognise more plainly than we are apt to do the surpassing value of manliness, honesty and pure domestic affection.' But while women managed to be womanly, the men do not strike me as having been at all manly. I am speaking of the middle classes. The nobility and the country gentry hunted and shot, around what Matthew Arnold called 'the great outposts of the Barbarians'; but the Philistines led a very cosseted existence. Even a war, the Crimean War, for instance, involved only the upper, the professional and the lower classes. The Victorian Age was incomparably secure—a placid interval between the reigns of the highwayman and the motor-car. Though cholera and typhus still recurred in the slums, and other epidemics killed many children (Archbishop Tait, when Dean of Carlisle, lost five young daughters in a month from scarlet fever), hygiene had banished smallpox and vastly reduced the death-rate of the comfortably-off adults. We who even in peace-time are familiar with the quotidian possibility of sudden death can hardly realise how rare was then such an occurence. *Has the motor-car led to increase in Coronaries? I think so.*

The novelists were indeed distraught by the difficulty of getting rid of characters whose survival made a happy ending impossible. Sometimes 'a putrid fever' could be used, but more often they devised boating accidents, poaching affrays, houses on fire, runaway horses and—invaluable recourse—the mill-dam. On one occasion Dickens was reduced to killing off an unwanted character by what he called 'spontaneous combustion'. The safety of life made for an unpleasing muffishness. What were called 'muffetees' enjoyed great popularity—knitted cuffs worn to defend the wrists; respirators also were in great demand—black pads held over the mouth by elastic. Even in hot weather, men wore clothes that were dark and thick; nor would they venture into a garden even for a few minutes without a hat. One gentleman recorded that he had not

51

paused to put on a hat when his child in the garden was in danger.

These womenly women and not so manly men formed jealously-guarded family groups. Cousins and sisters-in-law played an important part, but among outsiders only childhood friends were called by their Christian names.

A leading Victorian characteristic was violence of emotion, and notably violence of grief. The Queen herself was morbid in her response to bereavement, her preoccupation with what she called 'the dear remains', the positive gusto with which she abandoned herself to the rites of mourning. Indeed her subjects in general were, I believe, much more tearful and tender than we are. They were always talking in hushed voices. Doubtless two wars have forced us to adopt the odious habit of stoicism; doubtless too the Victorians were more often tempted than we are by hypocrisy. Yet I fancy that the English were genuinely more emotional in those days, as indeed they had been in earlier ages. The intellectuals who called for 'plain living and high thinking' had no need to add 'strong feeling'. Men were no more proud to be 'hard-boiled' than they were ashamed to be 'high-brow'. In part this was a relic of the preceding Age of Sensibility, and of the succeeding Romantic Movement, in part perhaps a product of security. This vehemence of feeling—perhaps one reason why Victorian literature is so noticeably superior to our own—was conspicuous in the realm of belief as well as in the domestic affections. The Victorians were always being harried by misgivings. An old story describes a visitor to a vicarage. 'And is it true that your dear Father has been offered a bishopric?' 'Yes, Papa is in his study praying for guidance, and Mamma is upstairs packing.' The prayers were not insincere, but excitement helped to blind men to their own deep motives. The passion imported into what we may consider trivial controversies was superlative. The minutiae of ecclesiastical ritual excited lifelong estrangements. A clergyman who lit the candles on his altar exposed himself to persecution. Bishops felt that death was preferable to the Deceased Wife's Sister Bill; yet all that this proposed was to legalise marriages that were licit in every other European country, where they were accepted alike by Catholic and Protestant theologians. Churchmen and dissenters decided that children must have no education rather than allow their rivals to increase their control of it. John Bright, for instance, voted against providing schools for children working in mills.

If the religious were bigoted, the sceptical were in deep mourning for their lost faith. Tennyson was uneasy, Clough quite miserable.

> We are most hopeless, who had once most hope,
> And most beliefless, that had once believed.

When geologists, biologists and textual critics adduced evidence that contradicted the literal truth of the Scriptures, the Victorians were dumbfounded. This seems very odd: we might suppose that Hume, Voltaire and Gibbon had never existed. The explanation, I suppose, is that the arguments of these men seemed shallow because they were expressed with wit, nay even with levity. The Victorians could be distressed only by writers like Strauss and Mill who were as solemn as themselves. Furthermore Darwin and the nineteenth century scientists were more subversive than the eighteenth century *philosophes*: not content to question miracles, they undermined the dignity of man. In Dr. Pusey's lectures on Daniel the Prophet, he reckoned that if the Flood had occurred at the time presumed by Ussher, the natural increase of the population would bring the world population to its actual estimated number. Instead of being created by Jehovah in B.C. 4004, six days after the creation of the world, Man was now exhibited as a late arrival, not to say an accident, cousin of the chimpanzee, second cousin of the crocodile. Nothing was fixed or permanent, the Earth was in flux and doomed to extinction. It is difficult for us to realise the shock that such novel conceptions inflicted even upon those who were not devout. The whole foundations of the universe seemed to be giving way. We are all familiar with the optimism of the early Victorians, Macaulay is the prime instance. The later Victorians changed their tune.

P.S. A recent book, *Everywhere Spoken Against*, by Valentine Cunningham, includes a lot of unfamiliar facts about the Victorian Dissenters and the pictures of them given by the leading novelists of the period from Thackeray to Hardy. When they portrayed Nonconformists, all of them except George Eliot and Mrs. Gaskell, we are told, were calumnious. So even was Hale White, a secondary author: he was a Congregationalist who knew his subject intimately, but ceased to attend chapel in his twenties. Possibly these novelists have coloured the views expressed in my essay.

C

Tennyson

We long have needed a new collected Tennyson including unpublished poems, revisions he made in the text and fuller annotation, to throw new light on the dating of the poems and the circumstances in which they were written. This is what Christopher Ricks now offers us. He prints them moreover in the order of their composition, so that for the first time we can follow the poet's development. The scholarship is tactful as well as thorough, precise and ingenious.

Tennyson's feelings were violent, too much so indeed in some of his work. He also denounced the purely aesthetic approach to literature. Yet study of this book confirms an old opinion of mine: he is above all an artist with a passion for beauty and for the musical language in which he reveals that passion—akin therefore to Theocritus, Virgil and Keats. He is at his best in lyrics, elegies, pictorial descriptions of Nature or the past, and (more surprisingly) in occasional verses addressed to his friends.

His concern with religion, morals and politics was strong, however, even in his twenties; and, alas, in the second half of his life (when, like most poets, he weakened in his inspiration) he grew increasingly didactic. Despite a sturdy sense of humour, his simplicity of heart allowed him to write sentimental or melodramatic monologues, which now seem ludicrous. The cleverest of our modern poets (W. H. Auden) has called him stupid—a verdict that would have staggered the many intellectuals who valued his friendship. The truth, I think, is that his brain was responsive and prehensile rather than penetrating or dominant.

This edition forms a complement to the richly detailed Life of the Laureate by Sir Charles Tennyson, his surviving grandson. Little Alfred began as the most precocious of children. At six he knew by heart the Latin of all the Horace Odes. At fourteen he wrote a comedy in Jacobean blank verse (*The Devil and the Lady*). The dazzling language makes it the most sustained achievement known to me by so young an author in any language.

A melancholiac, like his brothers and his tippling father, he took everything to heart, and was always over-sensitive. Professor Ricks proves that 'The Two Voices' (a superb poem of despair) was written before the event that has been thought its source—the death of Arthur Hallam.

We are also given a suppressed stanza from *In Memoriam* describing the poet and this adored friend at Cambridge together:

> They daily drank each other's breath
> With breast to breast in early years,
> They met with passion and with tears,
> Their every parting was a death.

This is likely to be misunderstood today; but after Hallam's death he wrote also: 'God will take him pure and good from his mother's lessons. Surely it would be better for him than to grow up such as I am.' Tennyson's feeling of guilt was probably due to religious doubt; and I think that his platonic love for Hallam would not have been so ardent, if he had been loose-living like other young men. Though he seems to have been fond of kissing, we don't know if he ever went further with anyone, except the wife he married when he was forty.

All poets have borrowed from their predecessors, and Tennyson more frequently than any other, from sources more numerous and more varied: he read omnivorously in five or six languages. Churton Collins, a critic who keenly admired him in the 1880s, showed how many of his phrases were echoes, and decided that he was 'not so much a poet of original genius as one whose mastery lay in assimilative skill and tireless artistry.' Tennyson therefore described him as 'a louse in the locks of literature'. The critic was mistaken about some of his borrowings, but on the whole I agree with his judgement. Christopher Ricks has unearthed further such parallels, and reveals also how often he borrowed from himself, putting to happier uses lines he had discarded from previous poems.

This volume is chiefly important, however, for its presentation of work by the poet that has remained unpublished—poems, fragments and variant readings from manuscripts and early editions. Trinity College, Cambridge, has refused (against the wishes of the present Lord Tennyson and Sir Charles) to allow any quotation from the papers given to it by the poet's eldest son. He made his veto perpetual; but it makes a definitive edition impossible and is sure to be removed before long.

The omissions and variants I have noted would fill two columns, and I can give a few examples. Here is part of a surprising industrial landscape omitted from *The Princess*:

> We crost into a land where mile-high towers
> Puff't out a night of smoke that drowsed the sun;
> Huge pistons rose and fell, and everywhere
> We heard the clank of chains, the creak of cranes.

Other omissions were wise, such as the lines from *Happy* (a poem bad enough even as printed): 'I never glanced at her full bust but wished myself the snake/ That bit the harlot bosom of that heathen by the Nile.' And almost all the verbal revisions are improvements. Tennyson was prepared to learn from his 'irresponsible, indolent reviewers' when they hit the target; and what sometimes failed him was his taste, not his ear. In *Tithonus* he changed 'And after many summers dies the rose' to 'After many a summer dies the swan'—a far finer music.

Here is an instance of two borrowings followed by a revision. In Thomson's *Seasons* he found 'The mellow bullfinch answers from the grove,' and in James Hurdis (a later eighteenth-century poet I had never heard of) 'And ouzel fluting with melodious pipe.' Tennyson combined these lines into 'The mellow ouzel fluted and aloft . . .' and finally sent to the printers 'The mellow ouzel fluted in the elm'—the 'l' and 'm' repeated in the final word perfecting the harmony both of vowels and consonants.

Tennyson, enshrined during his later life as the sanest, most right-thinking of Victorian prophets, became unfashionable after his death for the same reason. Then fifty years ago Harold Nicolson revived interest in him with a book that anticipated modern views of his character and poetry; and in 1950 Sir Charles Tennyson (who in his nineties has been delighting B.B.C. listeners with his talk) had the good sense and courage to reveal facts about his grandfather previously suppressed, though we need them to understand his career.

* * * *

Today the whirligig of taste has brought even the architecture and *bric-à-brac* of his period into fashion; and Professor Ricks, after producing a superb edition of his poems, offers us a penetrating book about the relationship between these and his personality, together with a delicate study of his versification.

Until the age of forty the poet was the victim of distressing circumstances, and also of melancholia. His father at the age of twelve had been disinherited in favour of a younger brother and forced to become a clergyman without any vocation. His eleven children, envious of their scornful, unjustly rich relations, had a straitened bringing-up in the Somersby rectory, pleasant but isolated and overcrowded.

At seven Alfred was sent to a boarding school for four years of misery, and then came home to be tutored in Latin and Greek by his father, whose rage at his disinheritance was driving him to the bottle, and who gradually became violent to the verge of insanity. Four of the poet's brothers were deeply neurotic; a fifth went mad at nineteen, and was confined in an asylum till his death some sixty years later.

The poet himself endured four terms of wretched loneliness at Cambridge, due presumably to his grim, shy manners and hippy appearance—long hair, untidy clothes, dirty linen. Then he found admiring friends there in a group of earnest, ambitious young intellectuals, notably Arthur Hallam, and won the gold medal for a prize poem. Yet he went down without a degree and with considerable debts. Loss of faith combined with fears of blindness and of hereditary madness drove him to brood on suicide.

His consolation was passionate love for natural beauty, for literature, for the composing of poetry—and for Hallam. The correspondence between the two young men was carefully destroyed by their relations, but *In Memoriam* revealed a depth of attachment that was to embarrass the poet's elder son. We must remember how successfully romanticism had extolled intensity of feeling.

We, and also the Augustans, seem hard-hearted compared with the Victorians, who luxuriated in affection as well as in grief. (The letters written in youth to Clough by Matthew Arnold are to our eyes curiously fervent.) Tennyson's love for Hallam in my view, remained absolutely chaste: for one thing, would not the language of *In Memoriam* have otherwise been more guarded?

Since I leant to the same conclusion about Henry James, some readers may suspect me as a starry-eyed whitewasher. On the contrary, I believe bisexuality to be commoner than is usually supposed. Christopher Ricks, let me add, after careful consideration of the *pros* and *cons* seems to agree with me about Tennyson.

Certainly he was delighted about his sister's engagement to Hallam, whose death three years later revived his thoughts of suicide. Then, as if in search of a substitute for his dead friend, he quickly fell in love with pretty Rose Baring. After encouraging him for a year or two, she—or her parents—chose to wait for a rich suitor. Almost at once he transferred his heart to Emily Sellwood, but the engagement was broken off, owing either to his religious doubts or their lack of money.

His newly rich grandfather had meanwhile died, and his will disappointed the senior branch of his family. His heir decided he was descended from the Plantagenets, and adopted the pretentious name of Tennyson d'Eyncourt. We are now given for the first time part of a comical letter from one of his sons.

I am very glad that we have changed our name, as it gives us a good position . . . besides which it will in a great measure keep us clear of the Somersby family which are quite hogs.

The split between the senior and cadet branches had now become total. Presumably that did not bother Alfred, but on top of all the other shocks he lost the whole of his small capital in a rash investment; and his poems, deeply admired by his friends and by a growing number of illustrious authors, had aroused brutal mockery in almost all the reviewers. Nor indeed did this exceptionally precocious poet win the applause of the critics and the general reader until he published *In Memoriam* at the age of forty. In the same month he married his Emily.

Henceforward ever-growing fame and prosperity elevated him into a public personage, a status seldom helpful to a writer's art. Christopher Ricks believes that his wife's solicitude may have saved his sanity. Other experts have suggested that she tamed his genius; but then most poets reach their apogee when comparatively young. His finest work had been inspired by landscape, sardonic humour and most usually by morbid feelings of yearning, misery, bereavement or guilt. Now he often wrote dramatic, narrative or didactic poetry, for which he was not gifted. I wish that in later life he had given us translations of his beloved

Theocritus and Virgil, instead of *The Idylls of the King* and the long poems on subjects unearthed at his request by his family and friends.

Yet many of those included beautiful passages, nor did he ever cease writing beautiful short poems. Moreover he displayed his mastery in a new type of Horatian verse that I particularly admire, such as the lines addressed to Virgil, to his wife (*The Daisy*), and to such friends as F. D. Maurice, Lord Dufferin, Lear and FitzGerald. *Pace* Auden, he was far from stupid: a number of his most intellectual contemporaries delighted in his talk. A strain of naivety, however, allowed him to publish a lot of sad stuff in his youth and his old age. His forte was not reasoning but versification, in the variety of which he outdid all our other poets.

Professor Ricks helps us to understand his work better than before with comments that are often witty as well as subtle, so subtle occasionally that they pass above my head. He quotes a few of the rare 'jawbreakers' that were left unrevised as well as many well-chosen specimens of his felicity in diction and in metre—which some puritanical critics condemn as too ingenious. They are never too ingenious for me.

> With further looking on — the kiss
> The woven arms — seem but to be
> Weak symbols of the settled bliss
> The comfort I have found in thee.
> But that God bless thee, dear, who wrought
> Two spirits to one equal mind;
> With blessings beyond hope or thought,
> With blessings which no words can find.

? origin.

Froude

How Froude would despise us English of today! Since his death in 1894 we have steadily been growing more humane—and (except when galvanised by German assaults) more lethargic. Lack of enterprise seems no less conspicuous among our scholars than among our exporters. Hitherto the only Life of Froude has been Herbert Paul's book, published fifty-six years ago. Now at last we are given a biography making proper use of his papers, and the author is an American.

He writes clearly and correctly. My only complaint is that he approaches his subject as the most uncritical of hero-worshippers. 'Happily the efforts of Froude's enemies to question the historical accuracy of his work has come,' we are told, 'to naught.' I cannot believe that any expert on the Reformation would endorse this statement. Freeman's attacks upon him were extravagant: he was indefatigable in research, but careless about detail, and all his books are inaccurate. Much worse, he was so blinded by prejudice that without conscious dishonesty he would, in order to bolster his case, employ any argument, however illogical, and swallow any evidence, however untrustworthy.

We are here told also that 'events have justified most of his positions' in regard to the politics of his time. Froude despised the Irish and the Indians as congenitally incapable of self-government, deplored the emancipation of Negroes, loathed democracy and applauded despotism, so long as the despot was not a Catholic. One may wonder what events have justified these Hitler-like 'positions.' After all, the Germans didn't win the war, did they?

Froude wrote an autobiography that breaks off when he is thirty-eight. This document (which Herbert Paul was allowed to summarise but not to quote) is printed for the first time in Mr. Dunn's book, occupying much of its space and giving it signal importance. Of all our nineteenth-century historians apart from Macaulay, Froude was the most popular and remains the most readable. His vivid personality presents moreover an exciting enigma. The key to his behaviour and beliefs must be sought in his early experiences.

Having lost his kindly mother at the age of two, he was brought —or rather crushed—up by his father, a prosperous, spartan, rigid and cold-hearted Archdeacon. His sisters were taught to despise him, and he had from infancy to endure also the deliberate cruelty of his eldest brother, Hurrell, one of the most brilliant, provocative and silly of Tractarian clergymen.

Despite his bad health he was sent at eleven to live in College at Westminster—'a den of wild animals'—where for over three years he was half-starved and outrageously bullied. His breeches were set on fire to make him dance, and he was often woken from sleep by cigars' burning holes in his face. A boy who had read all Homer twice in Greek at the age of ten was thus reduced to a stupid, quivering lump. The worthy Archdeacon, deciding therefore that he was not only a dolt but a coward and a liar, flogged him in the presence of the approving Hurrell, and threatened to make him work in a tannery.

The beastliness of such a family and such a school would have turned most boys into sullen rebels. Froude began once again to read, and (his brother having luckily died) got into Oriel. Then his election to a Fellowship obliged him to take deacon's orders, after which he quickly discovered his disbelief in traditional Christianity, published a novel on the subject and was forced to resign his Fellowship.

The pattern of his beliefs seems to have been fixed by the mixture of love and hatred he felt for his family: if there had been only hatred, he might have been less wrong-headed. At first he reacted: his loathing for Catholicism may have sprung from Hurrell's loathing for the Reformation. Moreover, he published a novel in his father's lifetime describing in detail the cruelties to which he had been submitted. Yet later he proclaimed that he had given the Archdeacon 'just cause' for displeasure, spoke of him with veneration and declared that he had never met anyone superior to Hurrell 'in excellencies of character and intellect.'

C*

Such testimonials to his tormentors seem to me not edifying but masochistic; and in effect his sufferings turned this otherwise intelligent man into a blinkered champion of authority. Froude commands our interest both as a dazzling writer and as a psychological oddity. He seems to have been a charming and amiable man whose opinions were perverted by a boyhood more hideous than Oliver Twist's.

We are entitled to laugh at the eminent Victorians: compared with the eighteenth-century thinkers or the Romantic poets, they do usually brim with naive prudery and solemn prejudice. But set them beside our own contemporaries—and what giants they appear! Take Froude: when half-way through his twelve volumes on Tudor England, and busy with research upon archives in Spain, he became the editor of *Fraser's Magazine*, and continued in this post until he had finished another book, *The English in Ireland*—after which the Government sent him travelling through South Africa to report upon the situation there. While finding most of his opinions rash or even odious, I am lost in admiration for the vigour, the brilliance and the variety of his achievements.

Froude at the age of thirty-nine produced the first instalment of his great history. Henceforward he enjoys fame, prosperity and the friendship of the illustrious. His wife dies, leaving him with three young children, and so he promptly marries a friend of hers who makes him happy for twelve years and then dies—after which he is tended by his daughter. He inspects Australia, New Zealand, the United States and the West Indies as well as South Africa; but his travels on the Continent are limited to Spain for research and to Norway for fishing. Having failed to become Regius Professor of History at Oxford in 1858, he obtains the chair in 1892, at the age of seventy-four, succeeding Freeman, the most persistent of his adversaries. Two years later he dies.

More interesting than any of this, however, is his relationship with Carlyle, who at the age of seventy lost his wife, and then survived for fourteen years. Froude looked after him with selfless devotion, and after his death edited his private papers (which had been entrusted to him) and wrote his biography. The revelations about his life, especially his behaviour to Mrs. Carlyle, came as a shock: poor Froude was denounced as a traitor and a ghoul. There were few, he complained, who had not turned their backs on him. But he was always prone to overstatement; and we are not told that the rumpus cost him any friendship that he valued.

His mistake, according to Mr. Dunn, was not revealing too much, but suppressing the most painful part of the story. True enough, but I think also that his feelings towards Carlyle were ambivalent. He venerated the memory of his father and his elder brother, Hurrell, despite (or perhaps partly because of) the monstrous brutality with which they had treated him as a boy. Carlyle, I believe, excited in him the same mixture of filial piety and underlying resentment. Mr. Dunn dismisses this notion (which I put forward in a review of his previous volume) with contempt. He blindly accepts Froude's later esteem for his father as reasonable, regardless of the horrid details in the autobiography. Next he resorts to an even wilder argument: 'Froude would have had as little faith in Freud as he had in spiritualism and similar beliefs.' In other words: 'Forget all discoveries about the subconscious: they are not the sort of thing that Froude cared about!'

My suggestion seems to be confirmed by two hitherto unpublished entries about Carlyle in Froude's journal for February, 1887.

'His character, when he was himself, was noble and generous; but he had absolutely no control over himself. He was wayward and violent, and perhaps at bottom believed himself a peculiar man who had a dispensation to have things his own way.'

'What my connection with Carlyle has cost me: my own prospects as a young man; later gave up *Fraser* because Carlyle wanted it for Allingham, and my work on Charles V so as to be free to write Carlyle's biography; then the ten years of worry before the book was finished, and the worry for the rest of my life.'

Hostile critics pounced upon a statement made by Froude when he was forty-five:

'It often seems to me as if History were like a child's box of letters, with which we can spell any word we please. We have only to pick out such letters as we want, arrange them as we like, and say nothing about those which do not suit our purpose.'

Twenty-two years later his view was phrased more judiciously in a talk with Churton Collins.

'He spoke with great contempt of the science of history . . . The basis of science lies in an exhaustive deduction from certain facts, and the facts of history can neither be exhaustively nor accurately ascertained.'

This seems to be an evident truth. In practice he sought pertinaciously for the facts, and then interpreted them with undisguised bias. I respect him all the more for that. Cannot the same be said of all the most enjoyable historians from Tacitus to Gibbon and Macaulay, Michelet and Taine?

All the same, Froude must sometimes dismay everyone, except I suppose Mr. Dunn. After reading Balzac's *Le Père Goriot*, he wanted to plunge into the sea to wash himself: 'The book seemed to me the worst ever written by a clever man . . . I object to being brought into the society of people in a book which I would shut my eyes rather than see in real life.' In one of his own books this sensitive soul pokes fun at a man because he was boiled alive by Henry VIII. Curious creatures, the eminent Victorians! Yes, but our contemporaries will doubtless seem equally bizarre a hundred years hence.

Bagehot

Despite the energetic and skilful efforts of Mr. St. John Stevas, Bagehot, except to specialists, is now little more than a name—which is apt to be mispronounced. (The g is soft as in 'badger'.) He was born in 1826, the son of a Somerset banker, who being a Unitarian sent him to Bristol College and University College, London. His career was uneventful. He failed in his only attempt to enter Parliament, nor do we know that he was ever in love with anyone except his own wife.

Her father, James Wilson, had made a fortune as a hatter, and ended as a Privy Councillor in charge of Indian finances. Meanwhile he had founded the *Economist*. Bagehot edited this austere journal from 1861 until his death in 1877, contributing two articles every week. He makes even the English Constitution a fascinating subject, such is the liveliness of his thought and style. In a book called *Lombard Street* he explained our banking system, and suggested reforms in it. *Physics and Politics* sought to apply to political life the Darwinian theory of natural selection, but it suffers from Bagehot's belief in the inheritance of acquired characteristics.

I should recommend, however, beginning with his *Literary and Biographical Studies*, the book that best reveals the wide play of a brilliant, most original and most un-Victorian mind. I can think of nobody at all like him except Lord Keynes, who also brimmed with highly individual notions about everything under the sun. Bagehot's last words were characteristic: 'Let me have my own fidgets.'

His account of the English Constitution in theory and practice, its virtues and its faults, displays Bagehot as second only to Macaulay in his gift for enlivening a dry subject. He illustrates his points with sketches of prominent men—King George III, Wellington, Lyndhurst and Palmerston, with criticisms of the American and French Constitutions, and with penetrating comments upon the English character and human nature in general. Since the first appearance of the book in 1867 the Constitution has been modified not only by legislation but by new precedents and customs. The summary of these changes offered by Mr. St. John Stevas seems to me valuable.

Bagehot described the sovereign authority in England as 'the diffused respectable higher middle class,' and deplored the notion of universal suffrage: the populace in his time was so barbarous. The parliamentary system worked well, in his opinion, only because party fervour was low and party discipline slight. He would be appalled by the subservience to the Whips now accepted, and by the elimination of Independent Members. The despotism of local party associations would leave him incredulous. He declared:

'Constituency government is the precise opposite of Parliamentary government. It is the government of immoderate persons far from the scene of action, instead of the government of moderate persons close to the scene of action.'

A local pundit has recently boasted, 'We don't care for Burke in Bournemouth.' They would care even less for Bagehot, if they had ever heard of him.

The essays about politicians here reprinted glitter with memorable verdicts: Brougham—'If he were a horse, nobody would buy him; with that eye no one could answer for his temper'; Peel—'No man has come so near our definition of a constitutional statesman —the powers of a first-rate man and the creed of a second-rate man'; Gladstone—'He believes, with all his heart and soul and strength, that there *is* such a thing as truth; he has the soul of a martyr with the intellect of an advocate'; Disraeli—'He has never had a political faith—he probably does not know what it means . . . Perhaps he has gained more than he has lost by the English not understanding him.' That verdict has been confirmed by the new information in the admirable biography by Lord Blake.

But in England, except perhaps at Oxford, epigrams are misdemeanours: the politician had better be a co-respondent than a wit; and so indeed had the writer who wishes to be taken seriously. Bagehot's infernal cleverness, however, cannot blind us to his heavenly good sense. He has been selected as the greatest (by which is meant the most representative) Victorian by Mr. G. M. Young, our chief authority upon the Victorian Age. I venture to take an opposite view. Bagehot lacked the two qualities I think most typical of the great Victorians: earnestness and that power of self-deception which foreigners mistake for hypocrisy. He has much in common with Sydney Smith, something with Lytton Strachey, precious little with Kingsley, John Bright or Ruskin.

> 'Since the time of Carlyle,' he wrote in a characteristic phrase, '"earnestness" has been a favourite virtue in literature, and it is customary to treat this wish to twist other people's belief into ours as if it were a part of the love of truth.'

But in fact, he continues, this wish fosters the persecuting impulse:

'It is most dangerous to be possessed with an idea . . . The less a man is conscious of inferior motives, the more likely he is to fancy that he is doing God service.'

Bagehot welcomed the deafness of the Victorian public to their prophets. 'The most essential mental quality for a free people, whose liberty is to be progressive, permanent, and on a large scale' is 'much stupidity.' Not being (like the English) stupid, the French—he thought—required an autocrat.

Modern men, especially statesmen (he maintained already in his time) were far too willing to burden themselves with responsibilities. Half their public actions, and a great many of their private actions, had better never have been: they should take a hint from Lord Melbourne, who would always ask: 'Can't you let it alone?' Bagehot advised politicians desirous of spreading their views to 'try a little pleasure.'

What he most admired both in statesmen and authors was 'an experiencing nature,' which he found in Shakespeare, Scott and Sydney Smith, but not in the younger Pitt, Guizot or Macaulay; and he thought this experiencing nature was usually associated with high spirits and an open, enjoying character.

Macaulay had declared his preference of dead authors to living men: 'With the dead there is no rivalry. In the dead there is no change . . . Demosthenes never comes unseasonably.' Bagehot riposted:

'Dreadful idea, having Demosthenes for an intimate friend!

He had pebbles in his mouth: he was always urging action: he spoke such good Greek: we cannot dwell on it—it is too much. Only a mind impassive to our daily life, unalive to bores and evils, to joys and sorrows, a prey to print, could imagine it.'

Who but Bagehot could have taken this tone in the Victorian heyday between the death of Sydney Smith and the arrival of Oscar Wilde? No one, I suggest, not even Disraeli.

Let me quote some of his other un-Victorian sayings:

'A man's mother is his misfortune, his wife is his fault.'
'At London dinners you talk nothing; between two pillars of crinoline you eat and are resigned.'
'The use of the University of Oxford is that no one over-read themselves there.'
'History is a view of one age taken by another.'
'You can say nothing favourable of the early Christians, except that they were Christians. We find no "form or comeliness" in them; no intellectual accomplishments, no caution in action, no discretion in understanding.'
'Nothing is more unpleasant than a virtuous person with a mean mind. A highly developed moral nature joined to an undeveloped artistic nature, and a very limited religious nature, is of necessity repulsive.'
'It has been said that at times every man wishes to be a man of the world, and even the most rigid critic must concede it to be nearly essential to a writer on real life and actual manners.'

I doubt whether the most rigid critics today would make that concession, but certainly what chiefly distinguishes Bagehot as a literary and political critic is his broad knowledge of the world. We find criticism of the same order in Johnson, in Hazlitt, and later in Desmond MacCarthy; but now it has become exceptional. Apart from Mr. V. S. Pritchett, how few living critics seem to have knocked around the world with 'the experiencing nature' that Bagehot admired and himself possessed!

'The reason why so few good books are written is that so few people that can write know anything. In general an author has always lived in a room, has read books, is acquainted with the styles and sentiments of the best authors, but is out of the way of employing his own eyes and ears. He has nothing to hear and nothing to see.'

Are not these words even more painfully to the point now than when they were written over a century ago?

His practicality, his belief in enjoyment and his total incapacity for humbug inform all his criticism. Apart from a famous essay contrasting the styles of Wordsworth, Tennyson and Browning, he is chiefly concerned with two questions about every author he discusses: What sort of fellow was he, and is his writing true to experience? Much as he admires Milton as a poet, he sees in him the typical puritan, who lacks humour and a knowledge of plain human nature, who cannot understand those temptations to which he is immune, is accustomed to think most men wrong, and to be dead-sure that he himself is invariably right. Again, 'it is most dangerous to be possessed with an idea' (on Shelley); and 'It is not desirable to take this world too much *au sérieux*: most persons will not; and the one in a thousand who will, should not' (on Clough). And here he is commenting on Shakespeare and expressing himself like Virginia Woolf: 'Taken as a whole, the universe is absurd . . . The soul ties its shoes; the mind washes its hands in a basin. All is incongruous.'

We can never be sure what he will say next. His irony is spontaneous. Visiting a friend with a park 'You've got the church in the grounds!' he exclaimed, 'I like that. It's well that the tenants shouldn't be *quite* sure that the landlord's power stops with this world.' (Will that be thought Victorian by anyone?) His literary criticism cannot be disentangled from his political convictions. At the age of twenty-six he defended Louis-Napoleon's *coup d'état*, of which he had been an eye-witness, thus profoundly shocking his fellow-Liberals. Today Conservatives will similarly deplore his belief that, if the English people deliberately accepted the position of a fourth-rate power, the national mind, conscience and strength would be improved. He had no patience with Imperialism, and also opposed our interference with the internal affairs of other countries.

> 'Criticism must be brief—not like poetry, because its interest is too intense to be sustained—but because its interest is too weak to be sustained.'

All too true; but Bagehot never lived up to his dictum. Most of his essays were written for quarterly reviews that wanted long articles; and like all their contributors he drove in the same point over and over again with a sledgehammer: nor did he ever learn to be concise in his shorter pieces. Modern reviewers suffer from confinement in a strait-jacket. Unlimited elbow-room can also prove a handicap: Bagehot is too copious. Despite this fault I find him, not indeed the most profound of Victorian critics, but the most delightful.

Enough has been quoted, I hope, to make my point: Bagehot did not possess, and could not endure, the earnestness typical of the great Victorians. He is never pompous or shrill, he never harps or nags. His realism and wit sometimes make him seem a cynic like Disraeli, but he was a man of principle, and also a man of heart, in deep sympathy with the mystical Nature-worship of Wordsworth and Shelley. His fault was writing too much and revising too little: many of his sentences could be easily improved. Yet no writer of his time had a sharper edge to his mind or more solid sense.

Newman (1948)

In the fineness of his prose John Henry Newman was surpassed by none of his contemporaries; his career, his character and the working of his mind, moreover, seem to me endlessly fascinating. But we can no longer expect the general reader to be familiar with the ecclesiastical controversies that provided the Victorians with so much excitement, and he is likely therefore to find many of Newman's preoccupations merely bizarre. To few outside a faithful minority of Anglicans has all this talk of Articles and Rubrics, of the Apostolical Succession and the Eastward Position, much more meaning than the quarrels of the Byzantine Greens and Blues. Allusions even to the Scriptures have become widely incomprehensible. Today bewilderment rather than alarm would be excited, for instance, by Newman's threat to ride over his opponents 'as Othniel prevailed over Chushan-Risathaim.' You cannot, however, begin to understand the intellectual climate of nineteenth century England without studying the Tractarians, and Newman in particular.

He remains an impenetrable enigma, though so much has been written about him. Apart from the *Apologia* and his vast correspondence, we have vivid, if not always trustworthy, accounts of him from Dean Church, Francis Newman, Thomas Mozley, Isaac Williams, Mark Pattison, Dean Lake and many others of his acquaintance. The official Life by Wilfrid Ward is one of the best biographies I know; and the delicate matter of his relations with Manning is presented with exemplary fairness in Abbot Butler's Life of Bishop Ullathorne. A little new material is now offered in *Newman and Bloxam, An Oxford Friendship*, by R. D. Middleton. The author is an Anglican clergyman commendable no less for his temper than for his scholarship; and the friendship he

71

describes formed a touching accompaniment to Newman's life.

In 1836 John Rouse Bloxam, a resident Fellow of Magdalen, aged twenty-nine, met Newman, who was six years older, in the newly consecrated church at Littlemore. He fell at once, and for ever, under that celebrated charm. What preachers, one wonders, could similarly enrapture Oxford today—not Mao himself, I think, even if he spoke there every week in a voice as seductive as Greta Garbo's. Newman penetrated to men's consciences with a power that was almost hypnotic. Bloxam offered to be curate of the Littlemore church, which was attached to St. Mary's, obtained this duty and worked under Newman for some three years. Sometimes he acted as messenger between Newman and Dr. Routh, who was for sixty-three years President of Magdalen. He was the only Head of a House who showed the great reformer any sympathy, and Newman dedicated to him in 1837 the Lectures on Romanism and Popular Protestantism 'with a respectful sense of his eminent services to the Church and with the prayer that what he witnesses to others may be his own support and protection in the day of account.' This is remarkable because, according to Thomas Mozley, the 'venerable' President notoriously neglected his duties, and the prayer in Newman's dedication was intended to remind him of ' "the day of account" in which he would want "support and protection" '.

Newman, after his submission to Rome, did his utmost to persuade Bloxam to follow him. He called on him by night in Magdalen, he invited him to Oscott: 'I must show you my Crucifix when you come, with a particle of the True Cross inclosed in the beam of it. Indulgences, too, are attached to the use of it. I trust it will convert you.' This may sound a tactless, as well as humourless, method of approaching a clergyman, since relics and indulgences are seldom the features of the Catholic Church that persons outside its fold find most engaging. Newman, however, was usually expert in adapting his arguments to the individual he was addressing; and Bloxam did, in fact, delight in what may be called the apparatus of devotion—in this respect differing from the founders of the Tractarian Movement. (Neither Keble nor Pusey nor Newman himself was a ritualist: it was the succeeding generation that delighted in manifesting the Oxford doctrines by the use of sacramental vestments and elaborate ceremonial, a provocative policy that has proved widely victorious.) Not even the promise of indulgences could make Bloxham budge from Magdalen. When he did leave, seventeen years later, it was for the college living at Upper Beeding in Sussex; and there he died, five months after Newman, in 1891.

He remained always a passionate admirer of Newman, cutting from newspapers every reference to him, corresponding with him, visiting him. In later years Newman felt an increasing tenderness towards the Church of England, not—as some have wished to believe—from any regret at having left it, but because he saw in the Establishment a barrier, however imperfect, against the rising tide of scepticism; and also because the hearts of the aged tend to turn to scenes associated with their hopeful youth. In a touching letter to Bloxam he writes: 'To old friends, like you, I have a chance of being seen, as I see myself, more in the past than in the present.' When he returned from receiving his Cardinal's hat in Rome, he went to see his erstwhile curate in his Sussex rectory before going home to Birmingham. Thereafter Bloxam paid several visits to Newman; and when he received the news of his friend's death he said the Roman Office of the Dead in Beeding church, while the bell tolled and the flag flew halfmast on the tower.

On one small matter, which concerns his probity, the book throws new light. In February 1870, Bloxam in a letter of birthday congratulations hinted very discreetly that he would be interested in Newman's opinion about the outcome of the great Vatican Council, and the answer was nothing if not sanguine. Untold good will, Newman proclaimed, would come from the Council, since it was bringing into personal acquaintance men from the most distant parts.

'Nor can I believe that so awful a visitation in the supernatural order, as a renewal of the day of Pentecost when it is granted them, will not make them all new men for the rest of their lives. They have come to Rome with antagonistic feelings, they will depart in the Peace of God. I don't think much will come of the movement for Papal Infallibility, though something very mild may be passed.'

Less than a month earlier he had written to Ullathorne that the Council infused into him little else than fear and dismay:

'I look with anxiety at the prospect of having to defend decisions which may not be difficult to my private judgment, but may be most difficult to defend logically in face of historical facts. What have we done to be treated as the Faithful never were treated before? Why should an aggressive and insolent faction be allowed to make the hearts of the just to mourn whom the Lord has not made sorrowful?'

Wilfrid Ward, with characteristic candour, printed both these letters, with the comment: 'It is to be observed that in writing to Anglican friends he emphasises the good which the Council was likely to effect.' At this point the reader of the biography had cause to cock an eyebrow: the Early Fathers might recommend 'economising' the truth, but did not Newman's change of language here amount to deliberate deceit? Mr. Middleton brings us some fresh evidence. Newman himself enters the box to account for his apparent inconsistency (an explanation to Bloxam was imperative because parts of the earlier, despondent letter had somehow seeped into print). In the interval—he explained—between writing the two contradictory accounts of his feelings, he had received from Ullathorne in Rome a letter about happenings there 'which dispelled all my fears. It was under the influence of that Letter that I wrote to you.'

This story I have found confirmed in Ullathorne's letter and in Newman's answer describing it as 'very tranquillizing.' Satisfactory as all this is to those of us who admire Newman, one further observation must be made. The letter to Bloxam, explaining that his fears had been dispelled in February, was written in April—by which time they had returned. (See letters dated March 20, March 27, and April 12, in Wilfrid Ward's *Life*.) It is rash to accuse Newman of telling lies, as Kingsley discovered. But while telling nothing but the truth, he did not always feel obliged to tell the whole truth—which of us does?—and he was not always unwilling to leave a false impression: one needs, therefore, to scrutinise his phraseology with particular attention. He persuaded himself that if careless readers were misled by his elaborately chosen words, it was their own fault. Mr. Gladstone acted upon the same unwisely legalistic principle. Since they both must have discovered that the average reader is careless, their indignation at the inevitable accusations of duplicity was ingenuous.

What makes the workings of Newman's mind singularly impenetrable is that both his scepticism and his credulity went to lengths that few of us can comprehend. He came near to being a solipsist; in any case he believed spontaneously and absolutely in the existence of only two beings, himself and God. His other beliefs, forming a colossal inverted pyramid, were based upon this, and not upon the evidence of his senses, which he thought could not be trusted to provide any substantial truth. Less defensible than this idealism, I suspect, was his scepticism about the validity of induction, which he made up for by a most exaggerated trust in what he called 'the illative sense,' a faculty which we now call 'the subconscious.' He was thus led to the most curious conclusions. He went out of his way to accept pious legends, never imposed upon the faithful and now discredited by them—such as the aeronautical journey of the Holy House of Loreto from Nazareth to the vicinity of Ancona, with a landing on the way in Dalmatia. He apparently conceived that he had better reason for believing this than most of us have for believing that Great Britain is an island. On the other hand, he was alive, earlier than the authorities of the Church, to the need for new methods of Christian apologetic. He sacrificed, moreover, his dearest earthly hopes rather than accept ultramontane theories that he considered dangerously novel. This rebuts, I consider, the common accusation that his beliefs were only the reflection of his wishes. The trouble was that his intellect and imagination alike moved in a realm of abstractions, upon which nothing so unrefined as common sense was allowed to intrude.

The disappointments that pursued him were so recurrent that he may be suspected of inviting them with some part of himself. He sometimes appears to have gone out of his way to antagonize not only the authorities in his Church, but his young followers. He quarrelled readily with those who disagreed with him, and while inspiring alarm he detested deference. The friendships that he formed and kept were more like loves, for his tenderness was equalled only be his occasional ferocity. From Dartington one summer he wrote to his mother: 'I should dissolve with essence of roses or be attenuated to an echo if I lived here.' (This is hard to reconcile with his odd declaration that he felt he would be a better and more religious man if he lived in Taormina.) Just as he was credulous because by nature sceptical, so he was ascetic, one may hazard, because by nature sensuous. Those who like their heroes simple should keep away from Newman no less than from Mr. Gladstone. On the other hand, even the deepest divergences in opinion and temperament fail to prevent some of us from finding in these intricate, not to say tortuous, spirits a profound and charming nobility.

*   *   *   *

The merits of a new book, *Young Mr. Newman*, by Maisie Ward impel me to return to its subject. What I want to consider this time is not so much his personality as some aspects of the movement in which he found himself the leader. A granddaughter of 'Ideal Ward' (a follower of Newman who when they had both submitted to Rome became his truculent antagonist), a daughter of Wilfrid Ward (Newman's devoted biographer), Miss Maisie Ward has written a valuable complement to her father's masterpiece, which—in obedience to the Cardinal's wishes—allowed little space to the first forty-three years of his life.

Too habitually writers of the Roman obedience treat Anglicanism with a condescension bordering upon malice: Miss Ward is always fair, and often generous. In her political comments similarly she appears more in accord with the Catholic intellectuals and statesmen of the Continent than with the reactionaries or froth-blowers who have tried to impose upon English Catholic thought so insular a flavour. Here is a remarkable passage:

> 'Often to-day we meet with the remark that Belloc's prophecy has been fufilled and that we are living in his servile state. But we are not. We are living in *a* servile state but quite a different one. In his vision part of the population was going to be enslaved to work for the other part. But to-day we are all enslaved to the state. Belloc in fact was looking backward rather than forward. His servile state existed: it was Disraeli's two nations. The factory hands were slaves of the owners, the villagers were slaves of the squires. And by this slavery they were being conditioned to be happy slaves of the state.'

The new material used in this book throws little light except upon Newman's relations with his family. It is surprising, however, to find that he of all men misquoted the Prayer Book, unconsciously twisting it to support his own Conservatism. (He wrote 'that state of life in which *it has pleased* God to call them' instead of '*it shall please*'). Miss Ward justly emphasises the melancholy, which she finds un-Catholic, conspicuous in Tractarian religion. All the leaders carried asceticism to lengths that would have been discouraged by an experienced spiritual director. They were, one notices, surrounded by the prematurely dying. (Was tuberculosis so usual in most families, or was there some causal connection between extreme piety and a tubercular strain?) Newman's two dearest friends, Bowden and Hurrell Froude, Froude's sister,

Pusey's daughter and wife, and Newman's beloved sister Mary: they all died young. Miss Ward might have quoted his singular reference to her sixteen years later:

'He led me forward by a series of Providences from the age of nineteen till twenty-seven. I *was* "the work of His hands," for He repeatedly and variously chastised me and at last to win me from the world, He took from me a dear sister—and just at the same time He gave me kind friends to teach me His way more perfectly.'

Was not Newman carrying self-centredness very far when he assumed that it was for his benefit that God deprived his sister of her life and her family of her presence? Such a view reminds me of the Port Royal hermit who wrote to his father, 'Monsieur mon père, Dieu s'étant servi de vous pour me mettre au monde . . .' Newman's attitude was perhaps partly a relic of his Evangelical period, upon which Miss Ward, like Mr. Christopher Dawson, lays great stress. She should, I think, have quoted, if only to disagree with it, Newman's declaration that he had never been 'a genuine Evangelical.'

Now let us consider the society that venerated Newman in his thirties, with such affection. The Anglo-Catholicism, into which Tractarianism evolved, has now for many decades inspired the most devoted and effective party in the Church of England. Its exponents have been characterised by the importance they attach to the seven Sacraments, by their use of pre-Reformation cere-monial, and—very often—by their advocacy of social reforms. The Oxford Movement, on the other hand, began with a Tory defence of Protestant property and privilege; nor did any of its leaders take an interest in ritual. Nineteen bishops out of twenty-one, it will be remembered, voted against the first reading of the great Reform Bill; and the first reformed House of Commons, which afterwards abolished slavery and passed the earliest Factory Act, began its career with a mild measure for redistributing all too little of the property unjustly held by that fat anomaly, the Church of Ireland. Thereupon John Keble, Fellow of Oriel and Professor of Poetry, denounced the Government as sacrile-gious from the pulpit of the University Church in a sermon humourlessly entitled *National Apostasy*. Another Fellow of Oriel, Newman, was equally extravagant: 'The gift of excom-munication,' he wrote, 'will not for ever remain unused. If I were a Bishop, the first thing I should do would be to excommunicate Lord Grey and half a dozen more, whose names it is almost a shame and a pollution for a Christian to mention.' These two, and a small group of sympathisers, then decided to expound in a series of tracts their high sense of the rights and powers attaching to the Anglican Church.

This entailed detecting grounds for its claims to superiority over alike the Papists and the Dissenters. The old High Church party were concerned rather with maintaining than with justifying the prerogatives of the Establishment. The Evangelicals and the Latitudinarians could offer no substantial reason why salvation should be sought among the Anglicans rather than among the Methodists: if their Low view of the Church had been traditional, two thousand clergy would not have left it in 1662 rather than accept the Act of Uniformity. In next to no time the Tractarians discovered that what appeared superficially to be a ramshackle Erastian contrivance, resulting from a series of compromises and rapacities, must really be the living Bride of Christ, endowed by Him through the Apostolical Succession with the most awful supernatural powers. Precedents for these claims could be found in the Caroline divines. But Churches like other societies evolve; and after the high-minded secession of the Nonjurors in 1689, the official mind of the Church of England (if such can be said to have existed) became emphatically Protestant and often Latitudinarian. Arians or Socinians such as Hoadly were consecrated as bishops; Laudian doctrines were more and more neglected save by a few Jacobites and scholars. When therefore the Tractarians pointed out that the Prayer Book enjoined fasting and daily services, that it insisted upon the doctrine of baptismal regeneration, that it provided for auricular confession and absolution, most churchmen were amazed, indignant and at a loss for an answer. When the Ninetieth Tract appeared, they could no longer contain themselves. This was written to show that the Forty-nine Articles had been so phrased as to admit a number of beliefs generally held to be papistical, including the doctrines of purgatory and the Sacrifice of the Mass. History, I think, justifies this argument: the Prayer Book was framed, not uncynically, to obtain the adherence of as many of His Majesty's subjects as possible. Tait, who was one of the first to protest officially against the Tract, soon came to see that subscription to the Articles entailed at least as much difficulty for Latitudinarians like himself as for those whom Thomas Arnold called 'the Oxford malignants.' The Evangelicals were less candid, because far less intellectual. Though they regularly disobeyed the Prayer Book, they were appalled by what they called the disloyalty of the Tractarians. To the detached observer it now seems that none of the three parties was in a position to attack the good faith of the others. Most of the bishops however, felt called upon to denounce the Tract; and its author, Newman, entered upon the five years of distressed uncertainty that ended with his submission to Rome.

The men who launched the Oxford Movement were to an extraordinary extent not only unworldly but ignorant of the world. Pusey had spent two years in German universities, three months in Paris; but the experience of the others was almost confined to Oxford (then a long journey from London) and to some sequestered rural parishes. Keble, for instance, was the son of a country parson and educated at home; he became an undergraduate before he was fifteen, obtained a double First and a fellowship before he was nineteen. His profound and touching piety went with a wilful blindness to the spirit of the age. He preferred not to hear what was unpleasant to him. At the same time he was a most painstaking parish priest, and suffered from the knowledge that he did not understand the difficulties of his flock, an ignorance that he blamed upon their refusal to come to confession. Newman, incomparably more powerful in intellect—and, incidentally, slightly inferior to his friends in social status—had read Gibbon and Hume and Tom Paine; but his innocence in matters of daily life remained always prodigious. He had settled in Birmingham, and he had the advantage of hearing confessions; yet in answer to a letter about Cardinal Manning's temperance crusade he declared—with a touch, I fancy, of self-satisfaction—that for his part he had no notion whether there were too many alehouses or too few.

The Tractarians, it is true, often animadverted upon the growing infidelity of the age: Cabinet Ministers, they complained, were no longer expected even to profess belief in the Atonement. To us, however, the Eighteen Thirties and Forties seem much more religious than either the preceding or succeeding period. According to Mr. G. M. Young, Lord Hatherton used to say that in 1810 only two gentlemen in Staffordshire had family prayers; in 1850 only two did not. On the other hand William Palmer gives the following account of the England into which the Tracts were launched:

79

'Allusions to God's being and providence became distasteful to the English parliament. They were voted ill-bred and superstitious; they were the subjects of ridicule as overmuch righteousness. Men were ashamed any longer to say family prayers, or to invoke the blessing of God upon their partaking of His gifts; the food which He alone had provided. The mention of His name was tabooed in polite circles.'

All this makes things difficult for the student of the age. A possible explanation is that while Evangelical, and then Tractarian, beliefs made the upper class more Christian than in Georgian times, scepticism began to percolate into the middle class.

Miss Ward aptly quotes R. H. Hutton's comment that the Tractarians lived 'more like a colony of immigrants than like a band of patriots who were reviving the old glories of their native land'; and she adds that 'they were living in an unreal world in which they were carrying all England with them on a tide of returning Catholicism.' Contemporaries of Macaulay, Mill, Disraeli, Mérimée and Sainte-Beuve, they lived in the company of Cyril of Alexandria and Chrysostom and Cyprian. (Newman wanted his nephew and godson christened Athanasius, but the parents were so perverse as to prefer Herbert.) The first Tract assumed not only that the bishops were likely to be martyrs but that they welcomed this prospect. Even among the dreaming spires of Oxford the Tractarians could hardly—one would have supposed—escape some closer glimpse of actuality: they had only to dine at any High Table save that of Oriel to meet a conglomeration of clergymen, plumpy with sirloins, rubicund with port, and blissfully unaware that they had been granted the staggering power of remitting sins and of turning bread and wine into the Body and Blood of Christ.

The point is that the Tractarians in order to defend the Church had to transform it so radically as to make it worth defending. If they had not lived 'in an unreal world,' they could hardly have essayed so seemingly impossible a task. And transform the Church they did to an astonishing degree, although the one man of genius among them, Newman, had been compelled by his conscience to become their antagonist. The bishops who condemned the Tracts, could they attend Eucharistic worship in their cathedrals today, would rub their eyes with vexed bewilderment.

Jowett

Hellenist, heretic, mentor to Viceroys and friend to poets, the famous Master of Balliol is now interesting chiefly as a Victorian character. Some of us also venerate him for the imprint he left upon his college. This may have been modified by some of his successors, but none of the young can love Balliol better than those who remember it when the elegant Strachan-Davidson was Master and such dedicated dons as Urquhart and Cyril Bailey maintained the traditions they had received from Jowett.

Though ashamed that the writing of this new biography should have been left to a Christ Church man, we must admit that in all other respects Sir Geoffrey Faber is admirably equipped for his task. Apart from a few slips in figures, his only fault is stinginess in *dicta* and anecdotes, which illuminate, even when legendary. In an urbane prose he reveals intimacy with the background, command of detail, psychological acumen and sympathy with his subject.

The official Life of Jowett by Abbott and Campbell is one of the better Victorian biographies, and will continue to be read for the delightful letters it contains. But Sir Geoffrey offers us important material that was either unavailable or unprintable sixty years ago, notably the massive correspondence with Florence Nightingale. She forbade Abbott and Campbell even to mention her friendship with Jowett, which was first revealed in the Life of her by Sir Edward Cook.

And here I must pick a final bone with Sir Geoffrey. This Life, he complains, was shamefully plagiarised in 'Eminent Victorians.' Let me point out that Strachey in his preface carefully commended Cook's biography for its exceptional merit, and explained that without it he could not have written his study of Florence Nightingale. If he was a plagiarist, so is Sir Geoffrey, who acknowledges his debt to Abbott and Campbell. Any stick now seems good enough for beating either Macaulay or Strachey: they cannot be forgiven for remaining so readable.

'Mine has been a happy life,' Jowett announced upon his death-bed. The gravest calamities he had had to face were a delay in becoming Master of Balliol and a prosecution for heresy that was immediately dismissed. His boyhood, however, had been unfortunate. The father, an Evangelical furrier, having failed in the family business, the mother with her younger children took refuge with a sister in Bath: and from the age of twelve poor Benjamin lived alone in lodgings as a day-boy at St. Paul's. Moreover his physique and temperament never became virile: with soft, baby hands, tiny feet, a tripping gait and a high-pitched voice he looked like a girl when young, and when old like a more intellectual Queen Victoria.

While he seems never to have been troubled by the flesh, deep emotion coloured his friendships, especially with Florence Nightingale and Robert Morier ('an agreeable young hulk' according to one of Jowett's uncomprehending friends).

As Sir Geoffrey points out, 'this close likeness in his feelings for two such utterly different persons of opposite sexes indicates an ambivalency of temperament which could not have been satisfied in wedlock.' We now learn, however, that he would in his early forties have proposed to the daughter of a Dean if he had been free to marry. He was not. In those days dons had to become clergymen, and with few exceptions forfeited their Fellowships by marriage. As a rule they did marry as soon as they could obtain a College living, and consequently most dons were youngish men (Sir Geoffrey explains) and not the crusty eccentrics immortalised in Tuckwell's reminiscences.

Jowett took in his stride the priesthood required by his vocation as college tutor. His feelings towards God no less than towards human beings could be described as a warm haze. He got into hot water for questioning the verbal inspiration of the Bible and, far worse, the Atonement (a central doctrine of traditional Christianity, Catholic and Protestant). He then turned from theology to Plato, and never revealed the extent of his scepticism. He had no firm belief in personal immortality or a personal God.

Sir Geoffrey seems to think such open-mindedness decent in a man receiving payment as an Anglican clergyman. I cannot help agreeing with Leslie Stephen, who attacked Jowett's position as untenable. A victim himself of the same uncertainties, he had abandoned his Orders and his Fellowship. Less likeable, I think, than Jowett, he had a more powerful intellect to guide his conscience. There was also a deeper difference between these two eminent Victorians: Jowett was gifted with a devout temperament. The Church, he fancied, could discard all supernatural doctrines, and still foster not only the ethics of altruism but a religiosity of feeling that he deeply valued.

One day he despondently asked himself whether he might not have attained real greatness had he been led by a nobler ideal than success in life; and his critics spoke of him as a worldly man who taught worldliness to his pupils. This seems to me unfair. Perhaps he too readily accepted worldly success as a test of merit: he cared passionately for the improvement of the world; and this, he thought, could seldom be furthered by the unsuccessful. He could not bear Balliol men to 'make a mess of their lives,' and was always urging them to improve their natural abilities by will-power and hard work: only thus could they attain the positions in which they could be most useful to their fellows. Such teaching sounds smug to modern ears. Dare I confess that I find it sensible, and admire Jowett for combining exceptional sense with exceptional goodness?

Sometimes he cowed young men into silence or felled them with a sudden snub, for he was shy (this is the traditional excuse for bad manners) and hated shyness in others because it evoked the same disability in himself. To black sheep he was indulgent.

'If a man were a peer, a profligate or a pauper,' somebody proclaimed, 'the Master would be sure to take him up.' (What he did not like, I deduce, was a prig.) To be thus taken up cannot have been an unmixed pleasure: 'A friendship once established meant for him that a friend should have no rest while any fault remained unreproved, any defect uncorrected.' Nevertheless his friends included not only Tennyson, Browning, George Eliot and Matthew Arnold, but such erratic characters as Swinburne and Symonds. His charm must have been enormous.

His humour also delights me. He loved money, he said, because it enabled him to do more mischief, and he loved mischief. Again, he thought that cunning required more character and self-control than was possessed by people of his time, including himself. Such talk can be misunderstood: what wonder that Jowett made enemies! To undergraduates in need, however, his generosity was magnificent, and he took infinite trouble on behalf of all his friends and the

College. His first act as Master was to improve the abominable food at Balliol: ascetic himself, he wished the College to earn 'a good reputation for eating and drinking.' He thus displayed the wisdom of the serpent, as commanded by the Gospel. Devoid of humbug and brimming with good sense, he seems to me a Victorian no less amiable than eminent.

Mark Pattison

We have been treated to four books about Ouida: no biographer has yet devoted a volume to Mark Pattison, a far better writer and also, in my eccentric opinion, a far more interesting character. Happily we have his Memoirs, which as a self-portrait of an English intellectual are surpassed only by Gibbon's Autobiography, and Newman's Apologia. The best and most objective account of him will be found in a new book.

Mr. V. H. H. Green, a Fellow of Lincoln, has written the history of his Senior Common Room from 1792 to 1884. Although I cannot help wishing that he had concentrated upon Pattison, the last and incomparably the most distinguished of the four Rectors whose reigns he describes, his plan enables him to display from its beginnings the reform of Oxford as it affected one college.

He has used a wealth of unpublished material, including Pattison's diaries; and he is polished in style as well as careful in scholarship. This history seems aimed chiefly at an academic audience, but the general reader will find it packed with lively details, and the account of Pattison is fascinating.

Rector Tatham represents unreformed Oxford at its most outrageous. He was elected in 1792, and the University had hardly changed during the fifty years since it had excited the censure of the youthful Gibbon. Potations, if not less dull, may have become less deep, but the rest of his famous indictment remained valid. Most Professors still made no pretence of teaching; examinations were a farce; and as for the Fellows, 'from the toil of reading, thinking, or writing, they had absolved their conscience.' Tatham, however, must be acquitted of torpor: boastful, opinionated and litigious, he earned his reputation as a controversialist by the fluency and truculence with which he defended Tory misrule and Anglican

85

intolerance. Hume, Priestley, Dissent and Catholic Emancipation excited his particular vituperation.

At Lincoln, one of the dimmest Colleges, he presided over eleven Fellows. Two of these did some teaching or lecturing; none could bother to officiate in chapel (a chaplain had to be hired); and as a rule only three were even resident. The others treated the College as a property in which they held shares, coming up merely to scrutinise the accounts and accept their dividends. They all had to be clergymen and unmarried, but they could hope for a College living that would forfeit their Fellowship but increase their income and permit connubial joys. Heads of Houses were allowed to marry; and the money-minded Tatham when over fifty selected a girl of humble birth. The father, a prosperous builder, stated her dowry in pounds: 'Make it guineas,' the Rector answered, 'and I'm your man.' He thus acquired a Xanthippe.

His reign was enlivened by continual disputes, and on one occasion he enlisted ducal gamekeepers to protect himself from enraged parishioners. We must not, however, underrate his piety: 'He once preached a sermon two and a half hours long . . . in the course of which he wished "all Jarman critics at the bottom of the Jarman Ocean".'

In 1839, five years after Tatham's death, Mark Pattison became a Fellow of Lincoln. He owed this post not to the intellectual powers that made him the greatest scholar in the Oxford of his time, but to his Yorkshire origin. (Fellowships then depended often upon birthplaces.) His father was a rector in Wensleydale, a gentleman but even more offensive than the father of the Brontës: after confinement in a mental home, he lived to plague his large family for thirty years. His cruelty to his daughters was extravagant. Mark, his eldest son, received no schooling, went as a commoner to Oriel and was there so ill taught that he obtained only a second. The three outstanding tutors to whom the College owed its unique reputation had just been dismissed by Provost Hawkins, who disliked their zeal even more than their immoderate doctrines. Their leader, Newman, obtained an enormous influence over Pattison, who all but followed him into the Roman Church. Instead his faith began to waver, and failed to withstand the disaster that soured him for the rest of his life.

This was his failure to become Rector of Lincoln in 1851. He had for several years been running the College under the insignificant Radford, on whose death he was promised the succession by a majority of the Fellows. A series of shameful and comical intrigues gave the post to one Thompson: a majority, including Pattison, 'voted for a man they regarded with loathing and contempt, to keep out a man they disliked even more.'

Academic life fosters an exorbitant lust for power, if we can believe C. P. Snow's persuasive novel, *The Masters*, and Pattison's anguish knew no limits. So learned a clergyman might be expected to find some solace, but (like Jowett in face of similar disappointment) he decided to sulk; and (unlike Jowett) he never recovered. Even his grammar collapsed under the shock: 'We have all here lost something, but no one has lost what I have lost—all their earthly hopes.' His diary brimmed with self-pity: nine years later he was still crying. 'My God, my God, why hast thou forsaken me?'

His defeat aggravated the faults by which it had been occasioned. Tactless, unsociable, morose, stingy, imperious and unforgiving, he complained that everyone was vulgar except his well-wishers, and even these excited his groundless suspicion. After ten years, however, he attained the Rectorship, and with it freedom to marry, of which he immediately availed himself. (How these Fellows, usually so unascetic in food and drink, managed their unwilling celibacy remains mysterious.) Pattison, who was now forty-eight, chose a bride of twenty-one, and *Middlemarch* was currently, if mistakenly, supposed to portray their union.

She soon complained of ill-health, which enabled her to spend most of her time away from him on the Continent. An intellectual herself, she delighted in his intellect; but from the first she had expressed 'the strongest aversion' from his embraces; and after fifteen years this aversion, she told him, could no longer be controlled. (She seems already to have been in love with Dilke, whom she eventually married.) Pattison was enraged, but soon found consolation in a clergyman's daughter who was forty years his junior. 'I must have my arms tightly round that dear waist,' he wrote to her, 'with infinite possibilities of kissing.' His wife, however, tended him during the pains and the furies of his last illness. He died in 1884 aged seventy.

A victim of heredity, poor Pattison was too maladjusted to behave with good sense or kindness. No scholar of his distinction has been more unproductive: his essays are enjoyable, but the *Life of Casaubon* is his one solid achievement. Even his Memoirs have appeared only in a truncated form, and Mr. Green does not tell us whether the original has survived. (The widow destroyed large parts of the diary.) As a brother Pattison was cruel, as Rector distant and ineffective. But at least he saw that the undergraduates were properly taught; and he must have been less odious than he paints himself, or he would never have won the affectionate esteem of a man so refined as Warde Fowler.

During two-thirds of his adult career he was living a lie, since he continued to celebrate the Holy Communion, when he had lost faith successively in the Church and in the existence of God. Honesty would have entailed expulsion from his darling Rectorship, for as late as 1882 the new statutes desired by the College, which allowed a layman to be Rector, were rejected by the House of Lords at the instigation of Bishop Christopher Wordsworth.

Churchmen and academics, supported by their fellow-Tories, struggled gamely to defend Oxford against all improvements. 'It seems it is necessary in the interests of the Church,' the sarcastic Pattison remarked, 'that the College endowments should be reserved for men of capacities and energies below the average.' The University, however, found an ingenious defence for every abuse: why seek to modify in any way the system devised in 1636, since the nature and faculties of the human mind had not changed in the interval?

When, despite the opposition of University and Colleges, Parliament enforced many of the overdue reforms demanded by Pattison, he remained as usual dissatisfied. The new Oxford realised not his ideal but Jowett's: it was not a centre of research and European culture, but a 'super-public-school,' devoted to teaching at the expense of learning. The life of this wonderfully gifted man was thus a long series of disappointments, public and private. Most of these, it may be said, came from his own faults, of which self-pity was not the least. But those who pity themselves deserve especial pity from others, since no practice is more dilapidating. It is wise moreover to assume that people—other people at any rate—cannot help being what they are.

P.S. A recent book, *Sister Dora*, by Jo Manton, recounts with exemplary skill, and for the first time, the career of one of Pattison's sisters. She devoted herself nobly to the medical care of sick and wounded workmen. Her brother treated her always with heartless contempt.

Ideal Ward

The reaction against the Victorian environment took a variety of shapes, among which Catholicism is prominent. Manning and Newman retained much fellow-feeling with their Protestant contemporaries. Wiseman, on the other hand, the exuberant and imposing Wiseman, was conspicuously un-Victorian. But then he had been born in Seville, and had lived from the age of sixteen to thirty-eight in Rome. Frederick Faber, again, was most un-Victorian, a conscious mutineer against the received ideas of his compatriots.[1] Unlike these, Ward was not Italianate, yet I find him at least equally dissident, and notably more interesting.

William George Ward was born in 1812. His father, the cadet of a landed family in the Isle of Wight, became known as a director of the Bank of England, a Tory M.P., and the best bat in the country. In the early eighteenth century the Wards had lived in Gibraltar, and W. G. Ward's great-grandmother was a Spanish lady 'of the Raphael family, which originated in Genoa'. The intensity and enthusiasm of temperament which characterised him may—his son suggested—derive from this Southern strain, which might (let me add) have been partly Jewish.

As a child Ward was notable for his candour, as well as his interest in mathematics, music and the drama. Taken to a children's party, he was heard to declare: 'I expected to find this a bore, and now that I am here I find it worse even than I thought.' At the age of eleven he entered Winchester as a commoner. Though clumsy at games, and without any interest in them, he was physically and morally too stalwart to be bullied. When he rose to be a prefect, he

[1] His devotion to the Madonna led him into theological indiscretions which Newman condemned most trenchantly. What Ward, who had chosen Faber as his confessor, thought of this incident remains obscure.

imposed discipline with such vigour as to provoke an insurrection, following which six boys were expelled. Referring in later life to the cruelty and immorality he had witnessed at Winchester, he remarked: 'If that isn't the nearest approach to hell of anything on earth, I know not what is.' His ambitions were already ecclesiastical, and he used to practise daydream episcopal signatures: 'Yrs faithfully, W. G. Winton' or 'W. G. Oxon'.

In 1830 he went up to Christ Church, where most of his energy was given to debates in the Union. In the *viva voce* for his degree he bewildered his examiner by parading, instead of trying to conceal, his inability to answer some of their questions. 'Take your time, Mr. Ward. You are nervous.' 'No, Sir, it's not nervousness; pure ignorance.' And soon he was answering in a resentful tone, as if the questions were impertinent. Though he obtained only a Second, the Warden of All Souls thought he might make a suitable Fellow, and asked him to dinner. He was not elected: 'He had not even taken the trouble,' said the Warden, 'to change his boots.' He obtained instead an Open Fellowship at Balliol.

His untempered frankness, his love of paradox and his brilliance in dialectic quickly made him a much-discussed figure in Oxford. To him everything was snow-white or coal-black. 'Intellect is a wretched gift, my dear Henry. Absolutely worthless. Now my intellect is in some respects almost infinite, yet I don't value it a bit.' Again, 'I have the mind of an archangel in the body of a rhinoceros.' Dean Church describes him as 'a singular and almost unique combination of the utmost abandon and readiness for argument with deep seriousness and reality of form and purpose, and with the dignity such reality gave.' He adored Italian opera, often interrupted theological discussion by trolling the *Largo al factotum*, and would heave his unwieldy form upon his knees to mime Don Giovanni, choosing some startled clergyman as his Zerlina. Jowett summed him up: 'Like Socrates in his dialectical powers, like Falstaff in his love of making fun.'

A close friend of Arthur Stanley, he was a devotee of Dr. Arnold, whom he found exemplary in his 'hatred of worldliness and strong sense of Christian equality among those in different situations.' Ward followed him in attacking 'the odiously unchristian way of both speaking and thinking of the poor, which, alas! we fear it cannot be denied pervades the upper and middle classes of Englishmen.' The other major influence upon the young don was J. S. Mill, in whom he recognised an intellect as potent in logic as his own.

Ward must have seemed the least likely of men to become a Tractarian.

The Oxford Movement is generally held to date from Keble's Sermon on National Apostasy, delivered in the Oxford University Church on July 14, 1833. This was a die-hard protest against the Government's eminently sensible bill for uniting some bishoprics in that shocking anomaly, the Established Church of Ireland. The next development was Newman's glorification of the Church of England as a *via media* between the equally grievous errors of Popery and Protestantism. Ward was temperamentally averse from the conservatism that considers the antiquity of an abuse as a sufficient excuse for it. Even more alien to him was the notion that wisdom could be found in the mean between two extremes. He detested moderation.[1] What can it be that converted this pupil of Arnold and Mill? The most likely answer seems to be the incomparable charm of Newman. If we are to believe the account given by a Mr. Price, Ward refused for a long while to hear Newman preach: 'Why should I go and listen to such myths?' He was at last cajoled into St. Mary's, and the sermon altered his life. Thereafter, when Newman's step was heard on the staircase, Ward's heart would begin to beat. Only a year before his death, after some twenty years of misunderstanding, estrangement and active antagonism, Ward told his son of a dream he had just woken from. 'He had found himself at a dinner-party next to a veiled lady who charmed him more and more as they talked. At last he exclaimed "I have never felt such charm in any conversation since I used to talk with John Henry Newman at Oxford!" "I am John Henry Newman," the lady replied, and raising her veil shewed the well-known face.' At the time of their sharpest differences, Ward wrote to Newman, 'I have never been able even approximately to replace you. If you will not laugh at the expression, I will say that I have felt myself an intellectual orphan.'[2]

The other force that attracted Ward into the Oxford Movement was Hurrell Froude's *Remains*, published in 1838. In these posthumous writings of an Anglican don he found a gusto for excess

[1] Despite his praise of the middle way, Newman was not thought moderate by his fellow clergymen.

[2] Ward's mother seems to have played little part in his emotional life. She teased him for being in love with his governess, who no doubt gave him what he failed to get from his mother. Newman, it appears, similarly drew upon Ward's filial emotions.

hardly inferior to his own. The Reformation was ostentatiously condemned; the Church of England, in this picture by one of her sons, emerged as not only heretical but dull. Ward jumped in his chair with excitement as he read the book, and at once became the extremist among the Tractarians, harassing Newman with awkard queries and remorseless deductions, dragging him, as might a boisterous child, at a painful pace towards a destination he preferred not to envisage. 'If any man be called "moderate" or "venerable", beware of him; if he is called both, you may be sure he is a scoundrel.' This *boutade* came from Ward's heart. So much for the *via media*. He could admit no logical resting-place on the long slope between atheism and the worship of relics. 'There goes Ward mystifying Clough,' a witness reported, 'and persuading him that he must believe *nothing* or accept the whole of Church doctrine.'

The Oxford Movement, like the Catholic Revival on the Continent, was a part of the Romantic Movement. The philosophers of the Enlightenment had tried to make men purely creatures of reason, and had failed,—necessarily, since they did not take into account some of the most valuable of human experiences. A Wordsworth and a Coleridge, excited by the solemn beauties of Nature to accept intimations of deity, were able to find a rationalisation of this feeling in the Church of England, just as Chateaubriand found it in the Church of Rome.[1] To those who were not poets, the Church of England seemed sunk in a complacent torpor. The expulsions from their livings of the High Church clergy by the Roundheads, of the Puritans in 1660, of the Nonjurors in 1689, and finally the breakaway of the Wesleyans, had successively purged the Church of enthusiasm. It had become, one might almost say, a department of the Civil Service, in which the younger sons of the nobility and gentry acquired handsome sinecures, while sweated curates did most of the work.[2] Forgetful of its past, the Establishment was now differentiated from the Nonconformist sects by its somnolence rather than by its doctrine. When therefore the Tract-

[1] Simultaneously Scott excited sympathy with the Middle Ages. 'Ecclesiastically Sir Walter ploughed, and Newman followed him with the seed-bag.' (*H. P. Liddon* by J. O. Johnson)

[2] During the eighteenth century the Catholic Church suffered a degeneration that was little less marked. Abbeys and even sees became appanages of noble houses, occupied often by youthful sceptics and libertines. The Roman Archbishop of Strasbourg maintained not only a pack of hounds but a *maîtresse en titre*. Nevertheless saintly lives continued to adorn both Churches.

arians claimed the Church of England as part of the Catholic Church, they seemed merely paradoxical. Of course the Establishment was Protestant: look at its services, look at its Articles! But if you did look, you discovered that the Book of Common Prayer was surprisingly close to the Missal and Breviary, upon which it was based. It clearly expounded the doctrine of Baptismal Regeneration, and provided for priestly absolution after auricular confession. The Communion Service certainly did not exclude the doctrine of the Real Presence; the service for the Consecration of Bishops suggested the doctrine of the Apostolical Succession. But, if the liturgy was in the main Catholic, surely the Articles were in the main Protestant? A careful inspection revealed that these gave loopholes for a wider interpretation. And this was what the notorious Tract XC set out to explain. Ward had worried Newman into writing it.

The tracts began in 1833 as pamphlets, to defend the Church against State encroachment, Popery and Methodism; soon they swelled into volumes, more erudite than concise, expounding the historic Catholicity of the Anglican Church, and thus claiming for it a dignity that disestablishment could never remove. Already in Tract I Newman refers, with characteristic irony, to the possibility of the English Bishops' being murdered by revolutionary mobs: 'Black event as it would be for the country, yet (as far as they are concerned) we could not wish them a more blessed termination of their course than the spoiling of their goods and martyrdom.'

Majestic in self-complacency, their cauliflower-wigs framing visages tumid with venison and port, their lawn-sleeves billowing over the black satin of their chimeres, lumbering in their coaches from their diocesan palaces to their London mansions, punctual in the House of Lords to vote against any reform however humane and overdue, the prelates of the Establishment turned the pages of the Tract with a bewilderment that quickly swelled into indignation. This jackanapes who wishes us to be robbed and murdered, some servitor turned curate, no doubt:—is he moonstruck or merely insolent? The Tract, you aver, was written by a Mr. Newman who is Fellow of Oriel and Rector of the University Church? Things are coming to a pretty pass. I must speak to my brother of Oxford.

It was the appearance of Tract XC that let loose the tempest. The Bishop of Oxford objected to it formally, and advised the suspension of the whole series. Deans of Colleges changed the dinner-hour in hall, so that undergraduates had to choose between

Newman's sermons and their meal. From one Palace after another came episcopal charges emphasising the Protestant character of the Established Church.

Ward weighed in with two pamphlets in defence of the Tract, which were nicely calculated to make matters worse. He went much further then Newman, saying plainly that it was proper to subscribe to the Articles in a 'non-natural' sense. He went out of his way also to parade an admiration for Romanism. Anglicans, he declared, were not obliged to maintain their superiority to Papists either in doctrine or in practice. It was, however, 'a labour of love' to remain in the Church of England 'in order to elevate its tone'.

> 'Let those whose love for her is lukewarm content themselves with mourning in private over her decayed condition; her true and faithful children will endeavour to awaken the minds of their brethren to a sense of her present degradation.'

Ward was justified in arguing, as Newman had, that the Articles were 'intended to be vague and to include persons of discordant sentiments.'[1] But what of the lethal contempt with which he spoke of the Church in which he held Orders? Pusey understated the facts when he complained that such pertness did not become so young a man. The Master of Balliol was flabbergasted. 'When I meet Ward and talk to him, I find him so amusing and agreeable that it is almost impossible to believe that he is the same man who says these *dreadful* things in print.' And to think that in his own college the undergraduates were listening to lectures upon logic from this 'most dangerous' person! The Master shuddered: 'What *heresy* may he not insinuate under the form of a syllogism!' To meet his wishes Ward amiably resigned his lectureship without a struggle.

He no longer believed in the validity of his priestly Orders.[2] He would still hear confessions, and pray with the penitents, but now refused to give absolution. Whether he continued to celebrate, or receive, Holy Communion remains obscure. Newman resigned the living of St. Mary's in September 1842, and retired to semi-monastic life with a few sympathetic disciples at Littlemore. During

[1] 'That the Articles were meant to keep as many Roman Catholics as possible within the Reformed Church' seemed to Mr. Gladstone 'an A.B.C. truth, almost a truism, of the reign of Elizabeth.'

[2] I cannot discover that any of the Carolines accepted the Eucharist as principal Anglican service and a Sunday obligation. Would anyone who did not accept this be considered as one of themselves by Anglo-Catholics today?

the two following years Ward and Pusey contested for his succession in the leadership of the Movement. This had now split into two. Ward never took any stock of the Caroline Divines, in whose theology Pusey found a precedent for his own. Indeed he differed from Newman no less than from Pusey in never feeling any affection for the Church of England— 'Old Mother Damnable', as he liked to call the institution in which he ministered. In a magazine called *The British Critic* he pursued his campaign of extravagances. Some of his arguments were trenchant.

> 'The idea that, to a Christian believing all the astonishing mysteries which are contained in the doctrine of the Incarnation, the further belief in the real presence, even as defined in the Tridentine decrees, is a serious tax on his credulity, is not tenable for one moment.'

This seems logically unanswerable, but does not allow for the obvious fact that men give far more easy credence to doctrines in which they have been brought up than to those with which they are unfamiliar.[1] Ward seemed usually less concerned to persuade than to exasperate. Thus he exalted the Italian schools at the expense of the English ones, and for the reason that in the former ecclesiastical espionage was customary. One may agree that English Public Schools could never have become as beastly as they often were, if the masters had had any notion of what was going on. It was typical of Ward to present an argument that had some force in language making it needlessly unacceptable.[2]

---

[1] Kingsley decided that Newman must be either a liar or a lunatic because he declared his belief in the doctrine of the Immaculate Conception. Yet it is more easy to believe that Mary was born without original sin than that the rest of mankind are born with it as a result of Adam's disobedience. Probably Kingsley had not troubled to discover the meaning of the doctrine he was denouncing, and supposed that it declared the mother of the Blessed Virgin to be herself a virgin.

[2] Newman, on the other hand, was later to pride himself on the absence of espionage at the Oratory School under his direction. But then he had not been to Winchester: he was educated in a large private school at Ealing. Years later Ward fulminated against classical studies which were almost unchallenged in English schools. Logic could see the subservience of consistency to custom comically exemplified in the spectacle of an ecclesiastic expounding to adolescents the legends of Pasiphae and Ganymede. In France the Abbé Gaume led a similar assault upon classical education. Ward went further, and deplored the unrestricted study by the young of any writer who implied 'some standard of praise and blame inconsistent with the Christian.'

All this was unspeakably trying for Dr. Pusey. The beloved Movement that it was his life work to promote was being discredited by Ward's taste for teasing. And now the Rev. William Palmer of Worcester College published a pamphlet against the Tracts for which he found in Ward's writings an abundance of ammunition. Ward set out upon a reply, which appeared in June 1844. This was entitled *The Ideal of a Christian Church Considered in Comparison with Existing Practice.* 'Well, Ward,' said the Master of Balliol, 'your book is like yourself, fat, awkward and ungainly.' The volume, which extended to over six hundred pages, had been written in a few months, and must have been a lot easier to write than to read.

It began with an exposition of the author's reasons for believing in Revelation. Ward was, in his own words, open to the irruption of philosophic doubt. Like Newman, and unlike most apologists, he was painfully aware, from his own experience, of the intellectual objections to revealed religion. 'Had I not been enthusiastically religious, I should have been enthusiastically profligate.' He followed Kant in holding that conscience was the primary informant in religious enquiry (a view which Mr. Gladstone, as a disciple of Bishop Butler, was to condemn as subjective). And upon this base he arrived at acceptance of the whole Catholic corpus of doctrine, constructing with what he took to be rigorous logic an edifice that others took to be as ill-founded as an inverted pyramid. A considerable part of the book is devoted to a vexing comparison between the Church of England as Ward knew it and the ideal of a Christian Church, in which he depicted the Roman Church as he believed it to be. Here are two quotations:

'To speak plainly, believing as I most firmly do, that ever since the schism of the sixteenth century the English Church has been swayed by a spirit of arrogance, self-contentment, and self-complacency, resembling rather an absolute infatuation than the imbecility of ordinary pride, which has stifled her energies, crippled her resources, frustrated all the efforts of her most devoted children to raise her from her existing degradation, I for one, however humble my position, will not be responsible for uttering one word or implying one opinion which shall tend to foster so outrageous a delusion.'

Having emphasised 'our Church's total neglect of her duties as a guardian and a witness to morality', he attributes to the Established

Church 'the grave and serious responsibility of that wide gulf of separation between rich and poor; that contrast of selfish and careless neglect on one side, with the union of rankling suspicion and hollow, cowardly servility on the other; which, (whatever honourable exceptions may exist) is now so actively and increasingly mischievous throughout our social system.' Then comes a reference to the hideous poverty and sweated child-labour revealed by Lord Ashley.

'Has the English Church at least exhibited the grace of humiliation and repentance? Has the blush of shame been visible on her cheek? Have her ministers sorrowfully and contritely confessed their unpardonable and sinful dereliction of duty, and taken on themselves bitter shame as fact after fact was brought into light? . . . Incredible as it might have appeared, the very conception would seem never to have occurred to them; with unruffled brow and complacent voice they have still repeated their insane watchwords. "pure and apostolical", "holy and venerable" Church, and have dared to speak of the corruptions of other Christian bodies, when they should rather have been in lowly and penitential abasement, mourning those of their own.'[1]

This seems the only moment in Ward's career when he revealed any conspicuous preoccupation with the physical conditions of the poor. An Anglican might reasonably retort with a reference to the social degradation visible in the two Sicilies, Spain and Spanish America. Did the clergy in these countries sorrowfully and contritely confess their unpardonable and sinful dereliction of duty? A Catholic—Father Ryder of the Oratory in his pamphlet *Idealism in Theology*—refutes Ward's argument with a reference to the French Church in the years before the Revolution.

The one consolation that Ward could discover was that the seeds of better things were beginning to sprout:

'We found, oh most joyful, most wonderful, most unexpected sight, the whole cycle of Roman doctrine gradually possessing numbers of English Churchmen.'

Such an opinion was designed to infuriate every loyal Anglican. It will be noticed, moreover, that it is expressed in an exclamatory style that is more Latin than English.

Mill considered *The Ideal* an epoch-making book. Mr. Gladstone remarked that it ill became a priest of the Church of England to speak of her, even if he thought of her, in terms so wanting in respect. 'The Master of Balliol was found pacing up and down his room, book in hand, quoting in accents of astonishment and horror some of its strongest expressions. "We are a corrupted Church!". "We are in a degraded position!". "We are to sue for pardon at the feet of Rome humbly!"; and then the word *humbly* he repeated in a yet deeper tone of horror.'

Evidently Ward liked nothing better than to shock. To the end there was something not adult in him. One can either deplore a surface frivolity such as was to crop up in another gifted convert G. K. Chesterton; or one can enjoy the mischievousness with which this *enfant terrible*, this outsize urchin, teased the solemn Victorians among whom he moved. This is not to deny that Ward was deeply in earnest. His whole life glows with utter unworldliness, with efficacious piety. To be more whole-hearted would be impossible. There is, however, a distinction between being earnest and being in earnest; and Ward differed from the mass of his educated contemporaries in England by choosing to express his most profound convictions in language so extravagant as often to appear ironical. Though he justly prided himself upon his logical powers, the position he assumed in *The Ideal* was logically indefensible. 'In subscribing to the Articles,' he wrote, 'I renounce no one Roman doctrine.' But behind all Roman doctrines lies the assertion that Catholics are subject to ecclesiastical authority. And who authorised Ward to remain an Anglican while holding all these Roman doctrines? Certainly no Anglican Bishop. Just as certainly, no Roman Bishop. Only, it seems, his own conscience— and this means that his position was immitigably Protestant.

In December 1844, six months after the publication of *The Ideal*, the Vice-Chancellor of Oxford gave notice of proceedings to be taken against it. Six passages were quoted as inconsistent with the Articles and with Ward's good faith in subscribing to these. It was proposed to deprive him of his degrees. It was further proposed to assert that the Articles must be accepted, not according to the subtle explanations devised in the Nineteenth Century, but according to the rigid definitions of the Sixteenth. Only a week's notice was given of this second proposal, which was obviously aimed at Tract XC; Mr. Gladstone opined that this was to treat Newman as worse than a dog, and that the plan presented an aspect of incredible wickedness.

George Moberly, headmaster of Winchester, afterwards Bishop

of Salisbury, protested promptly against both the threatened measures. He questioned the authority in these matters of the Oxford Convocation. Furthermore 'it seems highly scandalous that any degree of what is called Romanising should be visited more severely than the heretical statements affecting the foundations of the Faith, the Trinity and the Incarnation.' This was sound reasoning, but the Church of England was more indulgent to sceptics than to Romanisers. The Liberals in the Church of England were little better pleased than the Tractarians with the Vice-Chancellor's proposals. Tait, the Erastian who later became Primate, approved of proceedings against Ward as a Papist in a Reformed Church, but defended Ward's good faith and claimed some liberty in interpreting the Articles. The latitudinarian F. D. Maurice went straight to the point: 'After all, he signed the document about as honestly as the rest of the world.' Another latitudinarian, Arthur Stanley, wrote for Ward the peroration of his speech in self-defence, an appeal to all Anglicans who loved liberty. None of the Evangelicals seems to have had enough self-respect or decency to join in these objections, although the Prayer Book laid down doctrines they did not pretend to accept, and enjoined practices they refused to perform.

The proceedings were opened in February 1845. 'Shew me,' said Ward, 'how any of the recognised parties in the Church can subscribe in a natural sense, before you condemn me for subscribing in a non-natural.' But, being Ward, he was not content to stand on this unassailable defensive position. Over and over again he protested that he believed all the doctrines of the Roman Church. He made a series of sallies into the ranks of his judges. As *The Edinburgh Review* remarked, 'Every statement and overt inference that could offend their prejudices, irritate their vanity, or wound their self-respect was urged with the zeal of a candidate for martyrdom.' The result was inevitable.

The objectionable passages in *The Ideal* were censured by a majority of 777 to 391; and Ward was deprived of his degrees by a majority of 569 to 511. The proposal to condemn Tract XC did not come to the vote, because the Proctors exercised their right of veto. J. R. Bloxam, Fellow of Magdalen and a lifelong friend of Newman (though he remained an Anglican) records, perhaps not without satisfaction: 'It was a cold east wind that day, and ten or more members of Convocation who came up against him died of the journey.'

That afternoon Ward went to see Pusey. Though still a Fellow of Balliol, he had ceased to be a graduate. 'They can't expect me to wear an undergraduate's cap and gown. I suppose I must wear my Beaver.'

He went on to crack a series of jokes about the disputes likely to arise with the Master of Balliol. A voice was heard from the other end of the room: 'The situation seems to me, Mr. Ward, of the utmost gravity. It is indeed a serious crisis. Let us not at such a time give way to the spirit of levity or hilarity.' This Victorian voice was Manning's; and the first meeting between the two men who were to become such formidable allies reveals the depth of the temperamental gulf between them.

What Ward did as a first result of his condemnation was characteristically unexpected: he announced his engagement to be married. Keble and Pusey, though both of them had taken wives, were deeply pained. Ward had not changed his views about the obligation of clerical celibacy, but he had long since ceased to consider himself a priest. So married he was to a Miss Wingfield, a zealous Puseyite and the daughter of a Canon. Six months later he made his submission to Rome. One cannot well understand why so pious a man chose to continue so long without the support of the Sacraments. His conversion had to be precipitated by his wife. In the middle of copying an article in which he declared that the Church of Rome was the true Church, she broke down: 'I cannot stand it, I shall go and be received into the Catholic Church.'

Ward was the first in the procession of eminent Anglicans who were to submit to Rome.[1] A month later Newman made his submission, and with him three of his most attached disciples. Frederick Faber followed in the same year. Manning remained an Anglican till 1851. There were thousands of other converts during this period, many of them highly educated and belonging to the clergy or the nobility. This mass-movement excited hardly less

[1] As a result of Ward's condemnation, the Church of England had already in 1843 lost a clergyman named Sibthorp, who soon reverted to Canterbury and then back to Rome for good. There was also the Rev. A. D. Wackerbath. Earlier converts, though hardly to be described as eminent Anglicans, were Pugin, who was received in 1834, and Ambrose Lisle Mark Phillipps, who later saw fit to change his name to Phillipps de Lisle. He was received in 1825 at the age of thirteen; subsequently a vision was vouchsafed to him in the neighbourhood of his school. An eccentric and immoderate character, he devoted his abundant energies to the promotion of Gothic architecture and of a corporate reunion of the Church of England with the Church of Rome.

disturbance in the Church they reinforced than in the Church they deserted.

After three centuries of a persecution that had grown less and less severe, the adherents of 'the Old Religion' in England had become a deliberately unobtrusive body, hoping indeed for freedom from their remaining disabilities,[1] but at least equally anxious to avoid any action that might fan the embers of that anti-Catholic bigotry which had as recently as in 1780 burnt down their chapels and their houses. Though justly proud of their loyalty to the Church, they had no wish to renew the ancestral experience of martyrdom and forfeiture. The tepidity, moreover, which penetrated the Church of England in the Eighteenth Century had weakened the ardour also of the Catholic body. While still praying for the conversion of England, they seldom showed any confidence that their prayers would be answered. They were decidedly conservative in their religion, and little attracted by Continental innovations. Lacking diocesan bishops, they were governed by Vicars Apostolic. Not allowed into the English Universities, they were seldom conspicuous for concern with culture.[2]

A community thus comprehensibly hidebound had to digest numbers of converts, often learned, always enthusiastic and bursting with the missionary spirit. Bishop Wiseman might entertain glorious visions of England returning to the Faith. Many of the old Catholics seem to have found it all very upsetting. Five years after Ward's conversion, Wiseman, now a Cardinal, announced in typically flamboyant language the establishment in England of a Catholic hierarchy. There were screams of 'papal aggression' throughout the country, and Parliament made itself ridiculous by passing a bill, which was never enforced, forbidding the new Archbishop of Westminster to assume this title. Such was the first unpleasant result of all this proselytising. There followed a multitude of disputes within the Church about new-fangled devotions, Religious Orders, ritual and architecture. Pugin, seconded by Phillipps de Lisle, held that Gothic was the only style of building permissible to Catholics, and stigmatised as

---

[1] Catholic Emancipation 1829, Admission of Catholics to the Universities 1854.

[2] John Lingard, 1771–1851, a priest and a most distinguished historian, was almost the only Catholic Englishman of his generation to make any mark as an intellectual.

'pagan' the Italian classical and baroque styles in which old Catholics and converts alike often preferred to express their devotion to Rome. In England, as in the other enlightened regions of Europe, the revival of Catholicism excited acute controversy among believers about the attitude to be adopted towards contemporary thought, entailing questions political and historical as well as theological, a controversy focused eventually upon the powers of the Pope.

What in his new Communion was to be Ward's future? By marrying he had shewn his determination to be a layman. 'What is the province of the laity?' Monsignor Talbot enquired, long afterwards, in a celebrated letter, 'To hunt, to shoot, to entertain. These matters they understand, but to meddle with ecclesiastical matters they have no right at all . . .'[1] Doubtless Mgr Talbot would have admitted another function as within the province of the laity—to further Catholic interests politically. But Ward, having taken Anglican Orders, was ineligible for the House of Commons. Assuredly he had not become a Catholic in order to hunt or shoot or even to entertain. Theology, he felt, was the only study 'which to pursue is really to *live*; in following others one does but *vegetate*.' He therefore spent his first Catholic year deepening his theological knowledge; and for this purpose he went to live near St. Edmund's College, Ware, a Catholic seminary in which the students were not allowed even to see the newspapers. He commissioned Pugin to build for him a small house.

After the first meeting between this eccentric pair—in Ward's rooms at Balliol before his conversion—Pugin had exclaimed 'What an extraordinary thing that so glorious a man as Ward should be living in a room without mullions to the windows!' When told of this, Ward had asked 'What are mullions?' Now he insisted that some light and air should be allowed into the house that was being built for him. Pugin could not forgive the rejection of his beloved lancet windows. 'I assure you that if I had known that Mr. Ward would have turned out so badly, I would never have designed a respectable house for him. He ought not to be allowed in

---

[1] Mgr Talbot did not mean that these were the only duties incumbent upon the laity. He was feeling extremely cross because the leading laymen of England had just presented Newman with an address assuring him of their gratitude. His letter continued: 'There is, however, one exception to this rule, because he is really a theologian. I mean Dr. Ward.' Need I add that Dr. Ward had not signed the address to Newman?

the vicinity of so fine a screen.' (The chapel at St. Edmund's included a rood-screen designed by Pugin.) 'Who could have thought that the glorious man whom I knew at Oxford could have fallen so miserably low!' Some while later, when Ward attacked rood-screens as undevotional, Pugin wrote to him: 'I must plainly tell you that I consider you a greater enemy to true Christianity than the most rabid Exeter Hall fanatic.' Ward commented: 'I knew Pugin was strong on rood-screens; I didn't know he was so good a hand at rude letters.' Late in life he said: 'I have a very great sympathy with Pugin. He was very like me. He was a man of one idea, and so was I. His idea was Gothic architecture, mine was devotion to Rome.'

Four years after his conversion Ward, who had not been well-to-do, inherited from an uncle large estates in the Isle of Wight. Death, hardly less than sex, was a subject apt to lead the Victorians into triumphs of self-deception. But, so far from turning their eyes away from it, as we now incline to do, they loved—particularly the women—to dwell upon it, revelling with hushed voices in the pageantry of woe. It was a poor novel that did not proffer a death-bed or two. (The popularity of the detective-story today suggests that our preoccupation with death is equal to theirs, though expressed in toughness instead of in sentimentality.) To our cynical eyes they often appear morbid, so anxious were they not only to display but also to feel as much grief as possible. Ward, however, being in Tennyson's words 'grotesquely truthful', did not disguise from himself a wish that, when his uncle lay dying, the end might be speedy.

'He consulted a priest . . . as to how far his feeling was a faulty one. The priest suggested the customary considerations. "It is quite enough that you should feel a certain regret at your uncle's *death*," he said, "though you may be pleased to inherit his property." But Mr. Ward's candour was not to be beaten. "I feel no regret whatever at the prospect," he insisted. "Well, you must have a certain wish, quite apart from other consequences, that he might be spared."—"No, not the slightest. I never cared for him in the least."—"Your poor uncle has been suffering—your spirits fall a little at all events when you hear he is worse?"—"On the contrary, they rise." The priest began to fear that he was dealing with a reprobate. "Good heavens," he said suddenly, "you would not do anything to *hasten* his death, would you?" The roar of laughter with which his penitent received the question was sufficient answer.'

No less typical in their candour are some remarks he made later about his new situation.

'I am a large landed proprietor, and I rejoice in my thereby assured income as a means of securely prosecuting my physical or literary or philosophical studies. Otherwise I am profoundly uninterested in my estate. I cannot distinguish wheat from barley; I am quite indifferent to field sports. I have no tendency whatever towards personal relations with my agricultural dependants. Information reaches me that my agent has been acting with gross injustice to various of my tenants, and is endeavouring to stifle their complaints. What is my spontaneous impulse? Probably to invent some salve to my conscience as regards the tenants, and to plunge myself afresh in my favourite studies. I have no particular affection for my tenants any more than for any other farmers who happen to live in my neighbourhood and pursue their (to me utterly unintelligible) avocations. I can easily persuade myself, if I choose, that I may conscientiously ignore the information I have received, and continue without further enquiry to repose trust in my agent. On the other hand, if I am really conscientious, I am able by means of due thought to see clearly where my duty lies. Accordingly I put forth anti-impulsive effort. With sighing and weariness of heart I bid *adieu* to my studies for the necessary interval of painful and laborious enquiry.'[1]

A lack of what are hopefully called 'natural feelings' distinguished Ward as a father no less than as a landlord. Again, his frankness is strikingly un-Victorian. He is reported to have said of his children 'I am always informed when they are born, but know nothing more of them.' Thence he derived the following syllogism:

'I can have no affection for persons with whose character I am unacquainted; I know nothing of the character of my younger children; ergo, I can have no affection for them.'

[1] This passage occurs as an illustration of Ward's theory of 'anti-impulsive effort', in which he strangely thought to find an argument in favour of Free Will. The facts, however, are autobiographical, and reveal him as the least self-deceiving of men as well as highly conscientious.

When they grew up, he seems to have behaved to them uncommonly well. His other relations he avoided. 'The Wards,' he said, 'have always disagreed on every conceivable subject. Therefore I best agree with my family by differing from them.' Sometimes he arranged not to be on speaking terms; and, having achieved this pleasing condition with his brother, Henry, he once met him at the theatre, forgot the quarrel, and enjoyed a chat.

'Next morning came a letter from Henry Ward; "Dear William, in the hurry of the moment tonight I forgot that we had arranged to meet as strangers, and I write this lest you should misunderstand me, to say that I think we had better adhere to our arrangement; and I remain, dear William, your affectionate brother, Henry Ward." '

Ward replied, at once: 'Dear Henry, I too had forgotten our arrangement. I agree with you that we had better keep to it; and I remain, your affectionate brother, W. G. Ward.'

The peppery element in Ward may have come from the sluggishness of his liver, to remedy which he was obliged by his physician to ride for an hour every day. He loathed horses, and was always falling off. Eventually, the road proving too dangerous, he built for himself a riding-school on his estate, and another in London. (His income was £10,000 a year.) He never learnt even to rise in his stirrups, and his corpulence was such that a horse could not stand the strain for more than ten minutes: 'After every jolt the dead weight came down on the flanks of the animal, until after two or three circuits they quivered frightfully!' Six horses were therefore needed to give him the prescribed hour, and while his mount was changed, he would read or argue about theology. His dependence upon this regimen made it difficult for him to go away for more than thirty-six hours from the neighbourhood of one or other of his riding-schools.

In 1851 Ward became lecturer in Moral Philosophy at St. Edmund's College, and in the following year he became Professor of Dogmatic Theology. Some Catholics protested: it was unheard of for a layman to occupy such a position, but he had Wiseman's support. When the ecclesiastic who afterwards became Cardinal Vaughan was appointed Head of the College, he told Ward that he proposed to replace him with someone better qualified. Ward was content to exclaim: 'How very interesting! Yes, I quite see your point, most interesting! Thank you, thank you. So very kind of you to be so frank!' Vaughan changed his mind, and Ward remained at St. Edmund's till 1858, when he went to live on his estate. In 1863 he was invited by Wiseman to become editor of *The Dublin Review*; he consented, and thus was involved, not uncongenially, in every dispute that agitated Catholics during the next fifteen years.

Some account of the now unfamiliar battlefield imposes itself. The world was changing at a speed that then seemed vertiginous, and the Church was in disarray. Pius IX, after an ill-fated flirtation with political liberalism, had embarked upon a long-lived policy of hostility to the modern world. This excited increasing dismay among the intellectual Catholics in England, as in France and Germany. The fruitful, though disturbing, researches in biology and biblical criticism could not be met properly, they felt, with mere condemnation. If the Church did not digest so much of the new knowledge as was not definitely hostile to her doctrines, her hold upon all save the most uneducated would be in danger. There emerged therefore a 'progressive' party of Catholic scholars and statesmen, determined to voice the irresistible conclusions of their intellect, and certain that these could not prove inconsistent with Revelation rightly interpreted.

The English section of this party was headed by Sir John Acton, afterwards Lord Acton. His erudition was unequalled; his standards of intellectual integrity were formidable in their rigour; and his belief in liberty was little less absolute than his belief in God. (He went so far as to hold that all Dominicans lived in mortal sin, because they were committed to approval of the persecution of heretics.) He was utterly fearless, a close friend of Mr. Gladstone, and connected with many of the most illustrious families in Europe, his blood being more German than Italian, more Italian than French, more French than English. Like Ward, he was a layman; but he was not a convert; and, excessive as were some of his opinions, his upbringing as well as his erudition gave him an insight into the historical reality and practical workings of the Church, such as was never approached by Ward, who continued to see in it only his ideal. In *The Rambler* (afterwards *The Home and Foreign Review*) Acton conducted a bold campaign in defence of biblical criticism, historical objectivity, and political freedom, against the reactionary policy of Pio Nono. The Vatican, he considered, was losing the battle against infidelity by the backwardness of its apologetics. The Liberal Catholicism of which Acton was the chief English spokesman commanded on the Continent the sympathy in varying degrees of such eminent figures as Lacordaire, Dupanloup, Montalembert and Döllinger.

The adverse party, which claimed the support of the Holy Father, was championed with peculiar vehemence by Veuillot in France, by Ward and Manning in England.[1] Like many converts, Ward was from the first more Popish than the Pope. 'I should like a new papal bull every morning with my breakfast,' he declared. Such a view was absurdly alien to the traditional prudence of Catholic theologians. Ward disagreed with them also in holding that the existence of God could hardly be demonstrated by philosophical reasoning.[2] Having nevertheless managed to accept the premise that God existed, he argued that God must be good, that therefore He must want men to be saved, that therefore He must have founded the Church to tell them the truth, and that therefore at least one member of the Church, the Pope, must be able to furnish the right answer to every question. If his opinions were not quite so simple as they appear in my summary, they were decidedly more simple than the accepted teachings of the Church.

It was not from any English Catholic that Ward learnt this extravagant ultramontanism. In France, where the tyrannies successively of the Jacobins, of Napoleon, of Charles X and of Napoleon III had developed an addiction to untempered authority, a journal called *L'Univers* (edited by Louis Veuillot, a most gifted writer) was claiming for the Pope powers hitherto hardly dreamed of. Joseph de Maistre had inaugurated this school of thought, which drew from a great Catholic, Ozanam, the following indictment:

'It goes about looking for the boldest paradoxes, the most disputable propositions, provided they irritate the modern spirit. It presents the truth to men not by the side which attracts them, but by that which repels them. It does not propose to bring back unbelievers, but to stir up the passions of believers.'

These words might have been prompted by Ward's activities. He

---

[1] Manning was made Archbishop of Westminster in 1865. The appointment was a personal intervention by Pius IX, who heard a voice from Heaven saying—in Italian—'Put him there, put him there.' Such at least is the account given of the incident by Manning seventeen years later.

[2] At the end of his life Ward disowned this heretical opinion, which is called Fideism.

never descended, as Veuillot so often did, to grossly personal attacks upon the Catholics who disagreed with him, but a natural taste for excess gave to his language a violence that could not fail to wound. Though easily irritated, he was the least touchy of men, and he had not the imagination to realise that others were more sensitive. In his dealings with Newman there is an element of tragedy.

Newman's career in the Catholic Church was darkened by a series of heart-breaking disappointments. The authorities were not content to neglect the most distinguished intellect within their obedience. They repeatedly pressed him to undertake some task and, when he had become deeply implicated therein, left him in an untenable position. One cannot but be reminded of a cat playing with a mouse. Were these troubles due entirely to the machinations of his adversaries, or was there in him some indefinable quality that invited misfortune? 'Shall I tell you,' Manning said towards the end of his life, 'what has ruined that man's career? One thing only: Temper! Temper!! Temper!!!' Wiseman complained of Newman's 'intolerable arrogance'. He himself confessed: 'I have generally got on well with juniors, but not with superiors.' Nevertheless neither pride nor anger seems to me characteristic of Newman, unless one is to condemn as pride that honesty which prevented him from saying he was wrong when he believed he was right. A grain of hypocrisy is usually required for success within any large organisation. Newman lacked this; and when unjustly treated, took refuge in silence, instead of kissing the rod and acknowledging the justice of his opponents with a prudent affectation of humility. Some great saints have been able to feel gratitude to their tormentors. Lacking that so exceptional grace, Newman must be praised, I suggest, for not simulating this in order to edify. In any case Lytton Strachey's picture of him as a defenceless dove struck down by the predacious Manning is more dramatic than accurate. Of the two men Newman had far the sharper talons, though he seldom allowed himself to use them.[1]

In the acrimonious feuds that rent English Catholicism during the fifteen years before the Council of 1870, Newman occupied a central position, and suffered the customary fate of the moderate caught between two extremes. His hatred for liberalism was no

---

[1] Witness not only the *Apologia* in its original form but his letter to Mgr Talbot when invited to preach in Rome.

less hearty than Ward's.[1] He was however too wise to imagine that it could be combated by mere conservatism, and too expert in Church history to accept the Ultramontane innovations proposed by Ward and Veuillot. The mistrust, moreover, with which the Vatican treated him, became reciprocal.[2] During the first years after their conversion, he remained on excellent terms with Ward. As late as 1863, when he became editor of *The Dublin*, Ward invited him to contribute.[3] The invitation was not accepted: the disagreements between the two men had already become marked; and henceforward the gulf widened. Ward knew that Newman was in touch with Acton and Simpson, his adversaries on *The Home and Foreign*. From this followed the assumption that Newman shared their temerarious views, whereas in fact he continued to correspond with these champions of theological liberalism only in the hope of restraining their excesses. Agreeing with them, however, that the Church could not defeat criticism merely by ignoring it, he was concerned to provide an apologetic appropriate to the age.[4] This struck the ingenuous Ward as cowardly and anti-Roman. He was one of the most unreasonable opponents of Newman's scheme for establishing an Oratory at Oxford, and was largely responsible for the Vatican's refusal to allow Newman's return to the University City. 'Does it not seem queer,' Newman wrote in 1864, 'that the two persons now most opposed to me are Manning and Ward?' His opposition to them was about to become even more conspicuous, for the battle about Infallibility was now impending.

Questioned about the Catholic attitude to some other issue, Ward replied with characteristic candour: 'Opinions are divided, there are two views of which I, as usual, take the most bigoted.' About Papal Infallibility there were more than two views. Very few Catholic theologians denied it outright; many accepted it, but believed that to decree it would be inopportune; and the majority, while wishing it to be decreed, held that the limits within which Infallibility applied must be rigorously defined. Ward, however, had no patience with such reserves. In his son's words 'he reduced

[1] Liberalism in politics as well as in 'religion': 'No one can dislike the democratic principle more than I do.' *Letter to Duke of Norfolk.*

[2] One assignable reason for this distrust is that a letter to Rome from Newman in 1860 was not delivered by Wiseman and Manning.

[3] In this letter Ward wrote of himself: 'It is certainly a new phenomenon to have the editor of a quarterly profoundly ignorant of history, politics and literature.'

[4] *The Grammar of Assent* appeared in 1870.

to a minimum the necessity of guidance at the hands of theological experts, whether in determining the authority of a document or its obligatory explanation.' He never went quite so far as Veuillot, who most untheologically spoke of the Pope as directly 'inspired' by the Almighty, but his approach to the intricate problem was altogether too simple; and, following his bad example, let me summarise it altogether too simply: 'The more Bulls the better, and all of them infallible.'

Ward led a peculiarly sheltered life. He avoided the society of those who did not share his preoccupation with theology or else with metaphysics. He even kept visitors away from his house in the Isle of Wight, because he intended his sons to be priests, his daughters nuns. He was proud of his remoteness from ordinary interests: 'You will find me narrow and strong,' he warned a sub-editor of *The Dublin*, 'very narrow and very strong.' The extraordinary ignorance that resulted from this narrowness was revealed on a walk with Herbert Vaughan. 'What a fine beech tree!' the future Cardinal remarked. Ward was amazed. 'I knew,' he said, 'that you were a dogmatic theologian and an ascetic theologian and now I find that you are acquainted with all the minutiae of botany.'

Extreme unworldliness—but not unresponsiveness to nature— was a Tractarian characteristic, conspicuous also in Newman. (Manning, on the other hand, whose connection with the Oxford Movement had been short and ambiguous, was entirely at home in the great world.) When it was suggested in 1865 that Newman should go to Rome to explain his project for an Oxford Oratory, he exclaimed: 'What chance should *I* have with my broken Italian: they don't, they can't, talk Latin?' In the following year Ward was similarly pressed to visit Rome, and he too refused. 'But you love Rome so deeply,' said Manning. 'Yes,' he replied, 'my heart is very Roman, but my stomach is very English.' How typical, an enemy may comment, the bitterness, not to say the pride and petulance, of Newman, and the sturdy humour of Ward! Yes, but Ward could afford to be genial: it was not to calumniate him that Mgr Talbot scurried through the Vatican *coulisses* with a mouthful of lies.

None the less, Ward was wise, I suspect, to remain at home. In a figurative as well as a literal sense Rome might have turned his stomach. While still an Anglican with little personal experience of Catholicism, he had supposed that in *The Ideal of a Christian Church* he was describing the reality of the Roman Church. This was an illusion that could hardly have afflicted an educated man brought up as a Catholic. The Church Militant has never pretended to be perfect; even in the Pope infallibility must never be confused with impeccability. The consequent cynicism—or should one not say healthy realism?—with which devout Catholics sometimes speak of ecclesiastics, and in particular of the Curia, can shock and mislead innocent Protestants. Though the point is only hypothetical, I do not see how a visit to Rome could have failed to dismay Ward. Rome is cautious, dilatory, traditionally attached to compromise wherever possible; and such qualities were loathsome to him. What Italians admire as a *combinazione* would have struck him as an affront to logic. He was too little a man of the world to understand the practical prudence that has usually distinguished Vatican policy. His passionate love of Rome could be best preserved by absence.

His ignorance of the intellectual and spiritual climate in contemporary Rome was complemented by an almost equal ignorance of history. This led him to deny what was properly incontestable. Opinions 'not really true' have, as Newman pointed out, been universally accepted by the Church at a given time. Ward was acclaimed by Talbot as the only layman in England with the Roman spirit,[1] but in the controversy about Infallibility he went too far, and found himself obliged to withdraw a portion of his thesis as exaggerated.[2] Newman already accused him in a letter of making a Church within a Church: 'I protest not against your tenets but against what I call your schismatical spirit . . . I pray God that I may never denounce, as you do, what the Church has not denounced.'[3] In a letter to Manning Ward blamed Newman's influence for promoting, though unconsciously, both disloyalty to the Vicar of Christ and worldliness. He adds these extraordinary words: 'But unfortunately (as I think) Newman has slighted you in some degree; and this leads you possibly to magnify the Christian duty of forgiveness, while not adequately pondering on the Christian duty of protest.' Another Oratorian, Father Ryder, Manning's nephew by marriage, published in 1867 the first of three pamphlets

[1] He was also the only one to write to Rome (to Mgr Talbot) in support of Manning's elevation to the see of Westminster.

[2] Dupanloup, the leader of the French inopportunists, seized eagerly upon this retraction.

[3] Ward was, to quote his son, 'quite intolerable' in his theological criticisms of Newman. Talbot advised Manning to restrain these: he was alarmed at the disgust they excited in the laity.

answering Ward's extravagant articles about Infallibility. When Newman identified himself with this, Manning wrote to Talbot: 'This is opportune, but very sad.' How different would have been Ward's response to this occasion! I imagine him exclaiming: 'This time he has cut his own throat—splendid, splendid!'; and in this not a grain of ill will, whereas Manning's 'sadness' seems to me redolent of hypocrisy and malice. In his treatment of Newman Manning was so consistently ungenerous that one must suspect jealousy. Lytton Strachey shewed a culpable blindness to the evidence when he suggested that Manning's conversion was caused by ambition. It was in fact a triumph of conscience over worldliness. Yet love of power was his besetting sin, and all the more grievous because he persuaded himself that what he wanted, God wanted. 'In a quite unusual degree Manning was possessed of the idea that he was under the guidance of the Holy Ghost', and he thought therefore that opposition to himself must be displeasing to God. 'This frame of mind was, no doubt, a relic of the evangelical influence that played so strongly on Manning in his younger days.' (See Abbot Butler's *Ullathorne*.) But it is not easy to be fair to Manning: we know too much about him. Probably many of the men we most respect would cut a worse figure than he does, if their biographers had, like his, printed every private paper, however discreditable.

While the Council was sitting, a newspaper somehow procured and published a private letter by Newman to his Bishop, in which he denounced the extreme Ultramontanes as 'an insolent and aggressive faction.' What Ward made of this has not been disclosed. I doubt whether he felt any resentment. He might indeed have welcomed the epithets as a tribute to his leadership.

The Decree of Papal Infallibility, voted during a portentous thunderstorm, the day before the outbreak of the Franco-Prussian War, was worded cautiously enough to allay the more extravagant hopes and fears of the two parties in the Church. Newman was relieved to learn that the Supreme Pontiff should not proceed in judging in matters of faith, without counsel, deliberation and the use of scientific means. When the proceedings of the Council were published, the introduction and some of the annotations ran counter to certain of Ward's extravagances, but this was not until after his death. At the time he confessed to disappointment that the range of Infallibility had not been elucidated in the Decree; and when told by von Hügel of the view that the Council had made a clean sweep of the extreme Right as well as the extreme Left, he rushed out of his house bareheaded. This was a sign of uncontrollable agitation. Only when beside themselves, or faced with some hideous emergency, did the Victorians venture into their gardens without a hat. He could console himself with a Brief addressed to him by the Holy Father in July 1870, congratulating him upon the ability, knowledge, erudition and eloquence he had used in his labours to diffuse light, and lovingly imparting to him the Apostolic Benediction.

Ward lived to see a decline in the power of the party of which he was a leader. In 1874 Newman's high reputation among English Catholics was further enhanced by his *Letter to the Duke of Norfolk*, which incidentally stigmatised extreme ultramontanes as injurious to souls and virtually 'trampling on the little ones for whom Christ died.' After reading this, Ward had to take a double dose of chloral to get a tolerable night. 'Do you remember,' he wrote, 'Warren Hastings saying, when he heard Burke's speech, he for a moment thought himself a monster. Apply the parable and remember how enormously J. H. N. has always influenced my mind.' A letter from Ward to Newman in the following year, includes this passage:

'I am daily more and more convinced that my aim has been the true one; but I am also daily more and more convinced that I have fallen into grievous mistakes of judgment from time to time, whether as regards what I have said, or (much more) my way of saying it. I may say with the greatest sincerity that the one main cause of this has always appeared to me to be my breach with you. Never was a man more unfit than I to play any kind of first fiddle. You supplied exactly what I needed; corrected extravagances, corrected crudities, suggested opposite considerations, pointed out exaggerations of language, etc., etc.'

And he concluded, in italics, '*The whole colour of my life has changed*, I assure you, from the loss of your sympathy. But my gratitude for the past will ever remain intact.'

This looks like a pleasing finale to the stormy relation between two uncommonly good men. Alas, it must be noted that Ward lived for seven years longer, during which Newman was made a Cardinal; and that there is no trace of Ward's having sent to him any message of congratulation. The honour indeed not only marked the rehabilitation of Newman, but also implicitly rebuked Ward's many assaults upon his orthodoxy. Manning found it in his heart, when Newman died, to preach at the Requiem: 'We have lost our greatest witness for the Faith . . . The memories of an affectionate friendship of more than sixty years . . . beyond the power of all books has been the example of his humble and unworldly life . . . the greatest of our people . . .' 'Affectionate'! Has not Ward's silence a far sweeter smell?

Newman's elevation to the purple had been one of the first results of the death of Pius IX in 1878 and the succession of Leo XIII. In the previous year Manning was already complaining of his unpopularity in Rome and of the 'intrigues' in the Vatican. Now that he no longer had the Pope's ear, he began to complain about 'the essential injustice' of the procedure of the Holy Office: 'Their pride will not let them say after all that the earth moves.' The allusion to Galileo comes as a charming surprise from Manning; and soon we find him declaring that 'Pontiffs have no infallibility in the world of fact, except only dogmatic.' It is impossible not to be amused by these lamentations. Manning had for years claimed that since the Pope agreed with him, he must be right, and Newman must be wrong. Now he cites cases in which 'Rome was misled, went wrong, and had to revoke its decisions.'

What did Ward make of all this? Did his Ultramontanism lose any of its fervour, now that he no longer agreed with the Pope? We have not been told. His correspondence with Manning apparently has come to an end, except for formal letters in 1878 upon Ward's retirement from *The Dublin Review*. He did not live to witness Manning's enthusiasm for teetotalism, which would not have pleased him. He might, however, have welcomed the spirited championship of the poor that gave such lustre to the Cardinal's last years. One may doubt whether the two men, loyally as they worked together, ever cared for one another with anything that could be called personal friendship. Manning sought to deprive Newman of the offered Cardinal's Hat by a misrepresentation that may or may not have been deliberate. Ward's view of this deplorable incident has not been made known. Did this perhaps play a part in the coolness that appears to have overtaken his relation with Manning? That, I must emphasise, is only a conjecture springing from my high opinion of Ward's passionate love for honesty.

After 1870 Ward seldom indulged in assaults upon his fellow-Catholics. He may have felt that the Decree of Infallibility had definitively settled the issue with which he was most concerned.

Moreover a severe illness, in which he recognised 'the inauguration of old age', left him less combative, and perhaps also more aware of the pain given to many godly men by his zest in controversy. He still delighted in argument for its own sake and became one of the most active members of the Metaphysical Society, which was founded in 1869 to bring together in friendly debate representatives of the most varied schools of opinion. Among the members were J. S. Mill, Huxley, Tyndall, Morley, Bagehot, Tennyson, Mr. Gladstone, Thirlwall and several other bishops. Every month there was a meeting, at which a paper would be read, followed by a discussion. Manning, like Ward, enjoyed these meetings. Newman refused to join: indeed his delicacy was offended at the notion of such contact with unbelievers. He could not understand, he said, how Christians like Dean Church and the Archbishop of York, 'to say nothing of Cardinal Manning', could let Huxley read in their presence a paper intended to refute our Lord's Resurrection. In Ward's mind the one anxiety was that there should be no misunderstanding of his position. Huxley has left the following account:

'Dr. Ward took me aside and opened his mind thus: "You and I are on such friendly terms that I do not think it is right to let you remain in ignorance of something I wish to tell you." Rather alarmed at what this might portend, I begged him to say on. "Well, we Catholics hold that so and so (naming certain colleagues whose heresies were of a less deep hue than mine) are not guilty of absolutely unpardonable error; but your case is different, and I feel it unfair not to tell you so." Greatly relieved, I replied, without a moment's delay, perhaps too impulsively, "My dear Dr. Ward, if you don't mind, I don't", whereupon we parted with a hearty handshake; and intermitted neither friendship nor fighting henceforth ... He was before all things a chivalrous English gentleman.'

What impressed Ward's opponents in the Society was his unsurpassable candour. 'The most truthful man I ever knew was a strict Ultramontane,' Tennyson remarked. 'He was grotesquely truthful.' Ward paid a similar tribute to Mill, 'the fairest, the most truth-loving, the most generous of opponents.'

To make clear the width of the gulf separating Ward from most of his fellow-members of the Metaphysical Society, and indeed from almost all his Victorian contemporaries, nothing serves better than a quotation from a pamphlet he published in 1862, *On the Relation of Intellectual Power to Man's true Perfection.*

'The world awaits praise or blame to human actions, on some such principles as these—

Principle 1. If a man makes the main end of his life to consist in labouring to promote his own interior perfection and growth in God's love,— if he concentrates his chief energy in the performance of this work,—he must have a mean and contemptible spirit. Monasteries are the proper place for him: he is fit for nothing better.

Principle 2. Those who are worthy of our honour as highminded and spirited men have two main motives ever before their mind: a sensitive regard to their honour, and a keen sense of their personal dignity. Good Catholics would express this by saying— they must be actuated by vainglory and pride in an intense degree.

Principle 3. As their springs of action are worldly, so also are the external objects to which their action is directed. Some great temporal end—the exaltation of our country's temporal greatness or the achievement of her liberty—here is a pursuit worthy of men's high aspirations. He who should regard godlessness and worldliness as immeasurably greater evils than political weakness or subjection, is a poltroon unworthy of the name of patriot.'

Principle 4. Physical courage is a far greater virtue, at least in a man, than meekness or humility, or forgivingness.

Principle 5. Of all modes of life, the most irrational is that, wherein a man or a body of men separate from the world, that they may the more uninterruptedly contemplate their Creator. I might most easily add to this list; but I have said enough to indicate clearly what I mean. Such as these, I say, are the principles by which the world estimates human conduct; by which Lord Macaulay measures facts of the past, and the *Times* newspaper facts of the present. These principles are not categorically stated in worldly literature; they are treated as too obvious and undeniable to need explicit statement; and they underlie the whole award of praise and blame, expressed or implied by the mass of men, when contemplating the actions of their fellows. The Church, on the other hand, has no office more important than that of witnessing to and upholding consistently and prominently a moral standard in the extremest degree contrary to this.'

Here is a dissidence from Victorianism more pronounced than any other I have been able to discover. In no age, of course, not even when the cathedral of Chartres was rising heavenwards, or when Francis of Assisi was enlivening the Umbrian valleys with spiritual blossoms—in no age have the mass of men acted save on principles that Ward so justly denounces as the extreme contrary of the Christian ethos. The Victorians, however, accepted these principles more ostentatiously, as it were, than had hitherto been usual. Utilitarianism offered a far more defiant and far wider-spread rivalry to Christianity than the atheism of a Holbach. Ward indeed goes on to confess that even Catholics, like himself, often acted as if they held the Church's principles to be true for one half hour and false for the rest of the day. Is it unfair to comment that the Church has usually seemed more interested, as well as more successful, in its attacks upon lust than in its recommendations of humility?[1]

Not content with denigrating the sense of honour, physical courage and patriotism in the usual acceptation of the word, Ward was at pains to parade his disgust with the principle of toleration.[2] Here are a few words directed at the Victorian prejudice against the Inquisition, and against Innocent III as its founder:

'If, then, Catholicism be true, and if Catholics have the fullest ground for knowing it to be true, the one healthy, desirable and legitimate state of civil society is . . . that the civil ruler in all his highest and most admirable functions should be profoundly submissive to the Church's authority . . . In this respect, though by no means in others, the days of Innocent III are a kind of golden age, on which our eyes can reasonably look back with admiration and deep regret.'

Ward, I believe, was remarkably unimaginative. He followed whither his precious logic led him, all the better pleased when he arrived at what others would reject as the most grotesque of paradoxes. Was not Newman more dangerous than any teacher who did not pretend to be a Catholic? Must he therefore not have been—in 'a golden age'—Ward's first candidate for the stake? Yet it is

[1] Catholic Casuists have been surprisingly indulgent to the nobleman's sense of his 'honour', but Protestants have been much less concerned than Catholics for the virtue of humility.

[2] Ward received his first lesson in intolerance from Dr. Arnold, who said to him, 'I'ld give James Mill as much opportunity for advocating his opinions as is consistent with a journey to Botany Bay.'

E

quite evident that if Ward had seen his erstwhile friend contorted with agony as the first flames took the skin off his feet, he would have rushed forward not with a faggot but with a bucket of water. The danger of such a logician as Ward lies not in his own capacity for wickedness but in the readiness of others to act upon his preposterous deductions.

Ward died in 1882. Not long before the end, he remarked to a priest: 'There is one thing I long to see before I die.' A return of Vatican policy to the good old days of Pio Nono and Mgr Talbot? No, 'the Bancrofts at the Haymarket Theatre.' His passion for the play and the opera never deserted him. 'My working powers are getting so uncertain,' he remarked, picking up the Reminiscences of the playwright, Planché, 'that I find I have five different states of head, and keep a book for each. Kleutgen is for my best hours in the morning, Newman comes next, then Planché, then Trollope: and, when my head is good for nothing, I read a French play.' Sometimes he read six of these in one evening. His last recorded remark is characteristic and endearing. He was in great pain, and dictated to his servant an account of his sufferings 'so that others might know what they might have to go through.' Then he sweetly said: 'I fear that I am a great bore to everyone.'

Tennyson recited over his grave the poem by Shirley that ends:

> 'Only the actions of the just
> Smell sweet, and blossom in the dust.'

Then he composed the splendid epitaph:

> 'Farewell, whose living like I shall not find,
> —Whose faith and works were bells of full accord—
> My friend, the most unworldly of mankind,
> Most generous of all Ultramontanes, Ward.
> How subtle at tierce and quart of mind, with mind,
> How loyal in the following of thy Lord.'

The original version ran:

> 'Gone, lost to earth, whom lost I hope to find,
> Most liberal of all Ultramontanes, Ward.
> I knew thee most unworldly of mankind,
> Most subtle in tierce and quart of mind with mind,
> And hail the cross above thy hallowed sward,
> Mute symbol of thy service to the Lord.

The changes were improvements. It would be surprising if Ward ever used the word 'liberal' except pejoratively. In politics he was not anti-Liberal, although in 1865 he voted against his Catholic neighbour, Sir John Simeon, who was the Liberal candidate. He preferred a Protestant, who was fighting the election partly on anti-Popery, to a Catholic who was a friend of Newman and not an Ultramontane. To him Liberalism connoted the non-supernatural view of life. Newman was, I think, the only other eminent Victorian to treat earthly matters with such contempt. In his time most people in this country fancied, as they still do, that the heart of Christianity is to be found in the Golden Rule. But what differentiates Christianity from the pagan philosophies is that it makes duty towards God the first obligation, from which duty towards one's neighbour is only a derivative.

Carlyle

When Thomas Carlyle died in 1881 at eighty-five, he was deeply venerated here as both a prophet and an artist, more so indeed than any writer of English who had survived him, except perhaps Tennyson and Ruskin. Today he is less read, I believe, than any other of the supereminent Victorians. It is chiefly style that keeps books alive, and his style has become even more unacceptable than his ideas.

His gifts were extraordinary; and his best passages are gloriously vivid and rich in metaphor. But he adopted the vices of German Romanticism—obscurity, exaggeration, histrionic egocentricity and reckless verbosity. Although he spent thirteen years on his remarkable Life of Frederick the Great, the only person I know of who has got through it is Miss Nancy Mitford, who did so four times, finding it hilarious—and then wrote a book of her own on the same subject, because Carlyle had got his hero's character so hopelessly wrong.

His devout father, a stonemason who had become a farmer, by great sacrifices sent him at thirteen to Edinburgh University, for training as a minister; but, having lost his faith, young Tom became first a schoolmaster and then a private tutor. In 1821, at the age of twenty-five, he was introduced to Jane Welsh, five years his junior, the clever, spirited and by his standards elegant daughter of a physician. He lost his heart to her, while she admired him as far the most cultivated man she had ever met, and soon became, as it were, his pupil in their correspondence.

This reveals to us how incompatible they were in their characters and opinions. She explained that her love for him was an honest, serene affection, not a passion that clouded her judgment; and that she felt it her duty to society not to marry into a station inferior to her own. He wrote: 'It is the earnest, affectionate, warmhearted Jane that I *love*; the acute, sarcastic, clear-sighted, derisive Jane I can at best admire.' He also commended the bride of their friend Irving as 'certainly the very model of a wife, submissive, helpful, ever good-humoured, her sole object to be her husband's comforter and that of his friends.' That was not a model she could ever have followed: she was so lively and sharp-tongued. With dismay we watch the two of them converge despite such warnings, like the Titanic and the iceberg in the Hardy poem; and marry they did in October, 1826.

After their deaths, Froude, the historian, wrote a brilliant account of their lives and letters, which got him into a ghastly scrape: it was so candid. But if he had suppressed the material, there might now be little interest in Carlyle. In his opinion the marriage was never consummated. I fancy that it was, although the evidence is slight and contradictory. On his honeymoon Carlyle wrote to his mother: 'On the whole I have reason to say that I have been mercifully dealt with'—and that has been taken as an allusion to his wife's kindness about his impotence, although I feel sure that he was here expressing, not indeed with much enthusiasm, his gratitude to Providence. In any case they loved one another faithfully until her death, when he discovered with bitter remorse how deeply she had suffered from his self-centred blindness to her ill-health and other distresses.

From his father he had inherited a sulky reserve and a lack of tolerance; nor had he been brought up in his peasant home to treat women with any consideration, much as he adored his mother. The main trouble with the marriage, however, was that even before it both he and his wife were victims of chronic ill-health. In his own words:

'All the evils of life are as the small dust of the balance to a diseased stomach. It banishes all thought from your head, all love from your heart. It seems to pollute the very sanctuary of our being; it renders our suffering at once complete and contemptible.'

The same symptoms, dyspepsia and acute insomnia, afflicted Jane, who was prone also to colds, sore throats and influenzas. 'She seldom has a day of true health,' he wrote soon after the marriage. They therefore make me think of two plants, peas or scarlet runners, that need staking, and without it crush one another. How far their illnesses were neurotic we cannot know; but he died of old age at eighty-five, and she at sixty-five of a heart attack. They seem to have chosen a stodgy diet with little or no fruit and green vegetables; and they fought off biliousness with continual, violent purges, blue pills made of mercury, and also castor oil, of which he took a cup mixed with hot coffee in the middle of every morning—enough to ruin an excellent digestion. She also resorted often to morphia, and he occasionally. If modern painkillers and sedatives had been available, their lives, and his writings, might have been far less gloomy.

As things were, he became not only pathetic but comical, never ceasing to complain and to rail, denigrating almost every writer of his time. Wordsworth was intrinsically a small man, Coleridge full of moonshine, Keats (born in the same year as himself) a horrible sort of man, Macaulay and John Stuart Mill superficial, Lamb, Hazlitt and De Quincey contemptible, George Eliot much less gifted than Mrs. Carlyle. Verse, he decided, was now obsolete; its message was better given in prose.

He could not endure Mozart and Beethoven, disliked Gothic architecture, and dismissed all painting, except portraiture, as worthless. On top of all that, he hated or despised the Irish, the Jews, the Negroes (who ought never to have been emancipated) and the French—whose defeat by Prussia in 1871 was the one event in his lifetime that could excite his enthusiasm. Though he was always commending reverence as a virtue, he regretfully admitted to his brother his tyrannical scorn for other men.

His views of his own times were literally jaundiced: he saw trickery, quackery, anarchy, everywhere, except in Germany—and found the eighteenth century almost as bad. No writer on him, I think, has paid enough attention to his self-diagnosis. 'If this accursed burden of disease were cast away, nine-tenths of my faults and incapacities would pass away with it.'

The message he preached so repetitiously is simple, though vague. With a fanaticism rare in Deists he demanded aggressive faith in an impersonal First Cause which has implanted in us a knowledge of right and wrong. Our bounden duty is to obey this by working hard and remaining chaste, without even trying to be happy. The afterlife is one of the few matters on which he kept an open mind. About his disbelief in the Bible and in the dogmas of all Churches he is less explicit, thinking the scepticism of a Hume or a Gibbon further from the truth than any form of credulity.

Politically he started as a radical, with a just and then unusual indignation at the sufferings of the poor, caused largely by *laissez-faire*. Later he denounced every step towards democracy, and called for a dictatorship of the wise, without ever suggesting how that could be achieved. One can't help seeing in him a precursor of Hitler, who would probably have excited first his enthusiasm, then his invective.

*   *   *   *

If the historian of Frederick the Great is forgotten, the husband of Mrs. Carlyle continues to fascinate. When writing to or about her, he sheds fustian and bombast, revealing the strength of his humour and pathos.

Despite their mutual love and admiration, the Carlyles were a desperately ill-matched pair: it was as if D. H. Lawrence had taken to wife Katherine Mansfield. 'A good thing they married one another,' Browning is said to have remarked, 'Otherwise there might have been four unhappy persons instead of only two.' But I'm not sure that he was right. Unless impotent (as some believe), could not Carlyle have made a happy marriage with one of those soft-spoken, capable Victorian women who knew how to manage a house and a husband, taking masculine selfishness for granted? And could not Jane Welsh have made a contented and delightful wife for a man like Browning, who was considerate as well as clever, and who would have encouraged the use of her brilliant pen?

Perhaps—but only if an easier life had greatly improved their health, which seems likely enough. The illnesses at any rate of Mrs. Carlyle—endless colds, insomnia, neuralgia, fear of cancer and of insanity—seem to have been largely psychosomatic. An enjoyable new book by Mrs. Thea Holme gives a careful, detailed picture of her life with her husband in their Chelsea house.

When alone, she could offer herself the lighter diet she preferred; but she thought raw fruit dangerous and stopped Lady Ashburton's gardener from sending weekly parcels of country vegetables, fruit and flowers. Luxuries she called them, which cost too much to transport. (Perhaps she just did not wish to be beholden to a woman of whom she was jealous.) On top of his favourite remedies, she dosed herself for a while with chloroform and henbane.

There was seldom much other gaiety in her home. Her husband, like Proust, suffered tortures from noise: he was always groaning and railing and screaming about pianos, parrots, crowing cocks, organ-grinders, church-bells, distant railway whistles or the fireworks at Cremorne. He fussed terribly also about his clothes, which she had to buy for him: 'my husband would almost as soon have an affair with a mad dog as with a Cockney shopman.' But worst of all was her trouble with servants.

From the start of her marriage she always had one maid, and during her last six years two. (The house in Chelsea had eight rooms.) But as a rule the wretches quickly gave notice, or else had to be dismissed for sloth or dishonesty or drunkenness or mutiny—or for giving clandestine birth in the house when Mrs. Carlyle was ill in bed. During her thirty-two years in Cheyne Row she ran through thirty-four of them, although one stayed for ten years. It amazes me that she could get one to stay for ten days.

She always welcomed them with high hopes, and wished to make them her friends. Yes, but they had to carry water from the pump and fuel up three storeys, to cook by the light of one candle in a dark basement kitchen, and also to sleep there, although Carlyle in winter liked to use it as a smoking-room. The maid therefore had to lurk until late at night in the cold washroom next door, unable to get to bed, and obliged to rise at half past six the next morning. If domestic service is today unpopular, such employers as the Carlyles are largely to blame. Like boa-constrictors, they were unaware of the suffering they caused—which is still remembered by the great-grandchildren of their victims.

Mice, black beetles (one invaded the cook's ear) and epidemic bed-bugs were other worries with which poor Mrs. Carlyle had to cope. Worst of all was her husband's gloom, especially during the thirteen years of his work on *Frederick the Great*, the monstrous book that he himself came to hate before he had finished it. A psychologist might call both the Carlyles self-destructive: they brought upon themselves most of their illnesses, discomforts and anxieties—and are not on that account the less to be pitied. Both were well-meaning, even noble. But he, while always denouncing the weaknesses of his fellows, never learnt to control himself. He wasted his genius by not disciplining his style, and turned her into 'a frustrated artist' by incessant, needless demands upon her time and energy. Our sympathy goes to her in her lifetime, and to him after her death, when he was tormented by remorse.

Their domestic life as here described could be turned into what

M. Anouilh calls a *comédie grinçante* with humour sick enough to be popular. In an epilogue Carlyle learns that, though we never open *Frederick the Great*, we enjoy reading about his behaviour in the home—and he cannot visit upon us the vials of his wrath. That provides his Purgatory.

Two Fine Poets in Tandem (1959)

Saint-John Perse is a fascinating figure. No living poet enjoys a higher reputation in France; he has been translated into nine languages; and in England at any rate one of his long poems is known to readers of poetry because it was published here in 1931 together with a translation by Mr. Eliot. The new edition of this volume brings us some changes in the English text, a bibliography, and appreciations by Valery Larbaud, Hofmannsthal, Ungaretti and Lucien Fabre.

Mr. Eliot has translated no other poet, I believe, except Paul Valéry, and in his preface attributes to *Anabase* the same importance as to the later work of James Joyce— 'and this is a high estimate indeed.' He gives the reader, however, little guidance to its qualities, and provides no facts about the author (not even the date of his birth), assuming either that these are already known to us or that they are irrelevant.

Neither assumption seems to me well-founded, and this review must attempt to supply a little information, though I am far less qualified than Mr. Eliot to discuss M. Perse (whom I have never met) either as a poet or as a man. Let me recommend two books I have found useful: *Saint-John Perse* by Alain Bosquet and Roger Caillois's exemplary *Poétique de St.-John Perse*.

Even the names of the poet need elucidation. The pseudonym St.-J. Perse was adopted in 1924 (and the St.-J. first extended to St.-John in the original edition of the book under review). His previous poems had been signed 'Saintléger Léger'; and his true name is Marie-René Alexis Saint-Léger Léger. He was born in 1887 in Guadeloupe, the home for two centuries of his forbears on both sides, lawyers, planters and naval officers. At the age of eleven he was brought to France, went to school in Pau (where he met

Claudel and Jammes), then to Bordeaux University, where he studied Greek, philosophy and law. After two long visits to England (where he made friends with Conrad) he entered the Diplomatic Service in 1914.

During five years at the Peking Embassy he travelled widely in Central Asia, and also went in sailing-ships to Polynesia and Malaya. Back at the Quai d'Orsay, he worked under Briand, and was Permanent Under-Secretary from 1933 until May 1940, when he was denounced by the Right for his anti-Nazi policy. After the Armistice he escaped to the United States, whereupon Pétain deprived him of French citizenship and confiscated his property. Until recently he never returned to Europe (which may explain why he has not been elected to the Académie). He has now settled with his American wife near Toulon.

His first volume *Éloges* evokes his West Indian childhood; *Anabase* was the fruit of an expedition to the Gobi Desert; he composed *Exil* in America, suffering from loneliness while in his tortured France dignitaries were denouncing freedom—all of which preoccupations appear in the poem; but M. Perse has never written directly about his adult life. His latest and longest poem, *Amers* appeared in Paris in 1957, and with an English translation (*Seamarks*) last year, published by the admirable Bollingen Series in New York.

His writings are never easy to penetrate. Let me confess that my personal taste prefers the burnished concision of Mallarmé to the vaticinating of Whitman, Péguy or Claudel: and M. Perse writes always lengthily in free verse with a 'line' that may spread like a foaming breaker over fifty lines of print. This tempts one to read too fast; and in any case my poor English ear, which can catch rhymes and assonances, is apt to miss the alexandrines and octo-syllabics on which he bases his rhythmical structure. According to Mr. Eliot he is 'sometimes able to write poetry in what is called prose.' This has been achieved by Bossuet, Jeremy Taylor, Chateaubriand and Landor, but I am not sure that M. Perse ever crosses the unmappable frontier between the realms of verse and prose. Here is a passage displaying his texture at its most elaborate:

'Ce sont de grandes lignes calmes qui s'en vont à des bleuissements de vignes improbables. La terre en plus d'un point mûrit les violettes de l'orage; et ces fumées de sable qui s'élèvent au lieu des fleuves morts, comme des pans de siècle en voyage . . .'

Sont, vont; lignes, vigne; improbable, sable; bleuissements, pans; orage, voyage—such rhyming and a taste for concrete terms help to preserve M. Perse from the rhapsodic laxities of Claudel.

His obscurity comes chiefly from his images, often difficult in themselves and (as Mr. Eliot points out) with the links between them difficult to detect. The later poems still seem to me excessively opaque, but the more one reads *Anabase*, the more readily one can enjoy it. From a vast range of knowledge M. Perse draws upon a formidable vocabulary, including many technical terms, botanical, zoological and nautical. Some English readers must be familiar with *harfang, engoulevent, trocellaire, busaigle, phrygane, phasme, naissain* and *vaigrage*: I, alas, have to read with Harrap at my elbow, and also Littré, because (like Mallarmé) the poet enjoys using a word in its long-lost etymological sense. In *Anabase* a hat, for instance, has its brim 'seduced.'

Mr. Eliot by printing his translation opposite the original invites us usefully to scrutinise both of them word by word; and students of diction should compare also the English of the first edition with the revised text now given us. (There is moreover an intermediate rendering published in 1949.) M. Perse, who from the first collaborated with the translator, has been perfecting his mastery of English and is responsible for all the changes in this latest version. These usually make the translation more literal, and seem to me improvements. (One welcomes the removal of Mr. Eliot's 'camiknickers.') Sometimes the English defines a meaning that is left ambiguous in the French.

Old admirers of the translation will notice that a few of the more disconcerting phrases remain unmodified.

'*Mon cheval arrêté sous l'arbre plein de tourterelles, je siffle un sifflement si pur, qu'il n'est promesses à leurs rives que tiennent tous ces fleuves (Feuilles vivantes au matin sont à l'image de la gloire)* . . .'

'I have halted my horse by the tree of the doves. I whistle a note so sweet, shall the rivers break faith with their banks? (Living leaves in the morning fashioned in glory) . . .'

Do not such paraphrases make the meaning even more difficult? In another passage I fancied that a *fleuve sans destin* meant a river that like many in Asiatic deserts never reached the sea (or possibly one the ownership of which was undecided); but here it is still 'a meaningless river'—the sense of which eludes me. Again, 'prevarications' is retained to translate *prévarications*—possibly because M. Perse does not realise that the French meaning ('betrayal of trust') has been obsolete in English for centuries.

A perplexing word or phrase, when it has been agreed upon by two such pre-eminent poets as M. Perse and Mr. Eliot, interests the connoisseur of language no less than a crux in a classic. But anyone who has not read this poem in an earlier edition should at first neglect such details and surrender to the overwhelming impact of the poem as a whole. Though Mr. Eliot declares that his only aim is 'to assist the English-speaking reader who wishes to approach the French text,' readers without French will do well to enjoy the translation as a superb panorama in poetic prose. The setting is Central Asia at some unspecified period, perhaps a thousand years ago.

'Celebrations of open-air festivals for the name-day of great trees and public rites in honour of a pond; consecration of black stones perfectly round, discovery of springs in dead places, dedication of cloths held up on poles, at the gates of passes, and loud acclamations under the walls for the mutilation of adults in the sun, for the publication of bride-sheets!'

Memorable images abound:

'A child sorrowful as the death of apes—one that had an elder sister of great beauty—offered us a quail in a slipper of rose-coloured satin.'

'Tomorrow the festivals and tumults, the avenues planted with podded trees, and the dustman at dawn bearing away huge pieces of dead palm trees, fragment of giant wings . . .'

Anabase glorifies the founder of a city in the wilds who then longs for further discoveries—a symbol (it seems) of our appetites, conflicting but both of them noble, for civilisation and for adventure. Though his values never become explicit, M. Perse (like Gide) is a humanist who exalts fervour: to luxuriate in sadness is for him an unforgivable offence. We may doubt the reality of the phenomenal world (he suggests), and time turns everything to dust, but let us construct and cherish for so long as possible everything that can heighten the condition of mankind.

Cocteau (1950)

'When I shut my eyes and merely think, I can't believe that I am more than twenty-five years old'—thus John Henry Newman at the age of fifty-five. M. Jean Cocteau suffered at the same age from the same incredulity, even with his eyes open. Then, a couple of years ago, illness prevented him from shaving for a few days; a looking-glass told him that his beard was white; and to his astonishment—he had never been good at figures—he found out that he was fifty-six. Even those who have followed his work for thirty years or more may well share this astonishment, for he is something of a Peter Pan: has he not divided human beings into two classes—'*Il y a les poètes et les grandes personnes*'? Or we may put it that he has known, like some dapper snake, how to grow new skins serially, each of his published works being what Shakespeare calls 'a shining, chequer'd slough.' If we accept—and since M. Cocteau can, we must—the fact that he has reached canonical age, some attempt to weigh his so buoyant and volatile *oeuvre* seems to impose itself. This presents peculiar difficulties, for M. Cocteau is one of those, like Byron and Wilde, who have the art to float on the spirit of the age in which they live, as on a surf-rider's plank or in a glider on rising air-currents. It is easy for contemporaries to over-rate such artists, no less easy to disparage them unjustly.

Nineteen books of verse, seven novels, some sixteen books of criticism and confession, eleven plays, four films, several ballets, unnumbered drawings—yes, the critic has been provided with ample material by M. Cocteau, whom envy paints as a dandified chatterbox enslaved by drugs and irregular amours. In such calumnies, it must be added, he has been an accomplice; look at *Opium* and *Le livre blanc*, candours that he flourished like a bull-fighter's cloak; and most effective they have proved in distracting attention from the author's formidable, bourgeois industriousness.

There is altogether too much material rather than too little: M. Cocteau is not only a poet, a novelist, a critic, a dramatist, a film-director, a choreographer and a draughtsman: he is a public personality, indeed already a legend. Those who have heard him talk may claim even that his books are only the echoes or débris of his supreme conversation. In front of the bedizened Parisian booth he has been the most alluring of barkers, clamorous on behalf of lions so various as Picasso, Stravinsky, the musical 'Six,' Radiguet, Chirico, Bérard, Jean Desbordes, Jean Marais and Jean Genet—the criminal author of 'curious' books. (Dazzling as are the talents of this *halluciné*, it seems a trifle premature of M. Cocteau to place him over all other living French writers.) Dressmakers, restaurants, night-clubs have also won commendation from this arbiter of the elegances. Nor have his quarrels been less scintillating than his enthusiasms. The vilest denigration and the blindest idolatry conspire to conceal the real person: to be objective about him is as difficult for the Parisian as to be objective about M. Thorez or General de Gaulle.

Are we foreigners, then, better placed for pronouncing judgment? This must be doubted. The resolutely insular among us are likely to be quite baffled and therefore dismissive. (Superlative cleverness, of which M. Cocteau cannot be absolved even by his most ardent supporters, is hardly a quality that John Bull finds engaging.) Our batrachophiles, on the other hand, identify him with Paris as they do the Eiffel Tower; to judge him is to judge their past; he is the attar of a rose that suggests a thousand memories —the old *Boeuf sur le toit* in the Rue Boissy d'Anglas, the Fratellinis and Barbette, Sophoclean choruses spoken through a loudspeaker, Comte Étienne de Beaumont's 'Soirées de Paris', the eruption of Dada and surrealism, *vernissages* at both the Rosenbergs', Luna Park, the accordions of the still uninvaded Rue de Lappe, and the customary road south leading past the now demolished waterfront of Toulon to the Welcome Hotel on the battleship-embracing bay of Villefranche.

Let us begin by listening to counsel for the prosecution—M. Maurice Sachs, author of *Le Sabbat*, a scandalously brilliant book of reminiscences:

> '*Quel souvenir devions-nous garder de lui? Celui d'un illusioniste effrayant qui savait escamoter les coeurs et ne vous rendait qu'un lapin.*'

M. Sachs wrote with the hatred to be expected from a disillusioned worshipper, and most of the philippic of which I have quoted the conclusion is directed at the friend rather than the artist. Counsel for the defence is M. Roger Lannes, in a preface to an anthology of M. Cocteau's verse. Though he won the approval of his client, and has the good sense to deal not with the legend but with the books, he is too solemn to be effective; and, unlike the most skilled advocates, neither faces the gravest charges nor admits such small facts telling against him as are unescapable. Not that this matters: M. Cocteau's most eloquent champion will always be M. Cocteau. In book after book he goes on sticking up for himself; and, if he remains—as he believes—the most misunderstood of men, it is not for lack of explanation. (How rare it has become for any French writer to treat *le moi* as *haïssable*!) In his latest book, *La difficulté d'être*, M. Cocteau assembles a number of enchanting short essays on aesthetics, morals, his friends and his personality. Although, like all great *raconteurs*, he inclines to repeat himself, admirers of *Portraits-souvenirs* will here rediscover M. Cocteau's genius for evocation, notably in the sketches of Proust, Nijinsky and Apollinaire. The self-portrait reveals some significant *pentimenti*. The author, it appears, now lives 'like a monk,' and indeed has never had much experience of the pleasures of the flesh, though '*le monde en a décidé autrement*.' 'Who cares?' grunts the English reader, whether his crossness proceeds from pudor or from cynicism. M. Cocteau cares—that is the point. The decisions of '*le monde*' matter to him far more than we in our dowdy island can readily understand.

English writers and painters live as a rule privately, often kennelling themselves in the depths of the country. (There is no English word for *coterie*.) This does not prevent them from complaining of the indifference to the arts paraded here by the public in general, the fashionable world in particular. It is true that our poets now seldom mix with our dukes; but, bad as this must be for the dukes, it may be a blessing for the poets. Such a view need not proceed from inverted snobbery. (I suspect indeed that some regions of history, biography and criticism can be properly explored only by writers who are also men of the world.) Yet the high prestige of the artist in France exposes him to perpetual risks, not merely rivalries, slanders, intrigues, but—far more noxious— to social life, with the expense of spirit it entails, and to a morbid awareness of his audience. Between the wars M. Cocteau's Paris was the most stimulating and fruitfully cosmopolitan of capitals because the arts were there almost as fashionable as they had been in Quattrocento Florence or Cinquecento Venice. The trouble is that where the arts are fashionable, the artist is tempted to become over-responsive to fashion. He knows too intimately what '*le monde*' is saying; and he cares too much, because he knows that this world is remarkably unstupid, is dominated indeed by such persons as himself. The need to be *à la page* can thus become oppressive.

M. Cocteau has been for more than thirty years the glass of fashion, and we have the highest possible authority for considering this a term of praise. Until a hundred years ago it was most exceptional for a good artist not to be recognised as such, a healthy social condition which has been restored, one may think, in twentieth-century France, and partly through the energetic good taste of M. Cocteau. It is arguable indeed that he is a victim of his generosity, that his habit of launching fellow-artists has made him too conscious of the public on which he sought to impose them. More probably he was born histrionic, and already in the cradle cocked an eye at the audience for which he was crowing. (Again we are reminded of Byron and Wilde.) He is not least conscious of fashion when he ostentatiously runs counter to it. The titles of his first two books now seem prophetic of his career, *La lampe d'Aladin* (1909) and *Le prince frivole* (1910). Though he resents being labelled a magician, the word in both its senses applies to him. He is a poet who sometimes passes off conjuring for creation. Eusapia Palladino admitted that, when her paranormal powers failed, she resorted to trickery. Houdini, on the other hand, could never convince spiritualists that he was not a medium. M. Cocteau is the deftest of clairvoyants, the most uncanny of prestidigitators. He classifies his works as '*poésie*,' '*poésie de roman*,' '*poésie critique*,' '*poésie du théâtre*,' '*poésie graphique*' and '*poésie cinématographique*.' This is to indicate that his prose is poetry travelling incognito. His notion of the poetic, it must be confessed, would dismay Boileau and Wordsworth alike; Coleridge would allow him fancy, deny him imagination. In any case his career might be defined as one continuous campaign against the prosaic. Having entered a clinic to cure an addiction to opium, he wrote. '*Je ne suis pas un désintoxiqué fier de son effort. J'ai honte d'être chassé de ce monde auprès duquel la santé ressemble aux films ignobles où des ministres inaugurent une statue.*'

This can stand as an archetype of the prosaic: elderly politicans glum in seedy frock-coats uncovering a sham work of art. '*Dieu, que la vie est quotidienne!*' and to evade its dailiness (the term is used by our seventeenth-century divines) is the first need of the artist as of the saint. Has there ever been a masterpiece that could not justly be called 'escapist'?

M. Cocteau, it may be thought, has shown altogether too clean a pair of heels, has jettisoned the necessary to escape the commonplace. Prose, for him, has included the family (though he was a devoted son), the countryside, even the truth except when improbable. No newspaper tale is too tall for him to swallow; this most sophisticated of men is also, as he boasts, a simpleton; and when he scampered round the globe, sequined blinkers blinded him to almost everything that was not theatrical or odd. '*L'art*,' he declares enigmatically, '*ne vaut à mes yeux que s'il est la projection d'une morale*'; but what he means by a morality may puzzle even the least muscular of Christians. His work celebrates his fellow-feeling with truants from the norm; gypsies, sailors, schoolboys, vagabonds, actors ('sacred monsters' he calls them), airmen, invalids, impersonators, fortune-tellers, acrobats, self-destroyers, somnambulists, criminals, angels. '*Les êtres singuliers et leur actes asociaux sont le charme d'un monde pluriel qui les expulse*.' Love he can exalt, since it is a malady of the imagination, yet he prefers it to be equivocal, a perilous exaggeration of the affection between mother and son, sister and brother, friend and friend. Not only the poppy, but danger, the theatre, Catholicism, have been among his hiding-places from the humdrum. His latest asylum is the world of the film-makers; and this time perhaps he has fled too far, like some refugee from Paris in the summer of 1940 who would not take breath till he reached the Antipodes, and settled in the security of Pearl Island. Yet his first film is extraordinary.

Evidently the sexagenarian who insists upon remaining *avant-garde* risks resembling Pope's dancing dowagers: 'See round and round the ghosts of beauty glide/And haunt the places where their honour died.' As if to ward off such a fate, M. Cocteau, in some of his later works, has already rushed to meet the great public rather more than halfway. In *Les parents terribles* he gave satisfaction to the audiences that fed upon Henri Bataille and Bernstein. *L'aigle à deux têtes* is merely a vehicle for a young Sarah Bernhardt, who does not exist. The film, *La belle et la bête*, which has exquisite moments, is much less remarkable than the diary M. Cocteau kept while directing it: it reveals a most uncharacteristic heavy-fistedness, particularly in the excessive use of a hint from Mussorgsky: '*L'art de demain ce sera les statues qui bougent*.' *Renaud et Armide*, again, in spite of its beauties, is little but a display of virtuosity in writing alexandrines that recall now Racine, now Victor Hugo, now (alas) M. Cocteau's first master, Edmond Rostand. In the preface to it he tells us that he had noticed that '*l'époque allait venir où, loin de contredire la sottise, il s'agirait de contredire l'intelligence.*' Here is the same hypertrophied response to some ephemeral current that once made him condemn the Impressionists as *ennuyeux*. A contradiction of the intelligence is the last thing required by our besotted epoch. But skirts must now be long, just because they were short; and M. Cocteau must now be obvious, just because he was fine. Shall we next see him a candidate for the Académie? Or can we hope that skirts will soon again be short?

Orphée, *Les enfants terribles*, *La machine infernale*, *Plain-chant* and the *Essai de critique indirecte* may be thought the most telling and characteristic of M. Cocteau's works. I have been too deeply moved by these ever to dismiss their author as derivative or merely brilliant. Nor, when I re-read, is their spell less potent. In his fabulous gift for inventing images and detecting analogies we recognize the order of poetic wit that we venerate in our seventeenth-century Metaphysicals. On every page we are treated to some felicity such as '*Une ruine est un accident ralenti*' or '*Victor Hugo était un fou qui se croyait Victor Hugo.*' With similar rockets he ventured to illuminate even the legend of Oedipus—and triumphantly, though the spectator held his breath as if watching a trapeze-act without a safety-net. At the same time I wonder whether his most time-resisting works will not be those which he might list as '*poésie-comique.*' It is a vulgar tradition that pays more honour to the buskin than to the sock; and, if M. Cocteau has usually preferred tragic themes, he need not be thought to regard these as intrinsically superior. He has been a victim of bad health and of a fatality that has struck one favourite friend after another with premature death. While therefore obsessed with disaster, he has retained, he tells us, all his love—and capacity—for laughter. Can we not hope that he will again offer the advantage of this gift to the public as well as to his friends? *Manfred* and *Childe Harold*, *Salome* and *The Portrait of Dorian Gray*, have faded into period-pieces; *Don Juan* and *The Importance of Being Earnest* stay as fresh as when they were written. Perhaps M. Cocteau will in the same way be floated into immortality on the feather-light wings of *Le Potomak*, *Thomas l'imposteur* and such successors as he may yet give to these comic masterpieces.

Colette (1951)

When an Englishman finds himself with French friends he is sure
to be delighted, if sometimes also a little alarmed, by the vehemence
with which they will contend about the quality in every subject
discussed, from the Beaujolais and the Brie to Cimabue and Mr.
Churchill. A large proportion of the judgments put forward with
such wit, fire and apparent logic are the automatic reflection, he
will notice, of some system of ideas. The Mountain continues to
attack the Gironde *à propos* of André Breton; the hopeless legit-
imism of the *Blancs d'Espagne* is reflected in aversion from Dior or
Jean-Louis Barrault; the matter of vinegar in a salad dressing
renews the ancient cleavage between Fénelon and Bossuet.
However bracing the liveliness that results, an Englishman may
sometimes wistfully long to hear some merit allowed to Claudel
by a Radical, to Gide by a Communist, to Drieu la Rochelle by a
patriot, to Anatole France by anyone under 70. Should he confess
that he admires not only all of these, but Mauriac and Malraux and
Montherlant and Éluard and Jouhandeau and Simenon, he will be
overwhelmed by shouts of shocked incomprehension. One card,
however, he can safely play. Let him opine that nobody alive writes
better than Colette, and there will be reserves, of course, but no
hubbub. Her gifts, rare as they are, could not alone give her this
undisputed reputation: it is her detachment from all controversies,
whether political or aesthetic, that permits these gifts to be seen
without prejudice. If the Academy admitted women she would
long since have been elected. For she has become one of the traditional glories of France.

Colette—it seems affected to write 'Madame Colette' in discussing
the eminent writer rather than the woman—Colette has been little
appreciated in England. Our critics are chiefly to blame. Super-

latives have been rained upon writers so various as Jules Romains, Bernanos and Sartre. Few have paid careful attention to Colette. She is supremely a stylist, and an English equivalent of her style has eluded a dozen translators. Critics, however, often discuss writers who have not been translated into English even indifferently. Can it be that Colette is here still thought of as frivolous, not to say *grivoise*, the author of those *Claudine* books with which, over her husband's signature, she began her career? More probably the silence of English critics can be explained by the same cause as the applauding consensus of French critics. Colette is not occupied with ideas.

From the time of Descartes—one might say of Calvin—the French have gloried in the systematic character of their thought. In literature logic has been considered their habitual virtue, almost their monopoly. Poets and novelists have been conspicuous for the acumen with which, in defining individual instances, they have applied or deduced generalizations. Balzac and Proust, no less than La Rochefoucauld and La Bruyère, analyse men in order to define Man. This habit of mind has been so noticeable that another signal characteristic of the French has been often overlooked, though it is far more widespread—so much so that they themselves take it for granted. The French outdo all other European peoples (but probably not the Chinese and Japanese) in the intensity and refinement with which they commonly cultivate the pleasures of sense.

'*Les sens,*' says Buffon, '*sont des espèces d'instrument dont il faut apprendre à se servir.*' Yes, *apprendre*; but in our country the education of the senses is thought frivolous rather than obligatory. There are exceptions. We may train ourselves to recognise a Dow 1908 without incurring censure; and to tell the curlew from the whimbrel, the red eyebright from the lousewort, is positively commended. Any comparable connoisseurship in scents or sauces, in the cut of a dress or the texture of a skin, is dismissed as un-English, or at any rate unmanly. Across the Channel a refined taste in such matters is confined neither to one sex nor to one class. It is not merely that the French produce the best food, the best wine, the best clothes, the best scents and the best pictures. Everywhere the English traveller comes upon proofs of their fastidiousness. The cheese-stalls in a Savoyard market are set out with the same care for the eye as the shop windows in the rue du Faubourg St-Honoré. Your Paris taxi-driver will argue about the rival flavours of a *doyenné* pear and a *bon-chrétien* as if he lived on a fruit farm. (Probably his father or his sister does: family links with the peasantry have done much to save the sense of quality in city workers.) The making of love is discussed—and, we must presume, practised—with a solicitude such as we islanders reserve for dry flies and herbaceous borders. Hearing is the one sense that the French omit to cultivate. As a people, that is. Their composers reveal just the delicacy we admire in French products in the other arts; many of their folk-songs also are exquisite. But who can praise the common sounds of France, thundering, shrieking traffic, raised, raucous voices?

Here, then, is the realm that Colette explores, records and interprets with a fervour and a precision that are unsurpassed: the realm of the senses. Hardly less extraordinary is her remoteness from the realm of notions. By comparison, Jane Austen is an ideologist. Colette has written about politicians, never about politics. She was brought up without religion, she tells us; and from the absence of any other reference to it we may gather that to her it means nothing. Apart from her dramatic criticism, she seldom alludes to literature, music or painting. '*L'homme, c'est ma patrie,*' she has proclaimed; but he has to share her loyalty with the beast, the flower, the soil.

The connexion between Colette's life and her books, though exceptionally close, is not simple. The early editions of *Les vrilles de la vigne* include a chapter (suppressed in the *Oeuvres complètes*) wherein Colette protests against being identified with Claudine. Why, then, did she give the title *La maison de Claudine* to a later book about her mother and her childhood which is direct autobiography? The original Claudine might be described as a portrait of the youthful author, slightly romanticized by herself and then titivated under Willy's instructions to engage a lickerish public. In *La retraite sentimentale*, which is a continuation of the Claudine series written after the author had parted from Willy, she presents herself as a subsidiary character with the name 'Willette Collie.' The heroine of *La vagabonde* and *L'entrave* is called Renée Néré: in her character, if not in all her experiences, she seems to be a self-portrait; and when *La vagabonde* was dramatized Colette followed Laparcerie in the title role. *La naissance du jour*, she warns the reader, is a picture not so much of herself as of a model for herself. On the other hand, *Sido*, *Mes apprentissages* and *L'envers du Music-Hall* describe her youth without any pretence of fiction. Her last ten years are portrayed in four books, *Journal à rebours*, *De ma fenêtre*, *L'étoile vesper*, and *Le fanal bleu*. Between these two series there is a large part of her life, of which she has recounted only an episode here and there.

She was born in 1873, in Burgundy, a fertile province from which she retains a vigorous sounding of the letter 'r' and a piety towards wines whether choice or quotidian. Her grandmother was a quadroon—in the Southern States she would herself be regarded as coloured. Her mother was a magnificent character, and always her idol: a Belgian, she married twice, having a son and daughter by each husband. The youngest of these children is our author, who was christened Sidonie-Gabrielle. (Colette is her father's surname.) At the age of 20 she married Henri Gauthier-Villars: he was 14 years older than she, a witty, cultivated, avaricious, brutally selfish debauchee. With the pseudonym 'Willy' he signed a number of novels and a mass of periodical criticism, all written by 'ghosts,' among whom were the gifted Jean de Tinan and Marcel Boulestin.

Conscribed into the platoon that wrote for Willy's living, his wife produced *Claudine à l'école* (1900). To exploit the success won by the novel, Willy appeared everywhere with his wife and the young actress Polaire, identically dressed to represent its heroine. At their expense he gained all the publicity he hoped. Under his whip Colette wrote six further books for him to sign. One of these she has refused to acknowledge; the others now appear under her own name. Meanwhile she had written for her own satisfaction *Sept dialogues de bêtes* (1904), in which her peculiar sympathy with animals was deliciously revealed. In 1906 she left her husband, and for six years she earned her living as a mime, usually touring provincial music-halls. Severed from her beloved country sights and smells, in sour, airless dressing-rooms, in dingy, fly-blown hotel bedrooms, in cafés and railway carriages, she wrote *Les vrilles de la vigne* (1908) and *La vagabonde* (1911). Soon afterwards she married Henri de Jouvenel, a newspaper proprietor and politician, by whom she had a daughter in 1913. She began to work as a special reporter, describing boxing matches, murder trials and so forth for *Le Matin*. She was not allowed to sign this most accomplished prose with her own name: Claudine had made her reputation too doubtful for the readers of a popular and sensational newspaper.

Her books meanwhile were winning more and more admiration from the fastidious; and she enjoyed a resonant success with *Chéri*, published in 1920 and made into a play the following year. In 1925 came the entrancing short opera, *L'Enfant et les sortilèges*, which married the prose of Colette to the music of Ravel. Though busy from 1933 to 1938 with dramatic criticism (republished under the title *La jumelle noire*), she produced during these years four volumes of fiction and the memoirs called *Mes apprentissages*. Since then we have had five more books of stories, and four of reflection and reminiscence. Bed-ridden with arthritis, chronically in pain, Colette continues to work. She has always been not only an inspired artist but the most conscientious and steadfast of artisans.

When she began her career with Willy as taskmaster, he angrily crossed out several pages of what she had shown up, shouting '*Aurais-je épousé la dernière des lyriques?*' The sneer was a prophecy. By a pedestrian patience Colette was to scale the heights towards which the Comtesse de Noailles fluttered on her impetuous, fluent, Icarian pinions. It is rare, except in youth or at moments, to feel lyrical: rarest of all to translate such feeling into prose rather than verse. What writers of our time, we may ask ourselves, can be compared in the lyricism of their prose with Colette? In England, Virginia Woolf; in France, the youthful Gide, and then Proust. It is full-bloodedness that distinguishes Colette from these. A temperament all warmth has generated a style earthy, robust, weatherproof.

This style is at the same time intricate. Even the vocabulary is the most formidable that a foreign reader of French can encounter, except in such slangsters as Céline, Queneau and Jean Genet. She likes to deploy the names of obscure plants and archaic or provincial words on which Littré throws no light: *congai, deglinguer, varin, jouxtes, larnac, prasin, marchaon*. Open any of her books, moreover, and you come at once upon phrases that defy translation, though the meaning is clear. Let us take a *sors Colettiana*:

'*Une autre fois le renouveau fait songer à une rose immergée. Il brille sous l'eau, tout averses gaies, mousses crûes en quelques heures. D'un ongle vert, au bout d'une brande, s'égoutte sans fin une goutte, encore une goutte et toujours une goutte, qui alimente le chant des cascatelles souterraines. L'embryon est aqueux, l'herbe jute, l'écorce fend, l'argile sirupeuse trahit le pied. Mais une sourde lueur s'attache à chaque pli des eaux débordées, en un moment l'iris se dégaine, et la pluie est tiède. Au crépuscule la rivière fume comme un feu de fanes.*'

Such a passage illustrates her maxim: '*Le dessin musical et la phrase naissent du même couple évasif et immortel: la note, le rythme.*' She thus describes her daily labours: '*Je prends encore la plume pour commencer le jeu périlleux et décevant, pour saisir et fixer sous la pointe double et ployante, le châtoyant, le fugace, le passionnant adjectif.*' (She is too well-balanced to share Giraudoux's pernickety distaste for epithets.) Always she seeks to lend us the acuity of her own senses: her ear alert to catch '*la bave mijotante de la bûche humide qui bout même le long du chenet contre le marbre prise dans une toile d'araignée*'; her palate responsive not only to every fruit, every sauce, but to the taste of oak-leaves in the water of a forest-spring; her skin, tanned by delving in the sun-baked earth, yet so delicately aware of the damp leatheriness of a hydrangea-leaf, or the flutings on a fig, or the midsummer snow falling on geraniums still hot from the sun; her eye that nothing escapes, neither the faintest menace of dilapidation on an eyelid, nor a cat rifling the strawberry beds, nor the amenity radiating from the face of a husband who has just been unfaithful; above all, her nostrils feral in their keenness. She has always frequented what she describes, with an unfamiliar adjective, as '*la voie aromale*,' and has been glad to be called '*le romancier de l'odorat.*' This eagerness of the senses supplies energy to her genius. Often in her childhood, she recollects, '*il n'y avait d'urgent au monde que mon désir de posséder par les yeux les merveilles de la terre.*' Now that age has reft from her almost all the terrestrial nourishments, she finds that what has always been her pride is her chief consolation: '*Il me reste l'avidité.*'

The most immediately effective of her books and the most popular is *Chéri*, together with its sequel, *La fin de Chéri*. This does not imply that familiarity with it breeds contempt: thirty years after its publication it seems more brilliant than ever. Like *Manon Lescaut* and *Adolphe*, it is the classic rendering of a cardinal theme—in this case a passionate love between a very young man and a woman old enough to be his mother. Neither the carnality of the subject nor the turpitude of the setting calls for critical reserve. Colette handles them with candour and—some will think—with undue sympathy: of prurience there is none. Yet, the more fervent a reader's admiration for her books, the less likely is he to make this his favourite, so much is lacking of what he most admires: little of the countryside, no flowers, except the unrustic bouquets from expensive florists, no animals, and—worst of all—no direct revelation of Colette.

Chéri—this is one of its principal merits—is the picture of a closed world, in which no character except a boxing-instructor has the least aversion from venality. The *grandes cocottes* of fifty years ago have today taken on a pleasing picturesqueness. The flower-laden hats, the innumerable hooks and eyes inviting a leisurely disjunction, the petticoats frothing with lace and frills, the long sheath-like stays, the *art nouveau* dressing-tables, the carriages and high-stepping horses have become historical properties like the costumes and scenery of an opera. Vice, we may feel, has lost half its grossness by losing all its actuality. How sinister, nevertheless, are Chéri's mother and her parasites, indeed this whole world where money and the sexual allurements that earn money are the only interests. Chéri himself excites pity, yet his faithfulness in love is an obsession rather than a virtue. It is Léa, genial, generous, no less sensible than kind, who in spite of her professional past brings into the book the tonic freshness and soundness characteristic of Colette.

In some remote regions of Islam, it is said, a woman caught unveiled by a stranger will raise her skirt to cover her face. Of the same order is the pudicity in Colette. She conceals those feelings which others, when they write about themselves, hasten to unbare; the vanities and disappointments, the spurts of petulance, the ooze of self-pity. About her zest for physical love she makes no bones. She glories in a healthy appetite for peaches and for lips, for the curves of a bay and of a thigh or a breast, for the velvet on a dog's ear and on a youthful nape. English readers may sometimes be reminded of Cruft's, so expertly does she review the 'points' that make a body desirable. In *Ces plaisirs* (now renamed *Les purs et les impurs*) erotic divagations are treated with a cool familiarity. This is what she has observed, this is part of human nature. She accepts the facts, and with a readiness that amounts to complicity. She is happy that men and women should be so various, so incalculable, for it is her profession to be interested in character. Other novelists may disapprove the facts they delight to display (is there not a sensualist in Mauriac no less than a puritan in Gide?); Colette welcomes with open sympathy all that brings grist to her mill. *Chéri* and *Gigi* would not be the marvels they are, if their author had been too squeamish to put herself into the high-heeled shoes of Léa and Tante Alicia.

The novelist can ill afford to be dainty. Observation is not enough; and so he must project himself imaginatively into ignoble hearts, infect himself with feelings that produce evil and vulgar actions. He must have in him the seeds of the vices he describes. Not that this usually presents much difficulty. It was the weakness of Virginia Woolf that she remained the prisoner of her own distinction; most novelists have been adequately furnished with potential hatred, avarice and lust.

A country childhood enabled Colette to accept without surprise the animality in human nature; when this turned up in more devious forms among Willy's friends and in the music-hall, she was not disconcerted. A rare mixture of subtlety with downrightness has made her, it is apparent, an ideal and hardened confidante. Has any novelist been able to draw upon larger resources of fellow-feeling with both the sexes?

We do not know how Colette came to visit the world of rich, veteran mercenaries. She has described the evenings she used to spend in the house of La Belle Otero, whom she had met when they both were performing in music-halls. But this was an artist; and, whatever the youthful Charlotte Peloux and Lili may have exhibited upon the stage, it cannot have been talent. Yet *Chéri* and *Gigi* proclaim themselves the fruit of familiar knowledge. It is doubtful whether Colette has ever taken for her subject anything she has not closely observed. Some of the great novelists have been able to reconstruct a world from hearsay and their reading, with hardly any immediate contact. Presumably Colette lacks this type of imagination. '*Mon poème*,' she has remarked in a different context, '*mon poème est à ras la terre.*'.

She is, moreover, a *nouvelliste* rather than a novelist. Her longest book is her earliest; and since *L'Entrave*, 38 years ago, all her fiction has been comparatively brief, with a small cast of personages and the action confined to a short period. She has never attempted the novelist's most teasing task, which is to render duration. On the other hand, she has all the equipment of a storyteller. First, there is wide and lively experience. Everything vivid or passionate or eccentric engages her curiosity; and she can surrender herself in turn to gardening and the stage, to austerity and recklessness. Though she is habitually tender, and can be very grave, her humour is always on the *qui vive* and eager to break in. There are deliciously funny scenes in every one of her stories: *Le képi*, for instance, reveals her power to push a farcical situation to the point where it embraces pathos. Indeed, if her lyricism did not make a prior claim upon our applause, she would be placed among the first comic writers of her country.

In characterization she is masterly. Consider the portraits of her mother, of Willy, of Marguerite Moreno, even such miniatures as the Calvé or the Herriot; then the figures in her fiction, Julie de Carneilhan, Fred Peloux, Dufferein-Chautel, Mme Alvarez, the children in *Le blé qui lève*, the cat and dog in *Sept dialogues de bêtes*. No less noticeable is her gift for inventing situations, as in *La chatte, La lune de pluie, Chambre d'hôtel, La seconde, Le toutounier*, and *Bella Vista*. Upon these stories a course in the management of the medium could be based. Colette shines both in narrative and in dialogue; and she has a sure sense of when to move from one of these to the other. Her technique in fiction is so accomplished that it never obtrudes. The addict, however, is likely to consider that she herself is the most captivating of the characters she has portrayed, and to like best of her books those in which the auto-biography is undisguised: *Sido, Mes apprentissages, Journal à rebours, De ma fenêtre, L'étoile vesper*, and *Le fanal bleu*. In the last four of these, written during and after the war, her style becomes more obviously elaborate and individual than ever before, while remaining fine-fingered, exact and sapid.

The collected edition is exemplary. It is evident that M. Maurice Goudeket (whom Mme Colette married in 1935) has taken all precautions to make it scholarly. The bibliography will be invaluable to collectors. Four of Colette's books usually go to one volume, and there are fifteen volumes. Wiser than George Moore and Henry James, she has refrained from making more than slight cuts and modifications in the early works.

'*Elles garderont toutes les marques du temps, de l'erreur, de la hâte.*

Fraîches ici, plus loin tachées, que leurs macules attestent mon âge, mon long labeur, et l'honorable évolution qui transforment un écrivain hardi en critique timoré.'

Her admirers will cherish an edition that is not only handsome but so nearly complete. (*Histoires pour Bel Gazou* and *Supplément à Don Juan* seem the most notable absentees.) Here is a surprising richness of little-known material that has appeared, if at all, only in newspapers or extremely limited editions.

It is significant that in such occasional writings, some of them commissioned by a manufacturer or a shop, Colette strives for perfection no less than in her most ambitious books. Even when constrained to make her pot boil, she is unable to become perfunctory. Besides genius we find throughout her work what is now even rarer than genius, the conscientiousness of a passionate craftsman. Writers who denigrate pleasure have no excuse for slovenly language: if a man does not respond to the delightfulness of life, it should be no sacrifice to devote all his hours to the punctilio of his art. The industry of Colette, on the other hand, has entailed a heroic resistence to temptation. To scrutinize the quality conspicuous throughout this massive corpus excites our commiseration as well as our gratitude, so often must she have deprived herself of the joys she reveres in order to celebrate them with a more considered nicety.

Marcel Proust

Those of us who read each volume of the Proust novel (except the first) the moment it appeared, formed a happy band of enthusiasts, always swapping our latest impressions, a few even rash enough to shape their lives and loves by his standards. Yet, just as the height of Kangchenjunga is evident only from a distance, so the decades since his death have made his supreme genius more unmistakable, towering above other eminent novelists born about the same time, such as Wells, Bennett, Galsworthy, Baring and Maugham.

How welcome therefore the celebration of his hundredth birthday by an eleven of experts under the captaincy of Mr. Peter Quennell in a handsomely illustrated keepsake! The editor's essay makes an ideal guide for those who have not yet attempted the arduous ascent: he writes with such concision, elegance and penetration. Nor does he share the invaluable Mr. Painter's odd distrust of oral information. He has unearthed a few new details by talk with M. Jacques Porel, who knew Proust well, and from the Vicomte Charles de Noailles, who has many ties with the Proustian world, through his own family, and his wife's grandmother (a sitter for Oriane) and her stepfather, Francis de Croisset (whose name is echoed by Jacques du Rosier in *Le temps retrouvé*). I wish that the other contributors also had consulted surviving friends of Proust, notably M. Jacques de Lacretelle, the Comte Louis Gautier-Vignal and the Paul Morands.

I find *À la Recherche* gloriously life-enhancing in its extreme intelligence and beauty. It also becomes predominantly comic, often broadly so, with characters delirious in their infatuation, arrogance or rage. I must admit, however, that the comedy is frequently Swiftian, darkened by Proust's misanthropy.

Many of the generalisations are based upon his own quirks. After the age of twenty-five, he seems to have been physically attracted only by men, and by heterosexual men at that. He therefore decides that love is never reciprocal, and always poisoned by jealousy. Bisexuality for the same reason crops up eventually in an improbable number of personages. Again there is the assumption that unconscious memories, provoked by a tune or a flavour, must be far more revealing than ordinary recollections. Although we have all had such experiences, few of us, I believe, share Proust's belief in their importance. Anyone reading the novel for the first time should be warned that it is intensely subjective.

In Proust's view nobody can ever understand anyone else: personality is always so inconsistent, as well as so subject to continual changes by Time. Oddly enough, however, the greatest of all his gifts seems to me his characterisation, solid as well as subtle. He is equally inventive in the dramatic situations that display character. Again he surpasses all other novelists in his sensibility to the beauties of art as well as of Nature, and also in his induction of general laws from particular instances, following the French habit of La Bruyère and also of Balzac. Though Flaubert would have thought such considerations misplaced in a novel, Proust's are usually profound.

The world he created reminds us of the real Court depicted by Saint-Simon, but is not quite so narrow. The *petite bourgeoisie* and the populace are represented only by servants, one tailor and a few personages who have made their way into the company of the well-off. He provides, however, an almost sociological study of the distinctions apparent in the aristocracy and the upper *bourgeoisie*. We are shown the grand and witty Guermantes set, the intermediate circle of the déclassée Mme de Villeparisis, the Verdurins' little clan (two of its pillars tedious pedants, who surely could not have been admitted into a *salon* that included Anatole France), and the solid, self-sufficient professional class into which the narrator was born.

By the end of the book the only personages we are invited to respect (apart from the narrator's family, Swann and the Princesse de Parme) are Vinteuil, Elstir and Bergotte, who seem not so much individuals as idealised types of the composer, the painter and the novelist. The others, of whatever class, have been exposed as heartless, base, or at any rate silly. Proust expected his friends to be as generous in their affection (not their love) as he was himself, and they were always disappointing him. What won, and retained, his place in good society, I believe, was his wildly amusing talk.

*   *   *   *

The second volume of Mr. Painter's biography delights me. His research has been monumental. His judgment seems to me penetrating, and his style exemplary. A warning, however, may be needed: it is seldom wise to read the biography of a genius, if knowledge of his faults can weaken your enjoyment of his art.

Proust can stand the exposure of his character far better than, for instance, Pope, Rousseau, Beethoven, Dickens, Wagner or Tolstoy. He did suffer, it seems, from a strain of sadism (though I can't regard Maurice Sachs as a trustworthy witness). Also he sought to endear himself by extravagant presents or gross adulation; he cadged insensitively for flattering reviews or for votes, when he hoped for a literary prize. At the same time his sensibility made him as quick to take offence as a poor Victorian governess. It is more important to remember that he retained the admiring affection of all his closest friends. According to Georges de Lauris, who had known him for twenty years, 'never was so much goodness accompanied by so much intelligence.' Céleste Albaret, again, happily sacrificed eight years of her life to his service, 'his profound goodness reaching far deeper in him than anything that was imperfect.' Her account on a French television programme last year of his last hours was one of the most moving tributes I have ever heard.

He attacked Sainte-Beuve (a great blinkered critic, yes, but a great portraitist and social historian) for using the external features of a writer's life to explain his work: 'a book is the product of a different self from the one manifest in our habits, in society and in our vices.' Mr. Painter quotes this sentence, which he says might well give him pause as Proust's biographer. He then points out that we cannot fully understand *A la Recherche* (of all works of art) until we know 'the life in time of which it is a symbolic reconstruction on eternity.' That seems to me an evident truth: no other great novel is so autobiographical. How lucky therefore that its author's life is documented with singular fullness! In addition to a wealth of letters, many of them long, we have the reminiscences of him poured forth by a number of his friends. Mr. Painter has collated all this material with the novel, which he seems to know by heart. Thanks to his patience and ingenuity we can watch in detail the process of its creation.

The version composed in the years 1909–11 was rewritten and expanded to two and a half times its original length during the next nine years. Then Proust died, with the last two sections still unpublished, and *Le temps retrouvé* not yet properly assembled. In 1934 Professor Feuillerat wrote the first study of this expansion; and I think he deserves our gratitude, although Mr. Painter is severe upon him and further facts have been revealed in the masterly Pléiade edition.

There have been other good biographies of Proust—by Mr. Leon, for instance, or M. Maurois; but this book is far more thorough. It also offers a most acute analysis of his feelings: in particular towards his mother, a mixture of adoration, resentment and guilt. Mr. Painter's great achievement, however, is his detailed picture of the relation between the novel and its sources in the author's life. He reveals almost all the characters, places and situations as transpositions from personal experience. Proust was fascinated by the similar identification of the persons portrayed by Balzac.

In *A la Recherche* almost everything is an amalgam of several actualities. Balbec and its little railway, for instance, are modelled chiefly on Cabourg, but partly on Evian, with touches also of Dieppe and Trouville. We learn also that Oriane is taken from five women, Mme Verdurin from six, Odette from eight, Saint-Loup from nine young men, Vinteuil from seven composers, Bergotte from nine writers, Elstir from twelve painters. Though six men may have provided traits for Charlus, I think that the character portrays Robert de Montesquiou, as he might have been if promiscuous—which he was not (as we learn from the brilliant recent biography by M. Philippe Jullian). The shock of recognising himself, with such gross and uncharacteristic behaviour attributed to him, made him ill and is thought to have killed him.

Over and over again Proust wonderfully integrates details from his various sitters into a single convincing personage: Oriane and Mme Verdurin are as actual to us as our acquaintances. Yet there is one wretched failure. He was himself bisexual until the age of twenty-seven, after which he seems to have been attracted only by men. Out of prudence, however, he made the narrator, Marcel, strictly heterosexual which entailed wild improbabilities and inconsistencies. How could a girl with a bourgeois family live for years in his flat? And would he have been so obsessed with jealousy of her affairs with *girls*? A vital personage in the *Jeunes filles*, she becomes incredible and boring in *La prisonnière* and *Albertine disparue* because she is now based entirely upon young men loved by the author.

His picture of fashionable life seems to me unique. Mr. Painter thinks that the French nobility at that time had 'fashioned in miniature the last social culture our world has seen . . . In their drawing-rooms flourished a gay elegance, a fantastic individuality, a living interplay of mind, morals and emotions.' Yes, but chiefly, I suggest, because they opened these drawing-rooms to such delightful outsiders as Reynaldo Hahn, Cocteau and Proust himself. Montesquiou was indeed extremely clever and cultivated; but Proust had to borrow Oriane's wit from a Jewish *bourgeoise*, Mme Straus; and when the narrator gets to know her, she naturally turns out, as any duchess would, to be not a figure in a Gothic stained glass window but a woman with faults, like any other.

Even so, Proust's condemnation of the *beau monde* seems to me not only excessive but insincere: right up to his death he continued to find pleasure in the intelligence and kindness of his grand friends. But his novel was planned as a history of the disillusionment with the world that led Marcel to his vocation as a writer. At the end Proust smirches all the characters (except his mother and grand-mother), whatever their rank, with base motives or unlikely aberrations. (The cruel streak again?) Prodigiously intelligent and devoted to his friends, he condemns intelligence as futile and friendship as an illusion. In his view human beings exist only by our ideas of them; and this extreme subjectivity often makes his novel distort like the curved looking-glasses at a fair. Everyone is larger than life, or more comic, or (at first sight) more bewitching.

The portraiture is no less vigorous than in Balzac or Saint-Simon, and more subtle. No other novel abounds in such acute considerations upon all the arts. The style is a melodious labyrinth through which we wander amused and entranced. Proust's imaginary world therefore brings keener delight the more often it is revisited.

Anatole France (1957)

Forty years ago he was the most famous of living writers, certainly in France, probably in the world. He basked in the applause alike of the *élite* and of the great public. Even those who detested his opinions were obliged, if at all intelligent, to admire his style. Foreigners agreed with his compatriots that he was characteristically and deliciously French. The English, like every other civilised people, devoured his work both in the original and in translation.

Today he is generally despised, or else merely unknown. I can think of no other writer in our time who has fallen out of sight from so high a pinnacle. (Galsworthy never approached Anatole France in the estimation of the fastidious.) To have chosen him as an author to commend will expose me, I realise, to pity—above all in France. '*Ce pauvre Mortimer,*' I can hear my friends saying, '*évidemment il aime beaucoup notre littérature, mais sans y comprendre grand'chose: il se met maintenant à prôner Anatole France!*' Though a few of his books are still reprinted in cheap editions, they are thought as dowdy as hobble-skirts.

To overestimate the idols of one's youth is an amiable propensity, but this article has no such excuse. I read Anatole France in my nonage without enthusiasm: I was born too late. (Rémy de Gourmont, Maeterlinck and Gide were my early heroes.) I invite you to consider Anatole France, because I have recently reread most of his work with an enjoyment that has astonished me.

I saw him once, tall, white-bearded, with a crooked aquiline nose, but I never met him; and his character does not sound attractive. Like so many of the most celebrated writers, he seems to have been self-centred and inconsiderate. But then the most graphic and detailed account we have of him comes from his secretary, Brousson, whose Boswellising is brilliant rather than friendly or even accurate.

Now for a summary of his career. (Jacques Suffel is the best of his biographers.) Anatole Thibault was born in 1844. His father came from an extremely poor family in Anjou, joined the army, where he learnt to read, and started a small bookselling business in Paris. He then married a girl from Chartres, whose paternity was unknown. Anatole, their only child, went to a famous school but to no university. He scraped a living as a schoolmaster, a journalist and a publisher's reader. He won the friendship of the Parnassian poets, including Verlaine, and wrote poems in their style, which were published. He had changed his name from Thibault to France. At the age of thirty-two he obtained a post in the library of the Senate, which enabled him to marry. Four years later his first novel appeared. *Le crime de Sylvestre Bonnard*, a charmingly written, innocuous book, which was crowned by the Academy. Gradually he made his name by the distinction of his literary journalism, and gained admittance, despite his awkward bearing, to the salons of the hostesses then so powerful.

One of the most prominent of these was Mme Arman, whose husband assumed the additional name of de Caillavet. She was highly cultivated, energetic, brilliant, Jewish and unhappily married, with a son who was to become a popular and most amusing dramatist. She and France fell passionately in love. They were the same age, forty-four; and their liaison lasted till her death twenty-two years later. The girl he had married did not prove either intelligent or agreeable (his novel *Le mannequin d'osier* paints her as a narrow-minded termagant) and they had only one child, a daughter. He left his home, and was divorced, five years after the beginning of his affair with Mme Arman. She had taught him the manners of a gentleman. Now she assumed most of the duties and all the rights of a wife. She even wrote some of the articles he signed.

He used to work in his house in the mornings, go to luncheon in hers, and work there upstairs in the afternoon. Then, if she was receiving, he would put on his hat and coat, walk downstairs, and explain that as he was passing he had ventured to pay her a call. This routine became amusing to her guests. (Proust, who was a great protégé of hers, made M. de Norpois behave similarly in Mme de Villeparisis's house.) The eminent author was then commanded to talk; and the company listened in deferential silence to a discourse stuffed with anecdotes, epigrams and quotations, all carefully prepared beforehand.

Though Mme Arman's husband continued to live in the house and to dissipate her fortune, there was no secret about the liaison. She adored travel, and Anatole France accompanied her regularly to Italy and Greece. She infected him also with her passion for bric-à-brac. In Paris, in the provinces and abroad they would nose round antique shops almost every day. His house became crammed with Tanagra figures, Gothic madonnas, baroque vestments and reliquaries—not always genuine. He admired Rodin, but was blind to the marvellous painting of his contemporaries; and to all music he was deaf.

In England we do not expect a bookworm to be a rake, but Anatole France, like Sainte-Beuve, was both. Even in old age he expended a lot of time and energy upon the pursuit of women, who were sometimes unattractive and often venal. This was always getting him into hot water with Mme Arman, who found his *fredaines* undignified as well as wounding. With old age he became more capricious, and she more bossy. He was glad therefore to go without her (he was now sixty-five) on a lecture tour to South America. He then neglected even to answer her letters: he was so occupied with a middle-aged actress he had met in the ship. There were rumours, which he did not deny, that he was about to marry this siren; and Mme Arman attempted suicide. On his return they were reconciled, but she died within a year. He went to Italy, and everywhere was haunted by her memory.

'I see her at the corner of every street, sometimes still young and charming, sometimes old and so beloved . . . She would never give up anything. And now she has nothing, not even her rings. But now she misses nothing. When alive, she missed everything . . . I regret her, not for any happiness I expected at her hands: there was hardly any left to us, because of her character, my weaknesses and our circumstances, but in her I have lost my reason for existing, and—it seems—even the ability to remain alive.'

Her image, often angry, visited him also in his dreams. The scribbled diary of his grief is deeply moving: it sprang from the heart.

Within a year of Mme Arman's death Emma Laprévotte, who had been her second lady's-maid, was installed in his house. She was a simple, gentle being, aged thirty-nine, and not pretty: his choice of her came, I fancy, from a sort of strange fidelity to his ancient love. Ten years later he made her his wife and she survived him by six years. He had quarrelled long since with his daughter, Suzanne, but when she died took her only child, a son, to live in his house. He had many friends among the writers of his time (violent political differences could not destroy Barrès's affection for him); he had a variety of love affairs (an American killed herself when he broke with her: he was then a man of sixty-seven); but one may doubt whether he ever cared profoundly for anyone except Mme Arman.

Anatole France was forty-six before he acquired celebrity, or deserved it: I can think of no other famous author whose gifts matured so belatedly. He had always been industrious; he had earned the praise of the discriminating by his verse, his stories, his criticism. He had revealed charm and erudition, but little originality. He now produced *Thaïs*, a novel about a courtesan and a saint in early Christian Egypt; this made a prodigious hit, and henceforward he was one of the most successful of writers. In 1896 he was elected to the Academy in the nick of time: for within two years he had enraged all right-thinking people by supporting Zola in his championship of Dreyfus.

The Affair was the turning-point in his intellectual history. From early days he had been anti-clerical. This has been attributed to resentment against the priests at his school for giving prizes not to him but to boys who were better-born or prettier; but he was a natural sceptic. The wicked and transparent lies told by Dreyfus's opponents now turned him against the Army and the political Right. As a young man he had hated the Commune from watching its excesses; later he had for a short while been taken in by Boulanger, the would-be military dictator. The Affair led to an admiring friendship with Jaurès, the great socialist, whose views he adopted and never abandoned. The influence of Mme Arman as a Jewess upon his reactions to the Affair can easily be exaggerated: an ingrained contempt for falsehood and injustice was far more important; and this now gave his writings a passion they had previously lacked.

The German attack upon his country in 1914 rallied him to an orthodox patriotism; then the appalling losses led him, like Lord

Lansdowne, to champion a negotiated peace. The war fed his misanthropy; and in 1921 he gave his support to the newly-founded Communist Party as the only hope of bringing peace to the nations. The following year the Communist International demanded the exclusion of intellectual amateurs, and he ceased his contributions to their press. At about this time two tributes were offered to his celebrity: he received the Nobel Prize and the whole of his work was placed upon the Roman Index. In 1924 he died at the age of eighty.

A writer acclaimed by two generations is almost always rejected by the third; and a hundred years after a man's birth we are usually blind to his merits, unless he was underestimated in his lifetime, like Hopkins, Henry James and Mallarmé. (These are almost the only contemporaries of Anatole France who are still read with great enthusiasm.) The demolition-gang was already at work on the day of his funeral with an outrageous pamphlet entitled *Un cadavre*. This was signed by a brilliant group of young surrealists, including Breton, Aragon, Eluard and Drieu La Rochelle.

Their efforts were soon seconded by the nationalists and clericals, who had every reason to deplore Anatole France. Next, Paul Valéry, elected to replace him in the Academy and obliged therefore to pronounce an *éloge* on his predecessor, contrived to do this without once mentioning his name. He was denigrated also by Gide and Maurras, who agreed in little else; and he had been predeceased by the two among his juniors who most admired him, Péguy and Proust.

So far as I know, there is not yet any sign of a revival in his reputation. His indulgent hedonism seems shallow to the devotees of *Angst*. Horrified by the injustices and wars he witnessed, disillusioned, pessimistic to the point of misanthropy, Anatole France was nevertheless an enjoyer, living in an age happier than ours—at any rate for intellectuals. His language is now no better liked than the philosophy it so nicely reflects. Rivarol's dictum, '*Ce qui n'est pas clair n'est pas français*,' has been replaced by '*Ce qui est clair n'est pas profond*.'

His style is compared to the *faux Louis Quinze* favoured by the furniture makers of his period; and certainly it reveals the influence of Voltaire. But its colours and cadences are richer: he reminds me often of Renan, sometimes of Flaubert. And then there are always echoes of Greek and Latin writers. This is another (but unavowed) reason for his neglect by modern readers: they are seldom steeped, as he was, in classical literature, and therefore miss the allusions to it so frequent in his work. What novelist today would head a chapter, as he sometimes did, with a quotation in Greek?

He also inserted into his fiction long *pastiches* of Rabelais. This inveterate bookishness (which I find enchanting) vexes most readers today: they call for life in the raw and a colloquial style that is thought all the more powerful if it stammers. The wonder is that Anatole France was so widely enjoyed even in his own time. Cultured readers had been titillated by the bizarreries of the Goncourts and Huysmans; the great public had been bowled over by the Technicolor violence of the epical Zola. France's style remained pellucid, bland, seemingly direct. It abounds in surprises, but they lurk beneath an unruffled surface.

He was not by nature a novelist, yet he produced nearly twenty volumes that must be classed as fiction—more, if we include the semi-fictitious memories of childhood. He had neither the training nor the learning of an historian, yet far his longest book is devoted to Joan of Arc. He was not strictly even a critic, I think: the five volumes of *La vie littéraire* are delicious, but—as their title suggests —they are concerned with life rather than literature. Like Sainte-Beuve, he was moreover often imperceptive in his judgment of contemporary writing: classicism blinkered him to the contrasting virtues of Zola and Mallarmé.

How then are we to define him? The name of philosopher has been usurped by metaphysicians, though they are lovers often of systems rather than of wisdom; and so I suppose I must call him by the unsuitably forbidding name of sage. Whatever form his books take, their purpose is always to express judgments on the nature of man and society.

He was a most conscientious artist, taking endless pains to make his work agreeable to the reader. I can enjoy almost everything he wrote except *Le lys rouge* and *La rôtisserie de la Reine Pédauque*, but in *L'île des pingouins* and *La révolte des anges* I find the fantasy often mechanical and heavy-handed. The four volumes about M. Bergeret beginning with *L'orme du mail* form a single novel, partly about his marriage, partly about current politics: it is the most impassioned of his works. Though this makes it, I consider, his masterpiece, it is perhaps too topical for readers without some knowledge of the Third Republic.

I should therefore suggest their beginning with *Les dieux ont soif*: this incomparable picture of the French Revolution is also a penetrating diagnosis of revolution as such, a diagnosis confirmed by subsequent history. (Incidentally it is, I believe, the best novel ever produced by a man of sixty-seven.) Next, I urgently recommend *Les opinions de M. Jérôme Coignard*, which is not so much a novel as a conversation piece, a precursor of *South Wind*, *Crome Yellow* and Mr. Aubrey Menen's *Prevalence of Witches*. Anatole France is usually best when most discursive.

The view of life implicit in his fiction is expressed directly in *La vie littéraire* and in *Le jardin d'Epicure* (a medley of reflections). Beginning as a disciple of Darwin, Taine and Renan, he came to hold that everything is an illusion, and all belief an absurdity. Unlike the Buddha and Pyrrho, however, he never condemned or resisted the delights of intellectual curiosity or sensuous indulgence. He quotes Bernier, the seventeenth-century doctor and traveller: 'It is a sin to deprive oneself of any pleasure.'

His political beliefs, he admitted, were at variance with his absolute scepticism. Though too pessimistic as well as too incredulous ever to be convinced by Marx, he sometimes deliberately followed his heart instead of his head, accepting inconsistency as a part of the human condition. Often he reminds me of the eighteenth-century *moraliste*, Chamfort. Men, France considered, are essentially unreasonable, and nastier as a rule than they appear. But they must not be blamed for this (he never believed in free will), and our contempt for them should be tempered with benevolence: the wise man is governed by irony and compassion.

No, it is not as an original thinker that Antole France claims attention, but as an exquisitely civilised artist. His intelligence ranks him with Peacock, his style with Max Beerbohm. The outstanding quality of his writings is *agrément* (I do not know how to translate this into English: 'agreeableness' is too clumsy and not strong enough). He lays down a carpet for his readers, who are not so much dazzled by his cleverness as delighted by their own. This *agrément* is a social virtue that spread from the drawing-room to the library, from Mme de Sévigné to Montesquieu and d'Alembert, who lent charm even to jurisprudence and to mathematics. This quality is for the moment deeply unfashionable. Writers either pursue self-expression at the expense of communication, or else (especially if they be French) are 'engaged' and intent upon propaganda.

In the impenetrable human heart there certainly lurks a desire to be mystified, disgusted, alarmed, or even bullied. In most of us,

F*

however, the love of pleasure (in the ordinary sense) is more constant and more powerful. *Agrément*, therefore, is bound to be valued in the future as it was in the past; and soon, I am convinced, there will be a rediscovery of Anatole France.

Saint-Simon

A waspish, self-important little fusspot, hardly worth a mention except as the wearer of the highest heels at Court: such was the view of Saint-Simon held by most of those who knew him—and who are now remembered only because he took the trouble to describe them. Louis de Rouvroy (1675–1755) succeeded to his father's dukedom at the age of eighteen, and began almost at once to record what he saw or heard. The Memoirs as we know them seem to have been written in the years 1739 to 1749, but remained unpublished until the 1830s. By general agreement they are among the best in any language, and a supreme masterpiece of French prose.

Though uninterested in literature or the arts, and blinkered politically by idolatry of his own tiny class, Saint-Simon had a powerful mind, which he concentrated upon the workings of the human heart. Chaste and never in love, he thought the intelligence far superior to the senses in the pleasure it can give. His emotions, however, were violent, especially hatred and contempt. I believe it was to get these off his chest that he wrote his huge book, as well as to avenge himself and to instruct posterity. He made inquisitiveness his vocation, pouring forth his discoveries in a racing torrent of words, heedless of decorum. Combining the arts of the portrait-painter, the playwright and the novelist, he plunges us into the extraordinary world of the French Court, which he scrutinised for forty years.

As a man he is not likeable, but deserves respect: he was so courageous, so upright, so deeply attached to his wife (despite her mother's 'low birth') and to his friends. But what matters is his genius as a writer. He has imposed on almost all his readers his own view of everyone at all prominent at Versailles, beginning with superb portraits of the King and his clandestine wife, Mme de Maintenon. We can make allowance for his bias, which he never conceals. Although unjust to whole groups, such as the Jesuits and those bourgeois who had any power, he seems usually sound in his judgment of individuals, admitting the weakness of his friends and even the virtues of his enemies. His occasional mistakes of fact are never, I believe, deliberate. He gives us the truth (which he pursued with passion) as he saw it; and he was extremely clear-sighted. Like Balzac and Proust, on both of whom he had a deep influence, he makes us feel that we know his characters as if they had been in our own lives.

His magnificent descriptions of disasters and death beds must not blind us to his comic powers. The trouble is that often he now makes us laugh when he is most in earnest. Should both sides of a double door be opened to receive some prince? Which duchesses are entitled to sit on a stool in the King's presence? Ought not a magistrate to doff his bonnet when addressing a duke? How far down the body should a hat be lowered, when one meets a royal bastard? Such were the solemn questions that preoccupied the great French nobles, when their English equivalents were already substituting their rule for the monarch's. Protocol helped to console them for their loss of power, when they had been removed from their estates to cramped, slummy lodgings in the château of Versailles. In our unceremonious age their devotion to trivialities is hard to understand by any stretch of the imagination. Until recently some parallel might have been found in our public schools, with their regulations about which path one might use, which cap one might wear, whose arm one might take.

At the French Court the only privilege of practical value was easy access in private to the King, who could bestow office, rank, apartments and income upon oneself, one's relations and friends. Saint-Simon obtained such access to the Regent, but never to the King, whom he offended by his unguarded talk and taste for making trouble. In any case he cared far less for material advantage than for rank as such. Always on the *qui vive* for slights in a way that would now be thought vulgar, he felt personally affronted as a duke whenever any symbol of rank was in his view usurped. Even in a Court always deeply attentive to such matters his obsession with them was thought to be extravagant. Perhaps he suffered from some sense of inferiority. His ancestors, though noble for centuries, had remained obscure, until his father won the favour of Louis XIII, who gave him a dukedom, not for gallantry in battle but for trivial services in the hunting field.

Once we have come to terms with this foible, his Memoirs are irresistible; and Miss Lucy Norton, who has already given us a delightful series of excerpts from them in *Saint-Simon at Versailles*, is now producing a shortened version of the whole book in three volumes, the first of which has just appeared with a laudatory introduction by Sir Denis Brogan. She abridges drastically, omitting (I reckon) about seven-eighths of the original. But then the memoirs are of exorbitant length, and often tedious. I have never tried to fight my way right through them; but so far as I can judge, her selection is excellent.

She has turned the French into good English, wisely omitting the slang and the grammatical errors. Inevitably some of the colour has vanished: Saint-Simon's style is so idiosyncratic. How can one translate '*Leur sublime s'amalgama*'—his famous comment upon Fénelon and Mme Guyon? (She gives us 'Their visions merged' in which the irony is lost—not that I have anything much happier to suggest.) But her version catches the run of his prose, and is a glorious labour of love which provides intense enjoyment. Let me recommend also three modern French books that she mentions, *Saint-Simon et sa comédie humaine* by Jean de la Varende, *Saint-Simon par lui-même* by François-Regis Bastide and the brief *Sur Saint-Simon* by Emmanuel d'Astier: they ease our approach to an author who appears formidable and gradually becomes fascinating.

* * * *

Thanks to the personality, the vigour and the eloquence of Saint-Simon, the French Court during the years 1692 to 1723 is more intimately known than any other.

One longs for an equally dramatic and penetrating portrayal of Lorenzo dei Medici or Queen Elizabeth I with their relations, advisers and courtiers; but until well into the seventeenth century prose had not developed the requisite clarity, momentum or skill in psychological analysis. Nor has Saint-Simon been equalled by any subsequent writer of memoirs. Lord Hervey, delightful as he is, paints a far smaller picture of a far duller Court in much less detail.

The reader starting on this panorama should begin with Miss Norton's *Saint-Simon at Versailles* and then proceed to the three volumes, even more fascinating, of her further selections from the colossal work. It has never been translated into English without abridgement: Saint-Simon becomes so long-winded when carried away by his obsession with rank and protocol. (He believed that his *raison d'être* was being a duke, when in fact it was being a writer of genius.) Even so, the selection here made could have been twice as long without any sacrifice of quality.

Born almost midway between Fénelon and Voltaire, the Duke wrote in a style of his own, impulsive and often incorrect, which Miss Norton has turned into idiomatic, racy English, wisely breaking up, however, the sentences, sometimes meandering over a whole page, that so deeply influenced Proust.

This final volume begins after the death of Louis XIV with the accession of his little great-grandson and the Regency of the Duc d'Orléans. The King had outlived almost all his important contemporaries except Mme de Maintenon; and without him the interest of the book centres on Saint-Simon himself, who emerges from the *coulisses* to become, for the first time, prominent in the public eye. He had never been liked by the old King, whom he had boldly censured for his rash indulgence to his bastards and his wise employment of middle-class ministers.

Now power had come to the Regent, with whom Saint-Simon was linked by an old, mutual affection, despite the contrast between their characters—Orléans, a lazy, heavy-drinking, loose-living unbeliever, Saint-Simon devout, abstemious, chaste, passionately determined and absurdly prejudiced. Sometimes he reminds me of Dr. Johnson, whose gift for words cannot conceal his wrong-headedness.

Saint-Simon lacked political sense, and his chief aim was to see his fellow-noblemen restored to power. He expected his advice to be taken by the Regent, who indeed listened to it with seeming agreement but seldom acted on it. Instead he appalled his old friend by relying increasingly upon the low-born Abbé (afterward Cardinal) Dubois, a statesman of uncommon ability. Orléans did give Saint-Simon the thrill of his life by revoking the legitimisation of the late King's natural son, the Duc de Maine—who now had to concede precedence to the adorable Dukes. During humiliation of his arch-enemy

'Joy was nearly killing me. I was truly terrified of swooning, for my heart was swelling within me, and there seemed no room for it to expand . . . I had won; I was avenged; I wallowed in my vengeance.'

Not very edifying sentiments in so pious a Christian, but they made him exclaim, 'How far inferior are the pleasures of the senses to those of the mind!' If he had shared the Regent's taste for little actresses, he might have taken less pride in his vindictiveness.

Having prudently declined two important jobs, he got himself sent to Madrid as Ambassador Extraordinary, accompanying the Regent's daughter for her marriage to the heir to the King of Spain. He thus obtained grandeeships for himself and his elder son, and the Golden Fleece for his younger son, enormously raising the prestige of his family—'something they much needed,' as a contemporary noted.

The Memoirs end with the Regent's death in 1723, although Saint-Simon survived it for over twenty years. While doing full justice to a few fine characters such as Vauban, they fascinate us as a bitter, though also comical, indictment of the powerful for heartlessness, lust and rapacity.

Chanel

In this century dressmakers have far outshone other practitioners of the applied arts, such as cabinet-makers, silversmiths, designers of porcelain and of glass; and the most famous of these dressmakers has been Chanel (1883–1971). Though not so imaginative as Poiret or Balenciaga, she has a unique claim to historical importance: she did more than any feminist to promote the emancipation of women.

Their clothes, if fashionable, had for centuries made most forms of work impossible—long trains, panniers, crinolines,—and in the early years of this century tight-laced stays, whaleboned collars and skirts that swept the ground. Ladies could not even fasten or unfasten their dresses without help from their maids—or their lovers, who got a great kick, we are told, from undoing dozens of hooks and eyes. Such attire proclaimed that they could afford to be idle: it was the equivalent of the five-inch long nails in China.

Poiret had rejected the wasp-waist, but so far as I can discover his example was not generally followed. It was Chanel who launched the suit (and later the slacks) in which women could feel elegant when playing golf, driving a car, visiting their patients or customers and walking in the country or wet streets. The chief beneficiaries of that revolution have been not her rich clients, but the women and girls who must go out daily to work or to shop for their families. The best turned-out of these still usually wear clothes of the type she invented over fifty years ago. Why do some others prefer mini-skirts, even in winter, even if they have knock-knees or outsize legs?

Chanel's biographer, a journalist and broadcaster, has set himself a difficult task. He took tape-recordings of her talk, and gradually discovered the already notorious fact that she was a pathological liar, especially about her childhood. She pretended to be far younger than she was, said that she had only one sibling and that she was brought up without love by cousins of her dead mother in a beautiful house with servants, scented linen-cupboards and fresh napkins at every meal, while her father, a wine-merchant from a family in Béziers, sent money back from America.

This biography informs us that he was a pedlar of Savoyard origin, and that after his wife's death he consigned their two sons to the public authorities, and their three daughters, including Chanel, to his mother in Vichy, who sent them as charity children to an orphanage run by nuns at Moulins.

Here, at seventeen, Chanel became the mistress of a rich young cavalry officer in the garrison, Etienne Balsan. His service finished, he took her to his house near Compiègne, where he kept also a famous *cocotte*, Emilienne d'Alençon. Here she learnt to ride, started a hatshop, and after some years lost her heart to a young English friend of her protector's, Arthur Capel (always known as 'Boy'). Recriminations were followed by an agreement: the French-man gave her up, paying her off with a flat in Paris, where she could continue her millinery; and the Englishman provided her with a bank account. At this point let me intrude my own recollect-ions of Chanel.

Between the Wars I had a drink with her in her house in the rue Faubourg St. Honoré; but my memory (like a broken goldwasher's pan that often holds the mud and lets through the nuggets) retains nothing of this occasion except her glorious Coromandel screens. Then, perhaps ten years ago, the dearest of my old Parisian friends took me to luncheon in a Frenchman's house; and I made one of my *gaffes*, always unintentional, whatever people say.

We found an American couple waiting, like ourselves, for our host. I said I was a Londoner; the handsome lady said she lived in Los Angeles. 'Anything to do with the films?' I feebly murmured. I had failed to recognise the famous star, Rosalind Russell. Her companion, I believe, was a producer or scriptwriter. Then our host appeared, and Chanel. This biography says that she was beautiful as a girl; and certainly she had a lovely long neck and a svelte figure; but her chin was too large, her other features simian; and what had attracted so many lovers was always, I fancy, her verve, which indeed I found fascinating. She had kept her figure, but her face now was that of a gnarled, weather-beaten shepherd.

It soon became apparent that a meeting between the two ladies was the purpose of the luncheon: in a film about the great dressmaker's life the tall Miss Russell with her admirably feminine figure was to play the boyish little Chanel—who took one horrified look at her, and refused to speak anything but French, though the Americans spoke only English. The rest of us did some interpreting; but the moment the meal was over, they made an excuse and did a bunk.

Then Chanel, who was always a compulsive talker, and also had a liking for us English, took me aside, and spent over an hour telling me about the start of her career. Capel, she explained, thought she looked her best when riding in a man's sweater; and he begged her to wear the same sort of togs all the time instead of the cumbersome, fashionable clothes that were so unbecoming to her. Taking his advice, she made dresses of a new type not only for herself but for friends such as the actress, Gabrielle Dorziat—jerseys, cardigans and suits based on English masculine attire, with skirts well above the ankle.

She had the genius to make these seductively femine by such details as a single flower, cuffs, pale colours, pleated tweed skirts and masses of costume jewellery. Though this biography never suggests that Capel had any influence upon the style of her dressmaking, I believe that she was telling me the truth, because her fibs never seem to have redounded to the credit of anyone except herself.

In 1919 Capel, who had married, died in a motor-smash, and Chanel with new premises in the rue Cambon awoke to find herself famous. Her friendship with Misia Sert had by now alerted her to the world of the Russian Ballet, Stravinsky, Picasso, Cocteau and so on. (She later avenged herself on her benefactress by selling imitations in costume jewellery of her famous long diamond and gold chain). As tough in business as any tycoon, she made an ever-growing fortune, but never liked spending money even on herself. After an affair with a fascinating Grand Duke, she welcomed the jewels and extravagant luxury placed at her disposal by the Duke of Westminster, whom she described as the richest man in the world. The affair lasted for years, doubtless partly because he curbed his caprices, knowing that she could always afford to leave him. She was never a snob, let me add, and wanted *femmes du monde* to be her customers, not her friends.

At the outbreak of war in 1939, she shut her dressmaking business at once, but continued with the hugely profitable sale of her scents. She had always been anti-semitic; and her lawyer was Laval's son-in-law. Not surprisingly, she now chose as lover a German Baron. Mr. Haedrich suggests that she may have spied for the British, and a recent book, which has been withdrawn, that she spied for the Germans. I don't know that she collaborated (except in bed) more shockingly than lots of other French people who wanted to keep their business going.

In 1954 at the age of seventy-one she resumed dressmaking with outstanding success, particularly in the American market for ready-made clothes. She never deserted the style she had invented, went on working until her death seventeen years later and then was buried in Switzerland, where she had deposited her fortune.

She gave a large sum to Diaghilev when he was in need: she gave some help to her brothers and sent one of her nephews to a fashionable English school; she was kind to the poet Reverdy; and she seems to have been liked by many of her models. Otherwise rapacious, vindictive, jealous and totally egotistic, she exemplified the unwelcome truth that a good artist can be a shocking bad lot. Presumably her character can be blamed upon a childhood deprived of all affection.

This biography, which seeks to be indulgent, does not pretend to be scholarly, and much of the truth about her remains unknown. The translator has fallen into some well-known booby-traps, translating *misère*, which means 'destitution,' as 'misery,' and *timide*, which means 'shy,' as 'timid.' Timidity was never one of Chanel's defects.

P.S. A more recent biography, *L'Irrégulière* by Edmonde Charles-Roux, is much longer, and includes many new facts, but does not, I think, greatly alter the general impression left by Marcel Haedrich's portrait.

Bloomsbury

VIRGINIA WOOLF

At Leonard Woolf's request his wife's biography has been written by Mr. Quentin Bell. He, and he alone, is ideally equipped for the job. She and her *milieu* were familiar to him from childhood, his mother having been her adored sister Vanessa, who always remained closer to her than anyone else except her husband. What's more, Mr. Bell is a most accomplished writer, and also a widely cultivated man, who combines his mother's delight in the visible world with his aunt's curiosity about character, and his father's geniality and humour.

Critics who denounce the Bloomsbury set will also enjoy being shocked, because Mr. Bell lets some fresh cats out of the bag. Brought up with a horror of humbug and a belief in telling the whole truth, so far as it can be unearthed, he portrays even his parents with candour as well as affection. Such objectivity strikes me as wholly admirable.

In an early essay Virginia Stephen explained why the Lives of authors are peculiarly revealing.

> 'A writer is a writer from his cradle; in his dealings with the world, in his affections, in his attitudes to the thousand small things that happen between dawn and sunset, he shows the same point of view as that which he elaborates afterwards with a pen in his hand.'

This quotation justifies the method Mr. Bell has adopted. Yet surely the hours between sunset and dawn also can affect his point of view. In her case, Mr. Bell tells us, frigidity produced an incomprehension of sex that limited the range of her fiction.

He begins with Virginia's kinsfolk, on one side the Stephens, stern Evangelical administrators and jurists, and on the other the beautiful or gifted Pattle sisters. His large genealogical tree includes Thackeray, Mrs. Cameron the photographer, Lord Somers, Adeline Duchess of Bedford, John Addington Symonds, two historians, H. A. L. Fisher and F. W. Maitland, and the composer Vaughan Williams. Such was the varied background in which Virginia grew up.

She travelled as far as Turkey, and her fancy skimmed at the speed of light to landscapes and slums all over the place; yet her outward life was sheltered and unadventurous, nor was she ever converted to any dogmatism, religious or political. Born in 1882, she was given foreign governesses, learnt mathematics from her erudite father, Latin from her mother, Greek from a sister of Walter Pater. Readers of her wide-ranging criticism will be startled to learn that she always thought herself uneducated: how unfair, she complained, that, being a girl, she had not been sent, like her brothers, to Cambridge!

The real obstacle, I presume, was the delicacy of her health. In any case one may doubt whether studying for a degree would have made much difference. From her early twenties she and her sister saw a great deal of their brother Thoby's Cambridge chums, Clive Bell, Desmond MacCarthy and Lytton Strachey who, together with Maynard Keynes, Duncan Grant, Roger Fry and E. M. Forster became known as the Bloomsbury group (a term they always disliked). 'Deplorable, deplorable,' Henry James wailed, 'How could Vanessa and Virginia have picked up such friends?' Their father, who had been a friend of his, would have been appalled by the freedom of their talk and behaviour. These young men provided Virginia with the sort of talk that often proves more educative at a university than tutorials and lectures. Shy with them at first, she quickly earned their respect as well as their affection by the brilliance of her mind and the charm of her looks and her character. The kind, clever, stimulating Clive Bell (my closest friend in the set) was the first to recognise her signal gifts as a writer, when shown early drafts of *The Voyage Out*.

Of her literary friends she most admired Lytton Strachey, going so far as to accept his proposal of marriage, which he wisely withdrew at their next meeting. Yet envious fear of him as a rival author was always to keep her on her best behaviour with him; and her letters to him, Mr. Bell informs us, were the dullest and most pretentious she ever wrote. Unhappily they are the only ones that have yet been published.

Her essential traits were extreme devotion to her family, inexhaustible patience in perfecting her use of language, liveliness of imagination and the recurrent insanity which is here more fully described than ever before. This does not seem to have been inherited, though her father did suffer from the same excess of sensibility, which in him took the different form of peevishness and neurotic remorse. I believe that without a streak of madness, she—like Smart and Blake—might have been a less original and poetic author.

The first severe shock she suffered came from a half-brother twenty years older than herself, whose incestuous familiarities began when she was six and persisted after she was grown up. They gave her a horror of male sexuality. This led to a long platonic love for an older woman, and continued until, at twenty-six, she indulged in a passionate flirtation—not an affair—with her brother-in-law, Clive Bell. Later she accepted an *amitié amoureuse* with Vita Sackville-West.

A series of deaths in her family seems to have been damaging. Her first breakdown was at twelve when she lost her mother, the second, ten years later, when her father died. In the care of three nurses, she showed paranoiac distrust of her sister, thought that the birds were talking Greek, refused to eat and tried to kill herself by jumping out of the window, like Septimus in *Mrs. Dalloway*.

Though her elder brother's death and her sister's marriage brought her acute distress, she kept her sanity for the next four years, after which she remained ill for a whole summer, and had to spend five weeks in a nursing home, here described as 'a sort of polite madhouse for female lunatics.' Within eighteen months she was back there for a short 'rest cure.'

This was three months after a proposal of marriage from Leonard Woolf, who had just returned from seven years as an administrator in Ceylon. He confessed to her that he was selfish, jealous, cruel, lustful and a liar—faults he would never be able to control, if yoked to an inferior, submissive wife. (He did not mention what was generally thought his more noticeable failing, a stinginess due doubtless to poverty in boyhood.) She temporised, and after recovery from her breakdown, explained that she could not return his love until she knew him better: at present he was not physically attractive to her, and angered her by the strength of his desire, all the more so because he was a Jew and seemed to her so foreign. Within a month she realised that their characters were admirably matched, and that she had come to love him. He was always to prove the most devoted and protective of husbands.

Her first book, *The Voyage Out*, was not published until three years later; and in any case Mr. Bell has decided not to offer any explanation or assessment of her writings, although he hopes with good reason to throw light upon them by his account of her life and character. In this volume we see the conditions in which her gifts were evolved. As a child she was a voracious reader, with unrestricted access to her father's large library, and from the age of nine was contributing to a family newspaper edited by her elder siblings. At twenty-two she launched into print with reviews in a Church weekly, and soon afterwards in *The Times Literary Supplement*, for which she continued to write during the rest of her life. At twenty-five she began long years of work on *The Voyage Out*.

This seductive novel is more realistic than her mature fiction, although the descriptions of its main setting, Brazil, are recklessly remote from the facts. In a notebook written when she was twenty-six she outlined what was to become her characteristic method, the achievement of 'a symmetry by means of infinite discords, showing all the traces of the mind's passage through time . . . some kind of whole made from shivering fragments.'

In this she seems to have been influenced chiefly by Sterne (as later by Proust). Moreover from 1910 the painters in her circle, Vanessa Bell, Duncan Grant and Roger Fry, shared her distaste for realism: they were the first admirers here of the Post-Impressionists, the equivalent of whose approach to their art I detect in her later fiction. Its shimmering texture reminds me especially of Bonnard's pictures, in which curtains, chairs, carpets, flowers, fruits, dishes and dachshunds are just as important as the human figures, with which they have been blended in a design brimming with iridescent colour.

VIRGINIA AND LYTTON

The correspondence between Virginia Woolf and Lytton Strachey is of interest to their friends, but the general reader will find it less enlightening than Clive Bell's memoirs. Both authors enjoyed letter-writing, and they were intimate friends for twenty-five years. But they did not write to one another nearly so often as I should have expected. In their quality also the letters are often disappointing, because uncharacteristic.

The two authors, as the editorial preface explains, were a little wary of one another, and never felt so much at ease as they did when writing to people for whom they had less admiration and respect; hence a most unexpected touch of stiltedness or artificiality. This is not noticeable, I think, except in the earlier correspondence (as a rule a natural-seeming style can be achieved only by experienced authors). Yet the book as a whole may well give a misleading and unpleasant impression to anyone who did not know Mrs. Woolf and Strachey. They were loved not merely by a little clan of cronies: many people of the most varied sorts fell captive to their charm.

Certain of their qualities are little evident in these letters. She had, for instance, an extraordinary gift for eliciting confidences: the interest she showed in you made you feel you were more interesting than you had ever suspected. If she had not been naturally ascetic, she might have been the most irresistible of sirens. And he was conspicuous both for the violence of his moral convictions and for a warmth of feeling that won the hearts of all who inspired his affection, men and women, old and young. Instead of these endearing traits we find in the letters a vein of 'snootiness.' The mockery, especially hers, sometimes appears heartless and inhuman.

Let me quickly get over the worst—the passages about Lady Ottoline Morrell. (The victims of the authors' mockery are often disguised under false initials: her name is given.) She differed from the usual lion-hunting hostess: some curious insight enabled her to spot future celebrities long before they became celebrated. Unhappily she often displayed also a curious talent for alienating the persons she had taken up, chiefly, I believe, by demanding greater intimacy than they wished. Virginia Woolf and Lytton Strachey found her fascinating yet tiresome, and—though they still went to stay in her house—their letters about her are merciless.

The contemptuous tone in which they speak of persons they knew little, if at all, need not be taken very seriously. Writers, especially when they are young, are apt to be intolerant and satirical (I know I was). Virginia Woolf and Lytton Strachey had in addition an inherited sense of superiority. They thus took on some of the characteristics of the great Whig cousinage; and I was reminded of Emily Eden, for instance, by some of Virginia Woolf's jokes at the expense of persons she thought silly, stupid, on the make, ill-bred or merely antiquated.

Yes, but do not most of us, however unillustrious our ancestors, make uncharitable quips that would look odious in cold print? If ever these get published, it is usually when the victims have become remote and as it were personages in a novel. The ridicule that will offend in this book would be thought delicious if we found it in Voltaire or Horace Walpole.

The correspondence begins in 1906, when Virginia Stephen was twenty-four, and Lytton Strachey twenty-six. (They had known each other for some while, as he was a Cambridge friend of her elder brother.) They shared a circle of friends, a passion for literature and a grim assiduity in learning how to write. (His first book appeared in 1912, hers in 1915.) Like most writers who become friends, they had a great relish for one another's work, which did not prevent their noticing faults and pointing them out. He found her too romantic; she thought him too anxious to be entertaining. Each was the only critic, I fancy, whom the other feared.

The contrasts between them in character, imagination, style and taste add to the liveliness of the letters. The youthful Strachey abominates the Victorians as mouthing, bungling hypocrites 'but perhaps there really is a baroque charm in them which will be discovered by our great-great-grandchildren, as we have dis-covered the charm of Donne, who seemed intolerable to the eight-eenth century'; she defends the nineteenth century: 'It's a good deal hotter in the head than the eighteenth.' He is ecstatic about Saint-Simon as well as Racine and Voltaire; she exalts Peacock, Hardy and Dostoevsky—a trio revealing the width of her critical sympathy.

The comments on people are phrased with wonderful neatness. Strachey, who admires Henry James enormously but does not know him, is impressed by seeing him at the window of his Rye house—'so conscientious and worried and important—he was like an admirable tradesman trying his best to give satisfaction, infinitely solemn and polite.' Virginia Woolf makes charming fun of a young man (whom I seem to recognise): 'His modernity seems to me miraculous, as if he had already been to a lunch party which has not yet been given.' Delightful also the glimpses of seas, mountains, aquariums, clubs; and here, provoked by one of our island Augusts, is a typical burst of Stracheyesque nonsense:

'The ice carnival takes place this afternoon—and we shall all look charming in our furs, cutting figures of eight. Did you know that the Atlantic is often quite frozen over up here? The seals look so funny, sprawling almost among the glaciers, poor things—and then you should see the cormorants breaking the ice with their long bills and pulling out the jelly-fish—so cleverly!'

The editors of this correspondence have asked for trouble by publishing it 'as completely as possible.' This is what Virginia Woolf and Lytton Strachey would have wished—they were always enraged by any bowdlerisation—but it may lead to comical misunderstandings. He writes, for instance, that when he was talking to her sister about plans, 'she was very vague and perhaps drunk.' Doubtless some innocent readers will take this literally— just what one would expect of that horrid Bohemian set!

ROGER FRY

Sixty years ago artists so diverse as Cézanne and Seurat, Matisse and Picasso, were lumped together as bunglers, madmen or charlatans by our most prominent painters and critics, the chief exception being Roger Fry. The Post-Impressionist exhibitions he organised here in 1910 and 1912 excited gales of contemptuous laughter; yet they led a small group, mostly young, to paint, to buy or at least to enjoy work of the types he had revealed.

He is almost equally important as a propagandist for the older, then little-regarded, unrealistic arts of the Chinese, the Scythians, the Sassanians, the Moslems, the Copts, the Mayans, the Negroes and the Polynesians. Painting and sculpture, we must remember, were then still judged largely by the fidelity with which they reproduced the appearance of their subject-matter. Fry thus became a crucial figure in the history of our taste.

He still excites acute interest not only as a polemical and most persuasive writer on visual art, but as a hugely life-enhancing personality, and even as a gallant fighter against cruel circumstance. The Life of him published in 1940 by Virginia Woolf is beautifully written and based on intimate knowledge: in her illnesses she had found him the most imaginatively helpful of her friends; but she did not pretend to any knowledge of the art-historians' world, and had also to glide over some facts that might hurt the feelings of persons still alive. Mr. Denys Sutton now completes the picture with over 700 selected letters from Fry, and a long, masterly preface summarising his character and achievements.

He was born in 1866 of a Bristol family that began making chocolate in the eighteenth century and then accumulated a handsome Victorian fortune (although his own unearned income was never large). More significant, they had been Quakers since the foundation of that society; and as such his grandparents regarded not only the theatre but music as sinful. His father, a stern judge on the bench, once objected to a portrait in a house that he visited because the lady depicted had not been a model of chastity. From him Fry inherited a quick, lucid brain; but he seems to have found the atmosphere of his home oppressive. After a scientific education at Clifton and King's College, Cambridge, he was reluctantly allowed to attend an art school in Paris, where he showed no precocity and little interest in current French painting, though he was always to remain a passionate Francophile.

All his life, however, he thought of himself as primarily a painter, not as the outstanding critic that he proved; and he suffered bitterly from the inability of the public and of even his closest friends to admire his pictures.

In his thirtieth year he married a fellow-artist who gave him a son and a daughter, but she became increasingly insane for fifteen years, after which she had to live in a mental hospital. The laws of the time making divorce impossible, he had a series of amours, first and most passionate with Vanessa Bell (who after three years ended the affair, though their friendship remained close), then with an unbalanced Frenchwoman who killed herself, and finally with Helen Anrep, who brought him happiness for the nine years that remained to him.

Soon after his marriage he made himself an expert upon the Italian Old Masters, began to write criticism and became joint-editor of the newly-founded Burlington Magazine. In 1906 conscience unhappily forced him to decline the Directorship of the National Gallery, because a few days earlier he had accepted the less congenial post of curator of painting in the Metropolitan Museum of New York. In order to look after his invalid wife he resigned in 1908, but remained as advisor and purchaser for the museum.

We learn from his letters that in this capacity he suggested offering an old English lady £400 for a Breughel he believed to be worth at least £4,000. This is the only disreputable action I know of in his life, and possibly it might not be thought so in the museum world. After three years in this post Pierpont Morgan demanded for his own collection a picture that Fry had just bought for the Metropolitan. None of the trustees dared oppose the monstrous tycoon, and Fry was given the sack. A number of his purchases are now not thought to be by the artists to whom he attributed them; but I presume that all other experts in those days made similar mistakes.

Having now become an admirer, first of Renoir, then even more of Cézanne, he soon awoke to the importance of the Post-Impressionists, in whom he found that concern for composition and that disregard for realism which delighted him in Byzantine and Oriental art, in Giotto and Uccello.

After the two historic exhibitions of their pictures, he founded the Omega Workshops in which English artists produced decorative furniture, textiles and ceramics. There was a nasty row with Wyndham Lewis, already prone to persecution-mania. Moreover Fry's violent propaganda for Post-Impressionism had alienated several of his close friends, notably Will Rothenstein and even Berenson, who had long preceded him in applauding Cézanne and Matisse.

Taste was on the move, however. In 1914 Clive Bell, fifteen years his junior, published a widely-read book entitled *Art*, about the formal qualities that in his view were the only criteria for painting. Being neither a painter nor a trained art-historian, he has often been thought a mere populariser of Fry's opinions. In fact he had been quicker to notice Matisse and Picasso. He also rashly went much further than Fry in refusing any importance to the artist's subject-matter. His style being lively, his response to art spontaneous and acute, his writings won many admirers for the École de Paris; and so after the First War did the décors of the Diaghilev Ballet.

Like many of my generation, I was deeply influenced by both these critics, to whom I owe an immense debt. Although Fry thought me more frivolous than I believe myself to have been, he generously gave me one of his pictures which I still cherish—an amusing portrait of Queen Victoria in oils and *collage*. He thought himself too sceptical (and in profile he did resemble Erasmus): yet he often staggered his friends by his credulity. This was the obverse of his exemplary readiness to question any received idea, and also to revise his own judgments. Like all of us, he had his blind spots—notably a dislike for the Greek sculpture and drawing of the Periclean Age, for Turner and Delacroix, and for Paul Klee.

Enthusiasm sometimes made him impetuous, obstinate and even overbearing. Yet his trained sensibility to art was delicate, his curiosity indefatigable, his culture broad, his charm compelling, his character beautifully quixotic. In my view his virtues as an art-critic have been surpassed only by Kenneth Clark's.

His letters, graphic, humorous and occasionally touching, form a delightful self-portrait, and will interest everyone concerned with the taste and art of his period. They have been selected and edited with fine scholarship by Mr. Denys Sutton, whose preface and annotation contain a wealth of factual detail.

E. M. FORSTER (1968)

Respect, yes, and even reverence, but most of all I want to send affection to E. M. Forster for his birthday. More than the other eminent authors of our time, he prizes affection, and also excites it in his readers. He is in fine fettle, they will be glad to know. After reading a new book on India the other day, he wrote in his own hand an appreciative letter to its author.

What's more, in this, his ninetieth year, having got locked into the Cambridge Guildhall after a concert, he spent the whole night there alone without turning a hair. He also made his first flight in a glider, and then reported: 'There is absolutely nothing in it: you go up, and you come down.'

E. M. Forster complained once that André Gide was 'elusive, sometimes annoyingly so' —yet he is astonished if anyone describes him as elusive himself. All the same, none of my other friends seems to me so difficult to pin down: he peers at life from an angle entirely his own. In the 1950s he took me to a Marx Brothers film (the day before going into hospital for an operation he thought might kill him); and he never stopped chuckling. But he hadn't expected to, and chose this film merely for my pleasure. I remembered his saying to me years earlier, 'I don't care for the Marx Brothers: one wouldn't like to meet them, if one were mad.' Who else could have said that?

Let me jot down a few other sayings I find characteristic, whether from his talk or his writings. 'It's better to be superior than to kow-tow.' (This is notable because he detests presumption.) 'I ought to feel free, yet I can't keep my hat on in a church, even if no-one is looking.' (Most of us who have the same feeling would

177

never think of mentioning it, because we take it for granted.) 'He who knows too little often gets further than he who knows too much.' (To 'get further' here certainly refers to insight, not to material success.) 'The Englishman is unable to like anyone who can't knock him down.'

And here is a remark which I thought came from his book on the novel. It doesn't, and so I shan't get the phrasing right, but I am incapable of inventing it. Discussing Fanny Price in *Mansfield Park*, he said, 'Other people have described her as a white violet: she seems to me more like a mouse-trap.' I agree; and in Edmund Bertram she caught a fine fat mouse.

Yes, apart from his belief in truth, art, kindness and the individual, he is unpredictable. If you ask 'What is he really like?' no answer comes pat, or can be found in any of the books about him. 'Well, what does he look like?' Inconspicuous, I should say; and if you didn't know who he was, you probably wouldn't take him for an author, or indeed for anyone much out of the ordinary. The face is triangular, more like a cat's than a bull's or a horse's, with clever eyes and a sensuous mouth, half-hidden by a straggly moustache. His clothes would be a darkish, indefinite grey and a touch old-fashioned, with a cloth cap, which has now become unconventional.

Professor Trilling has called him worldly, which seems to mean merely that he doesn't turn a blind eye to facts he finds painful, such as differences in race and class. In the ordinary sense of the term he is the least worldly person I know. His Evangelical ancestors did themselves well in their Clapham mansion, its library designed by the younger Pitt, its huge garden, its hothouses full of grapes and nectarines. He too enjoys good food, but would never dream of going by himself to an expensive restaurant. He despises what he calls 'stodgy comfort' and lived till he was almost seventy in a house designed by his architect father that did not contain a single bathroom. The furniture in his rooms at King's is mostly mid-Victorian. There are family portraits, but hardly anything fine in the way of pictures, silver or porcelain. He treasures his books, but no other portable possessions, unless they are associated with his childhood. Literally and metaphorically, he travels light.

He has been gloriously munificent to his friends, and to such institutions as King's and the London Library, but never to himself. Cambridge he loves not only for its secluded beauty and its high thinking, but for its plain living. His fellow members of the secret society there known as the Apostles used always to write 'oxford' with a small 'o' (for all I know they still do); and he fancies there is something showy and therefore coarse in that university and its products—including, I am sure, myself, despite which he has managed to like me for many years.

He isn't self-conscious, and so I should call him not shy but reserved. It seems characteristic that he places only his initials before his surname on the title-page. His Christian names are Edward Morgan, yet I doubt whether anyone has ever called him Ted. He has always been known to his friends as Morgan; and when we referred to him as such in the old days, before he was world-famous, people used to think we were talking about the author of *Sparkenbroke*. He is diffident, superficially and within limits. Strangers presuming to be over-familiar with him would be inviting a quiet snub—which they probably wouldn't notice. He expects other people to possess the good manners of the heart, and is himself nothing if not considerate. But I don't think he is humble. 'I like being praised,' he said once with a smile, 'it is due to me.'

Humour indeed is the most constant quality in his talk: he is always laughing at himself, and affectionately at his friends. It keeps brimming over in his writings also, although so gently that it often passes unnoticed by learned critics. When he refers to the Taj Mahal as 'he (or she)' and attributes consciousness to a wood, a mountain or even a stone, he is playing, I think, with the Indian belief in pantheism. He talks similarly of the arty-crafty whose fingers 'bother' a piece of wood or metal into an ugly shape. To 'bother' anyone or anything is in his view deplorable. Finally I would refer anyone interested in what he is really like, to *The Hill of Devi*. This book of letters, mostly to his mother, is the most revealing, because the most unbuttoned, of his writings.*

From Patrick Wilkinson, a Fellow of King's in whose house he stayed for seven years, we get some details of his Cambridge life. Like many of the cleverest people I have known, he got only a second (in Classics and then in History). Over fifty years later as an Honorary Fellow (we learn) he opposed a suggested increase in the number of undergraduates at King's. 'Whereas in business generally expansion may be beneficial, it is harmful to our business, which is to produce civilised people.'

* The posthumously published stories in *The Life to Come* go further: they were written to excite himself, and seem to me feeble.

Again, we hear that when tactless undergraduates asked him why he had not written a novel for so long, he would answer patiently, 'Well, I hadn't anything more I wanted to say.' The truth is that since writing his last novel he has found a lot of splendid things to say, in no less than five volumes; but he underrates their value on the ground that they did not spring, like his fiction, from the subconscious. I believe, however, that the subconscious plays a part in almost all good writing, not least in biography and criticism.

Forster once declared, I believe, that the pains of composition were to him unknown. We must conclude, therefore, that he has found pleasure in re-writing: the changes he made in *A Passage to India* are so numerous. In the earliest version, for instance, Aziz and Adela (here called Janet) after entering the cave 'drift into one another's arms—then apart.' In a second version her breasts are touched by somebody. Only in the final text is there the possibility of a hallucination. Almost all the changes in phrasing are improvements. (He expunged, for instance, the obsolete word 'famigerated' which he had used in the wrong sense.) I regret, however, the loss of one bitter remark made to Adela by Mrs. Moore: 'You have succeeded in making everyone very kind to you, my dear. I wonder how long they will go on? People used to be kind to me.'

Among his fellow-writers Mr. Forster enjoys a prestige unequalled except by Mr. Eliot. Yet he has made no comparable revolution in technique or taste, and the last of his five novels came out almost forty years ago. The persistent growth of his reputation has been in great part due to his personal character and views, which are most directly revealed in two volumes of essays, reviews and broadcasts, *Abinger Harvest* and *Two Cheers for Democracy*.

Critics always find him deuced difficult to pin down. His mind never moves in a straight line; his opinions are always qualified by awareness of what can be said against them: his style is unemphatic and not quite so individual as his point of view. Moreover, he has been sparing of confidences about his private life. One critic has complained that he sometimes reveals inadequacy and immaturity by mistaking vagueness of vision for a virtue. But, surely, when he becomes evasive, it is because he hates to lay down the law and thinks that there are few questions plain enough to be given a plain answer.

'He is sometimes irritating,' his admirer, Mr. Trilling, complains, 'in his refusal to be great.' One sees what is meant: a deep-laid distaste for self-advertisement, pomposity and dogmatism has always prevented him from draping himself in the mantle of the seer or sage. D. H. Lawrence kindly remarked of him: 'He is not dead yet. I hope to see him pregnant with his own soul.' This spectacle Mr. Forster would never present: it would seem to him 'improper'—a word he often uses, although not about sex.

'It is a pity,' he once suggested, 'that Man cannot be at the same time impressive and truthful.' He therefore chose, one gathers, to be unimpressive. The two qualities don't seem to me incompatible; and I believe indeed that it is his truthfulness, even more than his art, that has made so deep an impression upon writers a generation younger than himself. On the other hand he is too subtle and unassuming to be a popular favourite, nor did he become a Nobel prize-winner.

Four points about Mr. Forster can be chosen as important. He was brought up in an upper-middle-class home with no other males in it. Although luckily a day-boy, he loathed his public school, which the masters grotesquely assured him was 'the world in miniature.' He lost his heart to his university, Cambridge, finding it 'the City of Friendship and Truth.' Then a modest independent income enabled him to educate himself further by travel instead of being forced into a job.

He has emphasised the necessity of 'connecting' the beast and the monk that live separated within us. We need to cultivate both the heart (or we shall become peevish) and the mind (or we shall live in a muddle). Love—by which he means desire as well as kindly feeling—and intellectual honesty are the two supremely valuable states of mind. The trouble, I think, is that they are not always easy to reconcile. Even if we can learn tolerance, how are we to remain spontaneous while striving to be considerate?

'If critics could only have a course on writers not thinking things out—a course of lectures!' His values, and his brave application of them to current problems, merit all the applause they have received; yet I wish critics would pay more attention to him as an artist. His novels, unlike Wells's propagandist fiction, can be enjoyed again and again for the sake of their humour and pathos, their shape and texture. He uses symbols rather as musicians use themes, but keeps them characteristically unobtrusive.

A Passage to India—even more unfair, I think, to the Indians than to the British—has too often been treated as an anti-Imperialist tract. It seems to me remarkable above all for the autor's handling of language, which here for the first time he perfected. His insight into Hindu pantheism, which will find sentience and divinity in plants and even stones, is expressed in prose that always moves with happy, easy-seeming grace, leaping sometimes into poetry. The previous novels, however, reveal more about the human heart, and also about their author.

One last word to any readers who do not know Mr. Forster's writings. Don't be too earnest in searching for his 'message'—which will gradually percolate. The author who has influenced him most deeply is Jane Austen; and even at his most serious he flickers with irony. His novels, though they embrace the tragic element in life, are fine social comedies of their time.

Abortion is an unspeakable crime against God and innocent human life. Would you **spiritually** adopt one baby in the womb **in danger of abortion?** Just pray that the life of the little one, whom you spiritually and mentally adopt, may be continued to birth and beyond its birth, so that this child may have its God-given right to life, and come to know, love and serve God on earth, and then be happy with him forever in heaven. This spiritual, mental adoption is simply a personal resolution to **pray daily,** at least once for a year, for a **particular child in the womb in danger of deliberate abortion.**

The following daily prayer is suggested : "Jesus, my Lord, through the intercession of Mary, Your Mother, who bore You so lovingly, and of Saint Joseph, strong man of faith, who protected You both, I pray to You for the life of the unborn child who is in danger of abortion, the one I have spiritually adopted. Please give to the parents of this particular child the grace and courage to bring it to the life You have destined for him, her."

During **your** earthly life this spiritually adopted child will be known to God. But, in eternal life, you will find a surprised happiness in each other's company.

†Imprimatur
†Thomas Muldoon
Auxiliary Bishop of Sydney, V.G.

From: The Blue Army of our Lady of Fatima, N.S.W., Australia.

With kind permission, printed and distributed in U.K. by P.S.R.S., Convent, Fishguard.

Krishnapher's Phenomenon

Ramakrishna (1836–1886) was a Hindu ascetic, teacher and mystic. A week before his death he admitted to his disciples that he was an avatar—not just a sharer in divinity but an incarnation of God. 'A saint is still a human being and an avatar is not. He takes human birth as an act of pure grace, for the good of humanity.'

Only about a dozen avatars have hitherto been born, it seems; and Mr. Christopher Isherwood believes, or is 'at least strongly inclined to believe,' that Ramakrishna was one of them. He invites us to approach his biography with open-minded curiosity, such as we should bring to the account of any other 'phenomenon'—by which he means 'something extraordinary and mysterious.' He offers Western readers the explanations they need, but modestly adds too few comments. A beautifully neat and intelligent writer, he has condensed material that seems to me unique. Has any Christian saint been described by eye-witnesses in such detail as this astonishing Hindu?

Gadadhar Chatterjee, whose name was later changed to Ramakrishna, was a Bengali born in a village seventy miles from Calcutta. His parents, pious Brahmins, had been favoured with annunciations of the birth to them of a god. A horoscope cast by his father prophesied that he would live in a temple, surrounded with disciples, found a new institution for religious teaching, and command reverence for generations to come. 'In later years' (Mr. Isherwood assures us) 'several well-known astrologers entirely confirmed his findings.'

The boy took no interest in secular learning; and his language was to remain always ungrammatical, sometimes gross. At sixteen he visited the new temple of Kali just outside Calcutta, which our author describes as impressive. (Less devout eyes are impressed chiefly by the hybrid ugliness of its style.) The little image worshipped here shows the goddess with a necklace of skulls, a girdle of severed arms and a decapitated head in one of her four hands. She is sticking out her tongue: 'some explain this as a gesture of coyness once common among Bengali countrywomen, others say she is licking up blood.'

Penetrated with love for Kali, Ramakrishna made the precincts of her temple his home for life. He would joke with her, coax her to eat, chuck her affectionately under the chin and even—to the horror of the devout—sleep on her bedstead. Yet she did not monopolise his devotion. By meditating upon Hanuman, the monkey-god, jumping instead of walking, and swishing his *dhoti* like a tail, he added an inch to his backbone. When he turned to Krishna, the handsome young god, he threw himself into the emotions of an infatuated girl, by wearing a bodice, a skirt, a valuable *sari*, gold ornaments and a wig. (As a boy he had wished to be reborn as a beautiful, long-haired child-widow, and soon afterwards revealed himself as a skilful female impersonator.) He enjoyed also a vision of Christ, who embraced him and then passed into his body.

When he was twenty-three, his mother arranged for him to marry. Apparently she feared that continence was driving him mad, and trusted that a wife would put things right. He agreed to this project, in order (it is thought) to prove his immunity to sexual temptation. His bride could not for some time realise either his mother's hopes or his own: she was only five. At thirteen she stayed with him for a few months, and at eighteen came to live for good in the temple, sometimes sharing his bed. The marriage, we learn, was never consummated. He had given up chewing betel-nuts, when told by a medium that they excited lust. Later he took to them again with no bad effects.

He lived totally absorbed in religion. 'An ordinary man,' he pointed out, 'could not have borne a quarter of that tremendous fervour. I had no sleep at all for six long years. My eyes lost the power of winking.' Meditation or even the sudden reminder of a goddess or god, was always sending him into ecstasy, during which he was almost, or totally, unaware of his surroundings, and might reel or get out of a carriage to dance with a drunken stranger. One such trance lasted for six months. A course of Tantric discipline left his body for some while emitting a golden lustre. 'People used to stare at the loveliness of my form. To escape public notice I had to wrap always a stout sheet round my body.'

Such unmistakable holiness naturally won him in due course a number of followers, some of whom he weaned from the world. (They had to seek him, for he never set out to find them.) His teaching, moreover, was attractive in its originality and imagery. He exalted complete detachment from the world; and whereas other *gurus* championed either monism or dualism, he embraced both these contradictory doctrines. 'God is one and many. He has forms, and yet again he is without form. Who knows how many other aspects he has!' Kali remained, however, the supreme object of his love. When a favourite disciple fell ill, it was to her that he turned.

'I prayed to Mother and vowed to offer her green coconut and sugar. I used to wake up early in the morning and weep before Mother, saying, 'Mother, please cure Keshab's illness. If Keshab doesn't go on living, who shall I talk to when I go to Calcutta?' That is why I vowed to Mother to offer her green coconut and sugar.'

The Master, who in his lifetime had often appeared in visions to his followers, continued to do so after his death. He told his widow, for instance, to become a spiritual teacher and not to discard her gold ornaments. Fourteen of his disciples now became monks living together without a Rule. The order thus founded has today over a hundred centres, including one here and one in the States.

With all my affection for Indian friends and relish for Indian art I cannot help being repelled by some aspects of Indian religion, in particular the worship of Kali. To honour this goddess and to edify her worshippers hundreds of young goats have their heads cut off in her Calcutta temple—a rite most unusual among the Hindus. Her festival, the Durga Puja, collected on the banks of the Ganges far the largest crowd I have ever seen, and I was horrified by their credulous idolatry. My prejudice may be dismissed as Victorian; but Mr. Isherwood strikes me as equally biased. Should he not change his name to Krishnapher?

Legends require time to grow, he tells us, and most of the tall stories about Ramakrishna were recorded by a high-minded eye-witness with a 'Western-agnostic' education: they therefore must be the truth, or else deliberate lies. But many of these stories, I consider, clearly reveal a craving for wonders and no critical sense. In our Western society facts are verifiable: to the pious Hindu everything material is illusory. Ramakrishna himself 'knew' that one of his doctors could cure patients by transferring their diseases to his own body; and one of his followers, he affirmed, could turn base metal into gold.

Mr. Isherwood's tongue often seems close to his cheek. He tells us, for instance, that a disciple hid a rupee in the Master's bed to test his proclaimed contempt for money; and no sooner had Ramakrishna touched the bed than he started back in physical pain, wondering what had happened to him. How, I wonder, could anyone expect him to be tempted by a small silver coin? His few simple needs were always provided for. However, when told about the test, he gave his approval.

Christians and agnostics cannot believe that he was divinely inspired. But no-one who reads this absorbing book, or the naïve hagiographies upon which it is based, is likely to question his total unworldliness or his intoxication with love for a goddess.

Firbank

Firbank (1886–1926) had a genius for comedy, yes; but he was also the oddest of fish. Today he is far more widely read, especially by the young, than ever before. He was born four months after D. H. Lawrence and died five years after him of the same disease. Although they have little else in common, let me rashly add that *Valmouth* and *Sorrow in Sunlight* are standing up to corrosion by time much better than *Lady Chatterley's Lover*—a feeble work by a tragically sick man, though it still attracts the prurient by its sensuality and the puritanical by its earnestness.

Argument about Firbank will make no converts: one finds him either futile or delicious. He has won handsome praise from eminent fellow-authors—E. M. Forster, Arthur Waley, Evelyn Waugh, Cyril Connolly, Anthony Powell and Philip Toynbee. As Jocelyn Brook pointed out no sort of moral purpose can be found in Firbank's work: the function of the very few allusions to morality is purely aesthetic. This limits the scope of his novels but adds to their originality. They could hardly be further from realism: the characters are comic marionettes with a curious life of their own.

Firbank loved his mother to excess, helped to look after his sister and was shrewd about his money, fending off all attempts to borrow it and pretending to be far less rich than he was. Otherwise he could be serious about nothing except beauty, his own patient writings and other works of art. He was incapable of abstract thought, and also one of the loneliest and most self-centred of men.

He had highly intelligent acquaintances who have left lively accounts of him—Lord Berners, Osbert Sitwell, J. K. Fletcher, Vyvyan Holland, Augustus John, Nancy Cunard and Harold

Nicolson (who portrayed him as Lambert Orme in *Some People*); but he never achieved a close or durable friendship. When he was about thirty-five I met him three or four times (not at parties, but *à deux* or *à trois*)—squirming, crimson-faced, incapable of communication because of shyness and drink. Though touchingly gratified to meet an enthusiast for his work, he spoke only in strangled and disjointed gasps of rapture, hilarity or dismay. I could not imagine how he managed to complete a book, or even to travel without an attendant.

His books poke airy fun at religiosity, snobbery, the kinks of carnality, and philistinism, while revealing also a poetic response to buildings and exotic landscapes. Often described as a butterfly, he seems to me more like a humming-bird hovering choosily from hibiscus to orchid. A belated decadent from the Nineties, he faintly anticipated the surrealists and is a master of 'high camp' —the ironical and histrionic exploitation not of artifice (which is to be found in almost all good writing from Homer onwards) but of artificiality. He learnt something from Beardsley's prose (which is far less comic) and also from the early, immature work of the now unjustly neglected Stella Benson.

In his miniature way he broke away, like Joyce and Virginia Woolf, from the traditional novel, and innovated by the reduction of narrative to a minimum. This technique reflected the inconsequence of his mind, which worked in images, not in terms of causation. He would jot sentences down on cards, polish them lovingly and then arrange them as it were in a mosaic or a pointillist painting.

His diction keeps deviating from the expected phrase. An ageing actress exclaims, 'I must urge my remains'; and 'an obedient ballet-skirt' is so described because it follows its wearer's movements. A coster despatching to an actress what Firbank might have described as a tight-frilled oeillade writes to her: 'I send you some red cars sweet and scenty fresh from Covent Garden, your true-gone Bill.' Such delicate touches make his writing iridescent as well as extravagant and wildly amusing.

Reading Firbank one must be on the *qui vive* for intentional eccentricities, yet the character in one of his novels who proclaims 'I love solecisms' is covering up, I believe, for the author's vagueness. Firbank misspells in seven languages; and these errors (unlike those of other bad spellers I have known) reveal deep ignorance. His grammar in English was reckless; and I doubt whether he could ever concentrate his mind upon any books except his own. He left Uppingham after only a term and a half, and somehow managed to spend five terms at Cambridge without taking any exam, even Little Go.

He loved the sound and shape of words, but did not always know or care about their meaning—'clerestory,' 'pietism' and 'béchamel sauce,' for instance (which he took to be a rare concoction, perhaps prepared—who knows—with *bêche-de-mer*). Whereas propagandists can afford to be slipshod, in a dandified style such trivial mistakes are vexatious. However, I am left wondering whether Firbank with a stronger and better-trained intellect could have achieved comedy so fantastic and so original.

His admirers differ about which of his books they like the best. I should recommend starting with *Valmouth* (the easiest to read) and going on to *Sorrow in Sunlight* (alternatively known as *Prancing Nigger*), which seems to me the best. *The Complete Ronald Firbank* (Duckworth) can be recommended: it contains all his best work and also two stories of little value, *Odette* and *Santal*, with an excellent introduction by Anthony Powell.

Miss Miriam Benkovitz has devoted long, arduous research to her biography of Firbank, unearthing a lot of new material. She has discovered that his mother was the daughter of an Anglo-Irish clergyman, that he spent four years at a prep-school, and that almost certainly he never visited Haiti (which has hitherto been thought the background of *Sorrow in Sunlight*). The letters she quotes, however, are surprisingly commonplace, nor are we given any new light on his interior life. Some of the facts she has uncovered are not worth printing: why tell us that a crammer who tutored him for a month took a third in Honour Mods?

Moreover she seems so unfamiliar with the Europe of his time that she might be writing about T'ang China. Her narrative goes wrong over a dozen names of persons and places, which she has obviously copied without checking them from Firbank's letters. What's much worse is her constant lack of humour. *The Eccentricities of Cardinal Pirelli* (she assures us) is a masterpiece not only of technique but of morality; and then she goes even further.

'The ideal of his novels is his concept of the spirit of Christ; the struggle in them is between the world and the spirit.'

If you believe that, you can believe anything.

Mother and Daughter

Nancy Cunard's recollections of George Moore begin when she was only four (he was her first friend) and finish some thirty years later when she was setting up his prose on her hand-press in Normandy.

She is able to give us only some of the many letters he wrote to her (the originals were lost in occupied France); and the sketches of him that she has drawn from memory may be slight, but they are deeply felt and vivid with amusement. A strangely assorted couple, one feels, but how fond they were of one another, and how finely she understood him!

Her mother was the great love of his life, a blonde Boucher nymph winged with gaiety and fantastic wit, who became a famous hostess, yet gave half of every night to serious reading. Miss Cunard presents Moore against the changing, too briefly evoked background of her own career. First there is Nevill Holt, the great castellated house in Leicestershire, where her father is Master of Hounds. Moore comes often from Dublin, plays lawn-tennis with Lady Randolph Churchill, reads the Lessons in church, questions footmen about cricket, mowers about scythes, and tells little Nancy to remember that yaffle is a prettier word than woodpecker, while she drags him on huge trudges and through the brambles in his London clothes and button boots.

Then at the age of eleven, when she is caught reading *Three Weeks* he defends her against governess and mother; and, because he enlarges so often on Manet's use of black and white, she is made to wear black patent-leather shoes and white socks.

A few years pass, and from Ebury Street he enlists her help for his anthology of 'pure poetry'; 'Sentiment passes away like the clouds,' he tells her, 'there is not a tear in Shakespeare' and she believes him, though she is already a poet. Next she is going to dances during the war; 'Tell me about your lovers,' he begs, meaning not *amants* but *amoureux*; and he begins to tell her of his ancient 'prowesses.' Soon she is contributing to *Wheels* and publishing her first volume which he reviews with a mixture of enthusiasm and admonition: 'A frail thing is genius, even as the soul, and will not survive the age of thirty if ample provision of talent be not made for it.'

Then she is living on the Ile Saint-Louis and he addresses to her a roundel, 'Summer has passed away, and loveliness is dead.' But not her loveliness, let me add, for her Paris was mine also; and I can see her, sleeved in African bracelets of ivory, laughing among the dear, dead friends she here evokes.

Moore arrives to find her among the young Dadaists and Surrealists; would that he had recounted this in his prose! He takes to young M. Aragon, so articulate and so good-looking, but cannot put up with the pictures on her blood-red walls by Chirico, Tanguy and Picabia. Ding-dong go the arguments about free verse ('Bad prose'), Mr. Eliot ('That cheerless soul'), Proust ('He writes like a man trying to plough a field with a pair of knitting needles') and *Ulysses* ('It cannot be a novel, for there is not a tree in it').

Physically he made Miss Cunard think of a 'distinguished carp' and also 'a debonair feline' (Mr. Charles Morgan has said 'a fiery sheep'). Yet 'I was a great dab at love,' he told her; and she rejects, I am sure with justice, the legend that his loves were imaginary. He responded with all his being to femininity; and when the age for loves was past, enchanting women rewarded him with tender affection. One of these said to Henry James: 'I hear you disapprove of my new friend George Moore?' 'Disapprove! Disapprove! To say that I disapprove would seem to imply that he *could* be approved of.' But then Moore was malicious even to the men he liked, and specially 'difficult'—as Miss Cunard admits—with young men. Not always, however; I could tell a story of his great kindness to me.

On only one point do I disagree with her; she accepts his statement that he had read Spinoza, Hume and Kant; and I cannot believe that he puzzled over any of them for more than a few pages: how many books—even by his most darling authors—did he ever read right to the end? Ignoramus, bounder, goose—he has been called all of these; and I think that his genius shows in the art with which he exploited his defects. All his life he could be astonished by the simplest facts, an 'innocency' that he prized. The 'I' of his books is one of the gloriously comic characters in our literature.

No writer has been more tireless in revising, more dedicated to his art. I believe him to be monstrously neglected. There is space only for a word to the young. Begin with *Esther Waters, Memoirs of My Dead Life* and *Hail and Farewell*; move on to *Avowals* and *Conversations in Ebury Street* (he is at his best when describing himself). Then, if you have learnt to love his voice, you may for its sake journey through *The Brook Kerith* and *Heloise and Abelard*, which stretch straight and level and quiet, league after league, like the tree-lined roads across the plain to Chartres.

Emerald Cunard (1872–1948) was a London hostess, her daughter Nancy a poet and a campaigner against injustice. Some prig will certainly ask why we should read a book about two such unimportant figures, thus echoing a protest made by Emerald herself. 'I haven't written anything. I haven't achieved anything. I have only been a friend to people. I should hate to go down to posterity. I don't deserve it.'

The importance brought by power or fame is in itself not so attractive, we feel, as force of personality; and we would rather read about Lady Holland or Mary Kingsley, for instance, than about such Prime Ministers as Addington or Aberdeen. The two Cunard ladies were nothing if not pointful.

An odd inverted snobbery, however, now despises hostesses as such. Witty Mme du Deffand, generous Mme Geoffrin, tender Mlle de Lespinasse—down with them all, and shame upon the intellectuals and painters who accepted their hospitality! Dare I suggest that hostesses survive even in Moscow, and will always play a part in any civilised society? They need not provide fine cooking and wines or enormous houses (though these are a great help); but they must have a gift for bringing together persons of differing ages and interests who might not otherwise meet. Let me gratefully name not only Emerald Cunard, but Margot Asquith, Ottoline Morrell, Sibyl Colefax, Violet Hammersley, Alice Wimborne, Ethel Sands, Mary Hutchinson, Maud Russell and Christabel Aberconway as hostesses, who introduced an obscure young reviewer to Winston Churchill, Curzon, Bernard Shaw, George Moore, Yeats, H. G. Wells, Max Beerbohm, Arnold Bennett and Somerset Maugham.

Emerald and Nancy were always angelic to me. I was indeed one of the few who continued to see them both after they had quarrelled. They were bound to quarrel just because they were so alike—seductive, widely-read, witty, fearless, wilful, self-confident and uninhibited. But in one respect what a contrast! Let me risk a paradox: Emerald's worldliness reinforced her natural amiability; Nancy's total unworldliness made her fiercely intolerant; and though far more gifted than her mother, she turned her later years into a desolation.

As a hostess Lady Cunard, who was called Maud not Emerald when I first met her, threw her net widely. She professed to choose men for their brains and women for their looks. In fact one also found at her table stupid men and plain women, for she knew how to bring out the best in everyone. People who had met her rarely, if at all, thought she was feather-headed because she chose to remain an *enfant terrible*. When introducing one to fellow-guests, she would gaily summarise one's claim to their attention. 'This is Lord Alington, my dear. He drives in a taxi at dawn from Paris to Rome, wearing evening dress and a gardenia, without any *luggage*,' or 'This is Mr. Evan Morgan, who looks like the poet Shelley, and whose mother makes birds' nests.' In fact she was highly cultivated, and spent most of every night reading in French as well as English.

From the many good things in this book, let me choose the story of the meeting she arranged between the Prince of Wales and Wyndham Lewis. The painter-poet (a paranoiac) alarmed her by producing a little pistol with a nacre handle, and placing it beside him on the dinner table. 'Was he going to assassinate the heir to the throne, or commit suicide or murder his hostess?' She quickly opened her bag and dropped the weapon inside, exclaiming: 'Oh! What an elegant object, is it loaded with black pearls?' a reference to the Duchess of Malfi's dying speech.

She was also a munificent patron of music and the drama, dashing to the rescue of her beloved Beecham, and even of James Joyce. She will probably be remembered longest, however, for the love she inspired in George Moore, out of fashion as he is at the moment. From their first meeting before her marriage until his death nearly forty years later he adored this 'sweet kind woman for her intellect and beauty.' 'You and you *alone* make me feel that I am alive' and again, 'You and Nancy are my realities—all the others are shadows.' What about her feelings? I presume that she was the unnamed mistress who said to him (if we may believe Yeats): 'I wish I had a slave to do this for me. I would not have to think of him afterwards.' She seems to have been born a devoted friend rather than a *grande amoureuse*.

Mothers who have been cold to their small children are seldom forgiven later. Nancy Cunard, while still in the schoolroom, shocked George Moore with the remark, 'I don't like Her Ladyship' (he would have been happier if she had said, 'I hate my mother'). Emerald became proud and also, I believe, deeply fond of her daughter when she grew up into a girl who enchanted her contemporaries by her beauty, her brains and her originality. But by then it was, alas, too late.

At twenty-six Nancy went to live in the artistic world of Paris, where the new Dadaist and Surrealist movements appealed to her deep rebelliousness. Louis Aragon (the finest French writer, I think, of his generation) fell passionately in love with her. I have never met anyone more fascinating than she was at that time. Two years later she started the Hours Press, which printed works by George Moore, Norman Douglas, Robert Graves, Aragon, Ezra Pound and Samuel Beckett. Then, turning like Aragon to Left-wing politics, she became a champion of the American Negroes, lived with one of them (a musician), published an odious, even maniacal, lampoon upon her disapproving mother and involved herself actively in the cause of the Spanish Republic. She continued to write poetry and love the arts. She produced a book on Norman Douglas, then the much better one on George Moore. But she had dwindled into a fanatic.

An American writer, Solita Solano, explains what went wrong. The minute glands that activate anger never left Nancy 'time to profit by the experience of love, guilt or remorse' (we are told). 'By nature she was loving, generous and true-blue; but her vast anger at injustice embraced the universe.'

Eventually this anger exploded into madness. Visiting her in a mental hospital, I found all the old charm and intelligence, although one had to steer her away from her delusions. After a few months she was again living her own life; and several friends, notably Solita Solano, Janet Flanner and John Banting, the painter, gave her selfless help; but her four remaining years were lonely, tempestuous and distraught.

Her tragic decline reminds me always of the famous Yeats poem about the Gore-Booth sisters. Her beauty ravaged, like theirs, by angry battling for a cause, she in turn grew 'withered, old and skeleton-gaunt,/An image of such politics.' The lines addressed to them may be whispered also by her friends:

> 'Dear shadows, now you know it all,
> All the folly of a fight
> With a common wrong or right.
> The innocent and the beautiful
> Have no enemy but time . . .'

Palinurus

Become infected with the virus of haste, and however gifted you may be, your writings will not last even the poor span of your own life. High-mindedness, truthfulness, missionary zeal have no strength to embalm; style alone resists the iniquity of oblivion. (Has any ill-written book survived two centuries, except the Greek Testament? And this becomes magnificent in the Vulgate and the Authorised Version.) But if you preach perfection to the young writer, *nonumque prematur in annum*, he will, if lettered, riposte with another schoolboy tag from the same source, *Vitae summa brevis spem nos vetat incohare longam*. Nine years indeed! Why, he may be killed tomorrow, before he is delivered of his message of salvation. So off to the printer goes the poem or the novel, and it sells as briskly as if every word in it had been painfully winnowed, the fall of every sentence rehearsed by a pernickety ear. Why vex oneself with considering posterity? Simplified spelling will soon come to make all old books impenetrable except to a few such specialists as now read Anglo-Saxon; and for that matter broadcasting may make obsolete the use of print. With all the resources of applied psychology at their disposal, the governments of the future should be able to extirpate the critical faculty which turns too easily from the arts to politics. Why, then, presume that posterity will possess good taste?

However unfounded this presumption, it has become habitual; and despite myself I cannot help imagining writers of hundreds of years hence poring over a Twentieth Century classic entitled *The Unquiet Grave*, and admiring in it the mirror of their own preoccupations. Most readers, now or in the future, will be only cross at what must strike them as morbid and anti-social. The artist has licence to amuse or to excite, but if he exposes his essential nonconformity he is asking to be persecuted. 'That's telling secrets,' was the arch reproof given by Hopkins to Patmore, who at once burnt the offending manuscript. The author of *The Unquiet Grave* is open to the same charge. Symmachus himself, cut off by the rising tides of Christianity and barbarism, was not more islanded and unfashionable.

Palinurus, the pilot in the *Aeneid*, fell into the sea, carrying with him the tiller and a part of the stern. Was the laziness of sleep to blame, or subconscious hatred, or the cruelty of the gods? Our author, believing that the only function of the writer is to produce a masterpiece, has for similarly obscure reasons neglected this starboard task; and his book is 'an experiment in self dismantling, a search for the obstruction which is blocking the flow from the well.' It provides a self-portrait, built of reflections and maxims upon religion, love, politics, nature and art, of quotations from congenial authors, and of remembrances from the author's past. A castaway thrown as jetsam on an enemy shore, Palinurus alternately bends over a rock-pool to confront his own image, and lifts a searching gaze to the horizons of the past and future. It is by copying out a number of passages that I can best warn the majority of readers against a book to which a fond few will addictedly return.

'When I consider what I believe, which I can do only by proceeding from what I do not believe, I seem in a minority of one,—and yet I know that there are hundreds like me: Liberals without a belief in progress, Democrats who despise their fellow-men, Pagans who live by Christian morals, Intellectuals who cannot find the intellect sufficient,—unsatisfied Materialists, we are as common as clay.'

But this predicament (less common than Palinurus supposes) is aggravated by a neurotic consciousness of guilt. 'Three faults, which are always found together and which infect every activity,— laziness, vanity, cowardice.' (Untrue, I suggest, since the brave and the industrious can be vain, and the modest cowardly.)

'When I contemplate the accumulation of guilt and remorse which, like a garbage-can, I carry through life, and which is fed not only by the lightest actions but by the most harmless pleasures, I feel Man to be of all living things the most biologically incompetent and ill-organised . . .'

He feeds his self-contempt with quotations from the most misanthropic of all great artists, Pascal, and looks for further enlightenment to Freud.

> 'The secret of happiness lies in the avoidance of Angst (anxiety, spleen, noia, guilt, fear, remorse, cafard). It is a mistake to consider happiness as a positive state. By removing Angst, the condition of all unhappiness, we are then prepared to receive any blessings to which we are entitled.'

But you generalise from yourself, we again protest, there are other unhappinesses beside *Angst*: but our author has gone on to particularise causes and temporary cures for *Angst*, to explain why it has become endemic.

> 'We live in such a desperate age that any happiness which we possess must be hidden like a deformity, for we know that, although our nature revolts, we can create only through what we suffer . . .
> Civilisation is maintained by a very few people in a small number of places, and we need only a few bombs and some prisons to blot it out altogether.
> The civilised are those who get more out of life than the uncivilised, and for this the uncivilised have not forgiven them. One by one, the Golden Apples of the West are shaken from the tree.'

Opium beckons, suicide tempts, till the author discovers his prototypes, Chamfort, victim of the same predicament, and Sainte-Beuve, who reveals the way of escape.

> 'I feel like a cringing dog kicked about in a crowd, which, running down an alley, finds there silence, an apprehension of revelation, and then round a corner comes suddenly upon a huge dark doggy statue, a canine colossus, from another age; awe-inspiring and faith-restoring, lending him courage and wishing him well.'

This fortifies him with courage to conjure his own past. 'Streets of Paris, pray for me; beaches in the sun, pray for me; ghosts of the lemurs, intercede for me; plane-tree and laurel rose, shade me; summer rain on quays of Toulon, wash me away.' And he rediscovers the possibility of happiness.

> 'July: Once more the bold Dragonfly of pleasure has brushed me with its wing. Divine Sainte-Beuve,—'L'épicurisme bien

compris,'—and Hume, the Northern Epicurus. Late June, July and early August, fruit-eating months when the English become callous, pleasure-ridden, amorous and Elizabethan. It is necessary. After the long suicidal winter Pleasure comes to rescue us from the desert island of the ego, and gives us two months' leave. Good-bye sick Pascal and his mouldy troup; gaunt Kierkegaard, hunch-backed Leopardi, wheezing Proust and limping Epictetus with his Open Door! Midsummer greetings to La Fontaine, Congreve, Aristippus, Horace and Voltaire! Goodbye, morning tears, "All-is-lost," never-again, doubt, despair! Welcome cheese-breathing hangovers, tipsy mornings for gargling poetry, asparagus afternoons, gull's-egg evenings, affection slopping over into gossip, who-was-there's and ring-a-ling! Taoism at last rewarded! "Flower of the Quince," . . . Hour of the Broad Bean.
If all the world loved pleasure as much as Palinurus there would be no wars.'

Imagination he defines as nostalgia for the past, the absent; and this nostalgia, cause of so much anguish, is also the source of art. Flaubert—Saint Flaubert—brings further illumination: *La mélancolie elle-même n'est qu'un souvenir qui s'ignore.* So our author uses the therapeutic powers of memory in a series of evocations, Paris, St.-Jean-de-Luz, the Ile de Gavrinis, Houlgate, Kitzbühel, Cannes.

'Early morning on the Mediterranean: bright air resinous with Aleppo pine, water spraying over the gleaming tarmac of the Route Nationale and darkly reflecting the spring-summer green of the planes; swifts wheeling round the oleanders, waiters unpiling the wicker chairs and scrubbing the café tables; armfuls of carnations in the flower-stalls, pyramids of aubergines and lemons, *rascasses* on the fishmonger's slab goggling among the wine-dark urchins; smell of brioches from the bakeries, sound of reed curtains jingling in the barber shops, clang of the tin kiosk opening for *Le Petit Var*. Rope-soles warming up on the cobbles by the harbour where the *Jean d'Agrève* prepares for a trip to the Islands and the Annamese boys scrub its brass-work. Now cooks from many yachts step ashore with their market-baskets, one-eyed cats scrounge among the fish-heads, while the hot sun refracts the dancing sea-glitter on the café awnings, and the sea becomes a green gin-fizz of stillness in whose depths a quiver of sprats charges and counter-charges in the pleasure of fishes.'

Yachts, gin-fizzes? The confessor and the commissar shake their puritanic heads. But needlessly. For how empty, how tiresome, were the yacht-owners; and the gin-fizzes were nothing but a link between the jealousies and frustrations that they banished and the hangover doldrums that they left behind. 'Art is memory; memory is re-enacted desire.' Add that art bowdlerises memory, and that memory is an Ophelia that turns hell itself to favour and to prettiness. The sweet past we yearn for was never present to us, and we enjoy the image of it as we never continuously enjoyed the reality. Anxious Palinurus has reached the same solace as wheezing Proust.

But he doesn't fail to hear the commissar.

'Well, which side are you on? The Corn Goddess or the Tractor? The Womb or the Bulldozer? Christ, Freud, Buddha, Bakunin, Baudelaire, or Marx, Watson, Pavlov, Stalin, Shaw, Wells, Beveridge and Bernal . . . We need men like you in the Group Age. Will you take your turn at the helm as you used to?'

Palinurus faces the challenge.

'And I answer a seven-fold "No" to your question: a physiological no, because I am not a cell, but myself. A biological no, because a specialised mutation from the norm indicates the richness and vitality of the species. A sociological no, because those who lack the herd-instinct are generally in advance of the herd, which is always conservative, stupid, intolerant and bourgeois. A psychological no, because those who have been all their lives used to intellectual isolation are those best fitted to remain isolated; they grow adjusted to their maladjustment. A political no, for England will remain the smallest of the great powers, and so must depend for her survival on qualitative standards. An aesthetic no, because the practice of literature is still best carried out through the individual unit. An ethical no, because I do not "find fulfilment through participation in the communal life of an organised group"—that is tyranny—but in the pursuit of art and knowledge and communion with the Bourgeois formalism of Nature. To sum up: I agree with Flaubert, "A mesure que l'humanité se perfectionne, l'homme se dégrade." '

And so we approach the conclusion.

'... nothing can be accomplished without fanaticism, and without serenity nothing can be enjoyed. Perfection of form or increase of knowledge, pursuit of fame or service to the community, love of God or god of Love,—we must select the Illusion which appeals to our temperament, and embrace it with passion, if we want to be happy. This is the last autumnal precept which Palinurus has salvaged from his receding nightmare. "*C'est là son fin mot.*" '

The book is rounded with an epilogue in which the Palinurus myth, which furnishes an elaborate but unobvious pattern to this record of a year, is discussed in mock-psychoanalytical style.

Neurosis vanishes, we are told, if once its causes are made real to the patient. Similarly Palinurus, in course of explaining why he has failed to be an artist, has produced a work of art. I have tried, like the authors of the notes in concert programmes, to select the more important recurring themes, and to sketch the construction. But the potency of the work depends upon development, variations, counterpoint, contrasts in tempo and texture, alternations of *pp* and *ff*. *The Unquiet Grave*, described by its author as 'a word cycle,' betrays throughout a solicitude for the *mot juste* such as seldom harasses writers born in this century: not an epithet or an adverb but has been selected as the happiest of a dozen candidates. Palinurus is enchantingly clever (and how much, much more habitable this island would become if cleverness were less despised). He is soaked in literature, Greek, Latin, French and English, blissfully responsive also to nature (particularly to beasts and fruits), to history, and to the visual arts. (Music he never mentions, yet the numinous which is a part of his quest is nowhere more manifest than in the constructions of an Orlando di Lasso, a Mozart and a Fauré.) He is above all conspicuous for the dire penetration of the gaze he turns upon himself. La Rochefoucauld and La Bruyère, his ancestors, doubtless learnt from the scrutiny of their own hearts, but they never confess as much. And the masters of autobiography, from Augustine to Rousseau and Gibbon, offer only portraits of a *persona*, the image that Man likes to present of himself. Elderly readers, otherwise the best qualified to relish the exquisitely mandarin style, may be put off by the author's use of the Freudian hypotheses; but it is this, I think, which gives such courage to his candour. Lacking

Grace to be either Catholic or Communist, Palinurus is doubly outflanked. His book, distressing and delicious, expounds the nature of that sacred monster, the artist. Another secret is out; something is added to what we have learnt from Flaubert and Renard and Gide. Trumpeting of the rogue elephant? Braying of the unfertile mule? Such will be the judgment of the innocent, the hearty, the devout and the envious. But some of us must welcome with wondering gratitude this unknown brother who catches the heart with his penetration into anxieties akin to our own. And when he tells of his vivid lemurs, his blessed journeys to the sun and his departed loves, we bless him for the tears of desiderium set free by his cadences in our too long resolutely arid eyes.

Picasso (1958)

By the time that a writer or painter has reached the age of seventy-six, we can as a rule discuss his works with a fair measure both of objectivity and of agreement; but Picasso at this age remains the subject of fierce debate—a debate that can divide individuals against themselves. I find myself in two minds about his achievements after following them with intense interest since 1918. He still seems to me the most puzzling figure in the history of the arts.

Roland Penrose's *Life and Work of Picasso* gives the best and fullest biography of the artist that I have read. The ancestors (perhaps in part Italian); the child, precocious in drawing, backward at his books; the penniless youth playing Box and Cox with the poet Max Jacob in a Paris bedroom; the early influences of Toulouse-Lautrec and Van Gogh; the friendships with Apollinaire and Jarry; the patronage of the perceptive Leo Stein and his energetic sister Gertrude; the constant returns to the source of his inspiration in Spain; the establishment of reputation and the escape from poverty at the age of twenty-five; then the ever-swelling fame that has long since transformed him into a myth—all these are here described clearly and in detail.

Writers about Picasso are apt to indulge in glozes more obscure than the works they profess to illuminate. Mr. Penrose is exceptionally unpretentious; and though his enthusiasm is evident, he does not offer many value-judgments. He describes every phase and activity in this spectacular career—paintings, drawings, ballet-designs, sculpture, ceramics and surrealist drama. Though I cannot share Mr. Penrose's respect for the playwright, Picasso can talk brilliantly, and this book is enlivened by a number of his sayings.

Mr. Penrose describes vividly the elaborate disorder that the artist likes to impose upon his homes.

'On the walls, unframed canvases and rare specimens of masks from the South Seas and Africa found themselves hanging between plaster mouldings wherever there happened to be a nail, interspersed with photos or scraps of paper with messages boldly written in crayon. With haphazard finality objects took their places round the rooms . . . Incongruous objects, crowded together, become more deeply hedged in by a forest of new-comers. Packing-cases are opened to see what is inside, then left packed. Flowers stand desiccated in their vases. Food, clothing, toys, books, lamps, presents of all descriptions, and objets d'art pile up on top of each other like the crusts of the earth. Yet strangely enough, in spite of all this there is no squalor.'

Picasso has the magician's gift of changing everything into something else, and is himself so protean as an artist that nobody can pin him down. According to Mr. Penrose (who often reveals great psychological acumen): 'His love of disguises prompts him to imagine himself in many different roles', the harlequin, the bull, the horse, the minotaur, the owl, the dove, the meditating lover, the bearded artist and even the child holding the candle are symbolic of Picasso himself.

Let me attempt to distinguish what I think are the truths about his work from the perplexities. No other artist known to us has been so prolific, so diverse, or so widely influential in his own lifetime; he is the finest draughtsman alive; and even the least successful of his paintings are unmistakably the work of a man with extraordinary powers.

So much seems to me as nearly certain as any judgment we can ever make about a living artist. On the other hand, even if the continuous changes in Picasso's style can be accepted, what are we to make of the contrasting moods? Is it possible to discover an integrated person behind the sentimentalist, the conjuror and the savage? And can the art issuing from all these moods be valid? Until these questions can be answered, it remains doubtful whether he is an artist comparable in achievement with the greatest of his predecessors, or one who more often than not has abused his gifts. Are we to trust our eyes or our brains? Both assure me that he is a genius. Looking at his works I am usually over-whelmed (nor do I understand how they can fail to excite anyone with a trained eye); but thinking about them, I find that admiration often becomes qualified by dismay.

Many painters and writers have made beautiful works out of repulsive subjects: Picasso enjoys making repulsive works out of beautiful subjects. It is always dangerous, I agree, for the critic to use the word 'beautiful,' because the beauty of an artifact often differs in character from the beauty of a natural object such as a child or a sunset. Awareness of this difference (which was largely disregarded by the philosophers and artists of classical Greece and Rome and of the Renaissance) has vastly enlarged the range of our artistic appreciation. It has also deflected Western art from a tradition familiar for centuries, thus widening the gulf between the artist and the general public. Many of the results, however, have been resplendent; and the questions I am asking about Picasso do not apply (let me emphasise) to the work of the other great painters of our time, such as Bonnard, Braque, and, best of all in my view, Matisse.

Many of Picasso's paintings, especially from the Negro, Cubist and Hellenistic periods between 1907 and 1926 seem to me superb; and at every period he has produced marvels. He draws with absolute authority, whether he uses a pen for outlines or smudges, a brush for calligraphy, a finger or thumb to adorn a dish. But already in the first years of the century in his Blue period such pictures as 'Maternity' and 'The Old Jew' strike me as blatant in their pursuit of expressiveness. Happily Picasso under the influence of Cézanne and primitive sculpture escaped from a possible quagmire of sentimentality to a solid foothold in disciplined form, until the demoniac strain in his temperament burst out in sinister paintings that seemed to depict non-figurative statues. In fact they were violently stylised renderings of women on a bathing-beach; and from this time onwards he has been largely occupied with transformations of the feminine face and body.

His feeling for women has always been intense (seven whom he has loved are named by Mr. Penrose, and three of these gave him children). He has portrayed their beauty in realistic and neo-classical pictures and drawings; and in 1932 he was expressing their voluptuous appeal in compositions constructed of curves; but for a long while his female models seem to have unleashed his destructive impulses. He enlarges their nostrils, redistributes their features and deforms their limbs with the brutality of the bull which in so many of his drawings tears the entrails from a horse.

These distortions are not formal expedients to strengthen a design: they are expressionist. In 'Guernica' they proclaim astonishment, terror and agony, as Mr. Penrose points out: he does not tell us what they signify in portraits of the beloved. High spirits, I suppose, not mockery and loathing; but Picasso, who as a man seems well-adjusted and genial, often paints as if he were a frenzied misanthrope, a second Swift. His massacre of women horrifies me as an outrage upon the human personality. Such painting may be thought a natural product of the world that invented Belsen and the Soviet labour-camps.

As a Communist Picasso ought to extol peace and to approve of violence; yet it would be foolish to seek in his political beliefs an explanation of his painting, which is frowned upon by the Kremlin. Like so many Western Communists, he seems to have joined the party because he is an idealist and a born rebel, not to say an anarchist. This is deeply unreasonable, but then most of his productions hurl defiance at logic. In the dazzling Clouzot film we saw him repeatedly change the subject-matter of a picture in the process of painting it. 'I don't know what's going on, I never do,' he said about an aquatint on which he was engaged. The new powers (Mr. Penrose explains) with which he has sought to endow the work of art 'are not the fruit of intellectual speculation: they are closely akin to the primitive heritage of art that has been overladen with convention and forgotten.'

The impact of this manifest Titan upon other artists everywhere has been measureless. He bears no direct blame for the vacuities of *tachisme* and action-painting; his works have always been translations of some visible object, even when one cannot be sure whether this is a guitar, a woman or a pipe. 'To deprive painting of all subject-matter and hence of all poetic allusions and symbols has always seemed to Picasso a form of castration.' Indirectly, however, he has done appalling damage by opening the floodgates; no other artist with such powers has taken such liberties. Since he can effectively make a bull's head from the saddle and handlebars of a bicycle, or a baboon's snout from a toy motor-car, other artists have come to believe that nothing is inadmissible.

We are sometimes told that we ought to welcome all the art produced by our gifted contemporaries: 'Whatever's new is right.' Such blind acceptance does not strike me as sensible. The painters most admired in the second half of the nineteenth century were led miserably astray by their taste for anecdotes and costume-pieces. It seems to me possible that many of the most admired painters today are similarly smothering their gifts by shrinking from the subject or any form of representation: seventy years hence they may seem as ill-advised as Landseer, Meissonier, Leighton and Bouguereau.

I cannot believe, however, that Picasso will be forgotten so long as Bosch, El Greco and Goya are remembered. Monster exalted or archangel ruined, he bestrides our waning world like a Colossus.

Far-Flung Festivities

The travel-addict will have visited some places for special occasions such as Holy Week in Seville and the Palio in Siena—the most spectacular survivals in Europe. Other celebrations one has come upon by mere chance; and here are a few that stick in my memory.

New Year's Eve at Tamatave. With two friends I had got up at 4.30 a.m. and flown there from Antananarivo, in order to spend the following day in a train crawling back to the capital through picturesque mountains. Tamatave, on the east coast of Madagascar, is its largest port, but quite a small place. Here more than anywhere else I realised why Lévi-Strauss, the most eloquent of anthropologists, called the tropics *tristes*. The inhabitants as well as the buildings seemed to be mouldered by the damp heat. The sun was beating down, but there seemed no place where we could bathe; and so we motored out to a botanical garden ten miles away, hoping for such wonders as one finds at Singapore and at Peradinya in Ceylon.

We did not find them, and soon were drenched to the skin by a blinding thunderstorm, after which we were given shelter and rum by a kindly gardener. Back in our modest hotel (which charged Ritz prices but would not change our travellers' cheques), we were told by the French manageress that there would be a grand *réveillon* supper at 10.30 to see the New Year in. Alas, we were too dispirited to attend what must have been the most Graham Greene of festivities. In the railway carriage the next day a young American naturalist took from a small bag the rare chameleons he had collected; and they clambered over us in the friendliest way, shooting out tongues as long as themselves to catch flies.

New Year's Day in Antigua. This was not the island in the

Leewards, but the old capital of Guatemala, which had been overwhelmed in 1773 by an earthquake and an eruption of mud from a volcano. It is now a most seductive little city in romantic mountain country with an ideal winter climate and astonishing sunsets in the brown tints of a Piazzetta painting. The Spaniards built Antigua on a grid plan (did they take the notion from the Aztecs?); and every street offers at each end green vistas of wooded slopes. There are over twenty baroque churches, two or three of them restored after the earthquake, the others roofless, overgrown, Piranesi ruins. In the profusion of their carved ornament they reminded me of Lecce in Apulia, which also belonged to the Spanish Empire.

A queue of devotees was waiting in the cathedral to embrace a large crucifix, with mothers pressing their infants against the body of Christ. During a delicious week I noticed just one other form of celebration: the post-office, which was the only place to sell stamps, remained shut because six days out of the seven were public holidays.

Mi-Carême in Pondicherry. When I was there, this was still a French possession, an enclave in the province of Madras. The Indians celebrated mid-Lent, although almost all of them Hindus, by prancing in procession through the streets, costumed for carnival as pierrots or eighteenth-century *marquises* (a piquant effect because here in South India they are extremely dark), while a few others had made themselves gorgeous to represent their gods, Siva perhaps or Hanuman. When they reached Government House, a charming Louis-Philippe building surrounded with two tiers of verandahs, they sang the Marseillaise.

They had good reason to enjoy being French. Pondicherry was a free port, which made life cheaper there than in the Republic of India; and alcohol was not prohibited. An easy livelihood was offered by the smuggling of gold and European goods into the surrounding province. Moreover, whenever famine struck this region, the French Government imported rice from Indo-China. If allowed a plebiscite, Pondicherry, I feel sure, would have chosen to remain French.

Aoi Matsura in Kyoto. This mid-May Hollyhock Festival is the most important in the Shinto calendar. The other day I was reading about it in Dr. Ivan Morris's noble edition of *The Pillow Book* by Sei Shonagon. The great Vestal used to go in procession to the shrine; everyone wore new clothes, yellowish green or deep violet; and hollyhocks were attached to pillars, blinds, hair and headdresses. Though I doubt whether the occasion retains much religious significance, there is still a procession in tenth-century costume, including halberd-bearers, pages, horsemen and imperial carriages drawn by oxen. The spectacle was of rare beauty, and fascinated me also as a pageant re-creating the world of Genji, the shining Prince.

Independence Day in St. Martinville, Louisiana. In New Orleans one July years ago I met the mayor of this little town, a hundred miles or more to the west. He was wearing a hand-painted tie displaying a bottle of the tabasco sauce he manufactured. I ought to visit his town, he told me; and there I discovered an America unlike anything I have seen elsewhere. The white people are Catholics, mostly descended from French Canadians we expelled from Nova Scotia in 1755. Their journey to exile in the deep South is described in Longfellow's 'Evangeline' and the heroine of the poem is commemorated by a statue in the St. Martinville churchyard. The older people here, I found, still spoke French (and so did the Negroes, but in a *patois* that I couldn't understand). The French in Nova Scotia were called 'Acadiens' and these descendants of theirs are known as Cajuns. The delta of the Mississippi where they settled is interspersed with *bayous*, marshy offshoots of the river; and the trees are festooned with Spanish Moss that looks like the cobwebs of some colossal, Science Fiction spider.

Though the feminine clothes down here were fashionable, the interiors of even the richest houses remained delightfully unaffected by current taste: enlarged oval portraits of grandparents hung above rocking-chairs and other nineteenth century furniture. At a party to celebrate Independence Day with a barbecue supper in the garden I was made wonderfully welcome as an Englishman—the first, I fancy, that some of the guests had ever met. The host was busy making frosted mint juleps and a pungent sauce for the grilled meat. We talked a lot about food, as if we had been in Burgundy or Savoy, and a little about the Civil War, which in the South must always be called 'The War between the States.' In this curious little French-speaking world, I felt more at home than in the great American cities, where so many of the inhabitants are by origin Russian or Polish.

The Durgapuja in Calcutta. Durga is one of the forms taken by Siva's consort Kali, the one Hindu deity honoured with animal sacrifices. During this festival in October, the people even in the poorest quarters subscribe to set up in tents or booths new, large images of the goddess with the male demon she vanquished at her feet. (The year I was there he was dressed as Tarzan in the old Hollywood films.) Flocks of the devout bring offerings for a week, after which the images are brought on lorries to the Hooghli, and dropped in its deep waters where they slowly sink.

Despite rain from a lingering monsoon the crowd, tight-packed upon the sloping slippery river-banks, was incomparably the largest in which I have ever found myself. I was scared by the superstitious excitement, and suddenly understood why our Victorian ancestors in India shuddered at idolatry. Mass-emotion I find horrid in itself, even when its irrationality does not seem dangerous—in a crowd, for instance, of unbelievers who sing *Abide with me* at a football match before they destroy the furnishings of railway trains. Festivities therefore must be on a fairly small scale if one is to remember them with enjoyment.

Back to Italy (1946)

Florence. A coin into the Trevi fountain, and then by jeep through Spoleto, Perugia and Arezzo. It was May Day, and everywhere we came on processions, red banners and gay red clothes. I haven't learnt much about Italian politics: this country provides so many more rewarding subjects for talk. I notice much less anxiety here than in France, much less passion than in Greece. Yet the Italians take an almost schoolboy delight in being able again to discuss politics. Rhetoric remains the traditional enemy: so many words, so few definitions. The Communists are obviously spending immense sums of money, the clergy are similarly lavishing a wealth of eloquence.

The road through Umbria and Tuscany showed blessedly little trace of the military tide that had swept over it. A few dull houses shelled on the outskirts of Perugia; and a signpost, fantastic among the Umbrian oleanders and olives, "To the Indian burning ghats". Almost every street in Arezzo has lost a house; but this, I noticed with surprised relief, hardly affects the impression made by this so refined and felicitous hill-town; and the churches have escaped. I spent a long while in San Francesco.

Every generation finds itself peculiarly responsive to one or two artists, and I share with my contemporaries a passionate devotion to Piero della Francesca and Cézanne (and Degas is another whom I worship almost uncritically). I note the fact, but have no explanation for it. When, oh when, shall we be given a history of taste? Ruskin says nothing about Piero except that he has a pretty name; Pater does not mention him. The twentieth century has placed him among the highest gods.

What has struck me most forcibly in Italian paintings, on this journey has been the interest of the artists in drama. Giotto, Fra

Angelico, Masaccio, Botticelli in his later years, Signorelli, Tintoret, the eclectics, all the baroque painters—how persistently they sought to display the telling gesture, the rapt or agonised expression of mouth and eye! Even Raphael in *The Transfiguration* is no less concerned with the dramatic significance of an up-stretched arm than with its function as a girder in his design. Even Piero—coolest, most recollected of painters—includes in his *Chosroes* a kneeling warrior whose grimace and outflung hand dramatize the terror of death. In this century we have become anaesthetized to such triumphs, or rather, when the later artists achieve them, we are more often than not repelled. All our critical talk is of design and handling, of tactile values or significant form. Because dramatic representation is not essential to good painting, we dismiss it as irrelevant; because it so often crops up in bad painting, we even deplore it as a vulgar disfigurement. (Which it often is: to enjoy the Raphael *Transfiguration* do we not have to overlook the histrionics in which the painter took such evident satisfaction?) This preoccupation of the Italian painters with the language of arm and eye came from belonging to a people among whom this language was vernacular. To us now it is alien, and we associate it chiefly with ham acting. In the eighteenth century the English, I feel sure, were as lavish with gestures as they were with tears. The nineteenth-century reaction against post-Raphael-ite painting and architecture, the twentieth-century exclusive zeal for purely formal elements in pictures, both reflect our lack of sympathy with gesticulation—the word itself is pejorative. But whenever two Italians meet, they renew the expressive movements studied and immortalised by their painters, and also their sculptors, centuries ago.

Every time I come to Florence I like it less. Yet it has not, like Rome, been vulgarly spoilt since I first knew it. The damage done by the Germans is indeed horrifying, all the bridges except the Ponte Vecchio destroyed, and a large part of the Borgo San Jacopo. (I wish Colonel Fuchs, who is alleged to be responsible, could be brought to trial for this outrage against Europe.) At the same time the damage is less than I had been told. I expected not to see one house standing of those which rise from the Arno between the Ponte Vecchio and the Ponte Santa Trinità; and I found that more than half of them had survived: the other central parts of Florence are intact.

Why, then, do I not like the place better? Is it that the palaces

H

are prison-like, that the churches incline to primness? (This last word I hardly dare to write, and yet is there not in Santo Spirito and San Lorenzo a sacrifice of emotion to intellect, of vitality to refinement?) In other Tuscan towns, however, my response to the Quattrocento is ungrudging. My liking for a city has now come to depend chiefly on one criterion: how pleasant is it to stroll in? This depends largely, of course, but not wholly, on the charm of the architecture. The narrow, traffic-crowded streets of Florence make walking a penance. London is nearly as bad; but almost all the centre of Paris is delightful; and Venice, with no wheeled traffic, is incomparable. There it is a pleasure even to lose one's way.

One must always return to Florence, for it has more good pictures in it than anywhere else. This time I have found the Uffizi shut, the interior having been damaged. San Marco, for some reason, is also inaccessible; but the Pitti is open, and some of the Uffizi pictures are there. The Carmine frescoes and the Michelangelo sculpture in the Sagrestia Nuova seem more majestic than ever in a world that is losing all sense of human majesty.

I made an expedition to Poggio a Cajano to see the Pontormo fresco, as seductive a decoration as any in the world. (And the Schifanoia, and the Villa at Maser, and the Villa Valmarana? Well, I like best the beauty I happen to be with, whichever it is. Incidentally, the supreme Masters seldom can bring themselves to sacrifice other and nobler virtues to decorativeness. The Arena Chapel, the Brancacci Chapel, the Choir of San Francesco at Arezzo, the Vatican *Stanze*, the Scuola di San Rocco, are none of them apt, judged merely as decoration. The two most obvious exceptions are the Botticelli frescoes in the Louvre and Raphael's *Galatea* in the Farnesina, but these are isolated panels, not entire schemes.) The Villa Reale has been slightly battered, and was being repaired. Admirable the determination with which the Italians are setting themselves to restore. In the Valdarno I was struck by the massive viaducts of brick or masonry that had already been rebuilt, and in one town hundreds of new houses.

On the road to Poggio a Cajano, I twice stopped to ask the way, and I was tempted to do so again, so beautifully smiling was the politeness of the answers. The manners of the Tuscan *contadini* reveal a deeper civilisation, a fuller humanity, than those of any other people I have encountered. And the landscape they have moulded reflects the same virtues. Not only do the villas and farms in the environs of Florence embellish the view, but the country itself is as it were exquisitely mannered: Man is responsible for the cypresses that punctuate the hillsides, but the gentleness of the mountainous skyline shows Nature at her most well-bred. (This has been further softened by men planting trees: the horizon is drawn at Athens with a single penstroke, at Florence with a brush.) Yes, one must always return to Florence while one has eyes to see with, for the sake not only of the paintings, sculpture and buildings but of the country around and its inhabitants. Here one can feel proud of belonging to the human race. In Florence itself the waiters and barbers walk straight out of Botticelli's pictures, every face is vivid with character.

Staying with Berenson in his villa a few miles outside the city, I find a crimson rose and a scarlet carnation side by side upon my breakfast tray; and as I dress I watch gardeners picking up armfuls of azalea petals that have fallen in the night. There is a prodigious library in the villa, masterpieces by Domenico Veneziano, Lorenzetti, Signorelli and Cima, Chinese bronzes of the furthest refinement, and some of the best talk I have known for years. If I tear myself from the terraced garden, I am on a hillside striped with cypresses. (Some of them, I notice for the first time, carry, low down and isolated, a branch that rises like a sapling in the same steepled form as the tree, and that suggests a small crane clinging to its mother's breast, or is it a kangaroo stretching its neck from the pouch?) Young wheat and vines and olive trees concert their various greens. Here I have refound the *vrai plaisir de vivre*.

Venice. From Florence I took the Futa Pass, crossing what was the Gothic line. Villages with not a house left habitable, Pianora almost a Cassino. In Bologna some houses have gone, but the general impression is unspoiled. San Petronio intact, also Santo Stefano with its seven churches growing out of one another like multiplying cells. Ferrara, the Municipio burnt out, but walls standing; the Castello intact. (Alas, no time to visit the Schifanoia.) Padua, the Santo intact; and inside it, to my astonished delight, one of the Mantegna frescoes from the Eremitani; and I learn that there is another that was moved to the safety of the Cà d'Oro. This is wonderful news, for these Mantegnas show, at its finest, the early Renaissance intoxication with the notion of ancient Rome. (The only comparable expression of this was the Rimini Temple, which has been made a ruin.) Tea in Asolo, with a view over the

Veneto, the campaniles like lead-pencils promising St. Mark's. Then, skirting Treviso, where seven thousand people were killed in a useless air-raid—they had come out in the streets, as usual, to watch delightedly our bombers on their way to cross the Alps—I came to the Lagoon.

During these long, onerous, insular years, my thoughts have kept returning to Venice. (Odd how Man likes to confuse emotion with intellect: 'I was thinking of you', one says to the beloved, alike in English and French, when one means 'I was feeling about you'.) I have never seen the sun reflected from the Thames on the underside of a leaning tree without remembering the stripes of light dappling the arches of the Venetian bridges. As I drove across the bridge from Mestre in the dark, I wondered whether my crystallization would not end in disappointment. Surely Venice could not be as beautiful as my image of it. But it is, it is! And I knew this the moment that I again reached the Canal, saw the scimitar prows bobbing above its ripples of black and gold, heard on its containing walls the heavy slap of water.

I have the wonderful luck to be staying, the guest of a most intelligent Englishman, whom I had not previously met, in the Casetta Rossa, a little house with a garden on the Canal, almost opposite the unfinished palace Venier dei Leoni. Walking in a bewilderment of delight and recognition to the Piazza, I found the square beside Santa Maria del Giglio cluttered with rubble. Had there after all been a bomb in the heart of Venice? No, this was the remains of an air-raid shelter; and in other *campi* I found the shelters still standing, shaped like Nissen huts, but in concrete. Venice was in fact bombed by the Allies, but only the dreary Marittima dock, and with exemplary precision. A German munition ship blew up and, very strangely, the frescoes in the Labia Palace, which is not near the dock, were damaged—a largish patch gone beneath Cleopatra's pearl and one of the figures on the balcony. It might have been much worse, for nothing else of importance has suffered.

The shops are as full as ever of stuff for tourists to buy, glass, tortoiseshell, beads, lace, but there are no tourists except the British troops on leave, with vermilion knees showing below their shorts. The chairs at Florian's are nine-tenths of them empty, and the price of a cup of coffee is indeed forbidding, three times higher than in Rome. The Army has requisitioned some of the Canal steamers, and by a most unlucky whim painted them red, green and white. (One must be glad, I suppose, that the design is taken from the Italian flag and not the Union Jack.) I can find no other change in Venice. Yes, I am forgetting that the Palazzo Vendramin, where Wagner died, has been turned into a gaming house. It is called the Casino, though this is the Italian word for a brothel, and the Italians are careful to give it the French pronunciation, accenting each syllable equally. Also, since I was last here, the lamp-posts have been removed from the Piazza. The new illumination, from searchlights on top of buildings, is an affront.

Pottering in the labyrinth of alleys, up and down the steps of bridges, to pay my homage to favourite churches, Santa Maria Formosa, San Francesco della Vigna, San Giovanni in Bragora, the Madonna dell' Orto, the Gesuiti, I think of all the friends who have been with me in Venice. As one grows older the places one has known the best become peopled with ghosts and, not least, with the ghosts of one's own dead selves. When I first came here, there was an old-established colony of English and Americans: Mrs. Curtis at the Palazzo Barbaro, where Henry James and Sargent used to stay with her (I remember her telling me the story that Henry James took from her to make *The Aspern Papers*); Mrs. Eden in her garden on the Giudecca; the Princesse Edmond de Polignac, surrounded with musicians, herself a brilliant painter as well as a pianist, and with an unexpected passion for golf; Sir Hubert Miller, a gloriously Proustian character with a hundred gilt baroque angels in his dining-room; and Mrs. Johnstone at the Palazzo Contarini with the most beautiful of Venetian gardens, looking across the lagoon towards Murano. Everyone wanted to see this, and she received so many royal persons that she caught their arrogance without catching the politeness under which they disguise it. An American Jewess, married to a painter whose works one was never allowed to see, she had been converted to Catholicism; and her piety, which could not disenvenom her tongue, obliged her to tear from her Prousts, before they were bound, every page referring to M. de Charlus. I suppose he reminded her too exactly of some of her fellow-Venetians. Yet she was an uncommonly clever woman, and I wish that today I could ring her bell and wait, as I used to do, for a quarter of an hour, while the butler discovered whether she would condescend to give me audience.

If I had a gift for fiction, and a better memory, I should write a novel about this vanished Venetian colony. It was quite different from the scallywag Capriote outpost described by Norman Douglas and Compton Mackenzie; but here, too, the expatriates, secure from the overshadowing that would have been their fate in London or Paris, could luxuriate into exorbitant personalities. Their quarrels were epic: gondoliers rowed wearily from palace to palace carrying declarations of war. Then, in the Twenties, this little society, which had welcomed the cultivated pilgrim, began to find the Piazza noisy with invaders whom it was hard to overlook, though they did not know the Frari from the Miracoli, and did not give a fig for the hierarchy of old residents. Venice in summer became fashionable with the pleasure-loving rich: bathing and backgammon at the Lido, fabulous fancy-dress parties in the hired palaces. The colony hated all that. Convenient it might be to let your apartment for a fabulous rent, but you returned to find your servants spoiled by the vulgar profuseness of your tenants. Venice, you complained, was being desecrated by this frivolity. In fact, Venice was merely recovering an ancient function. Read Casanova, or for that matter Voltaire, and you see that it was the Monte Carlo of the eighteenth century.

Not only in Venice and Florence and Rome, but in every pleasant place from Rapallo to Taormina, there used to be, when first I came to Italy, colonies of English. They ransacked the ancient shops for painted furniture, they made lovely gardens, they attended the English Church. And there were pensions murmurous with ladies interchanging advice about their watercolours before retiring to brew tea in their bedrooms. All these, colonists or regular migrants, knew the Italians, and therefore loved them. (If sometimes they loved them in the fullest sense of the term, the reciprocal benefit was all the more marked.) But Fascism arrived, and though the Italians almost all remained charming to us, fewer and fewer English were to be seen in the hotels. The older colonists died, and were not replaced. Whereas thirty years ago no Englishman was thought tolerably cultivated if he did not know Italy, now few of my friends under forty have been here. This does more than destroy Anglo-Italian understanding: it coarsens English civilization; and the kindness with which I have been received everywhere by the Italians convinces me that they long, as I do, for the connection to be renewed.

Milan. Leaving Venice for Milan, I felt like Adam expelled from his happy seat in Paradise, or Titus leaving Bérénice! (*Je l'aime, je le fuis: Titus m'aime, il me quitte.*) I stopped on the way to look at

Vicenza, Verona and Brescia. From all accounts the 'pattern bombing' of Vicenza was a waste of good explosive, and on what a target! Is any city more packed with splendid architecture? But even here, not through precision bombing, but by marvellous luck, the damage is much less hideous than I feared. The basilica roofless and burnt out, but its façades hardly hurt: the Loggia del Capitano, the Museo Civico, the Palazzo Thiene, and the exquisite Teatro Olimpico untouched. Verona has lost its medieval bridge, but no harm has come to the Piazza dell' Erbe, the Piazza dei Signori, the Scaliger tombs or Santo Zeno.

Everywhere rumour has exaggerated the extent of the destruction. You are told that there is not a column left of some masterpiece, and you find that not a column has been damaged. Human beings have fallen in love with disaster, have become addicts of calamity. Individuals and classes and nations are the same. They boast competitively of their sufferings. 'We had the Germans', 'We had the bombs', 'We are worse fed than you', 'Your tuberculosis rate is lower than ours', 'Your capital city is intact', 'Your inflation is not so great as ours', 'We were occupied', 'We fought alone', 'My son was killed', 'My daughters were tortured', 'I was in a concentration camp'. That such statements are often agonizingly true may excuse them but cannot make them commendable. The old-fashioned *parvenu* pride in prosperity is far preferable to this new ostentation with which, like mendicants, we parade our sores.

Whereas self-conceit is more comic than noxious, self-pity stifles pity for others. No vice is more easy to fall into, more difficult to throw off. Which of us cannot bring tears to his eyes by thinking how unfairly he has been treated? Give way to a taste for the luxury of woe, and you will never emerge into the simplicity of joy: self-pity destroys self-help. For the first time since the Renaissance, the mind of Western Europe has lost faith in the possibility, and—far graver—in the desirability, of happiness. The stoicism required in total war has lately degenerated into an even more odious disposition, a grotesque and paralysing masochism. Christianity at its most ascetic retains a solid foundation of hedonism, inviting us to sacrifice earthly pleasures to attain those which are eternal and infinite. The glumness now fashionable is gratuitous, not a means but an end in itself. Nothing is now more important than to rehabilitate the notion of pleasure— and, as an inseparable concomitant, the notion of quality.

Exaggeration of war damage has deflected me into this homily, which is not directed especially at the Italians. On the whole, their vitality, their native sense and good manners, encourage them to carry their troubles gaily. They may be thought to carry their disinvolture even to excess. '*He* was fool enough to drag us into this war; why should *we* suffer more than we already have?' Few of them conceive that a people has any responsibility for its government. Is this the result of twenty years of fascism; and, before that, of governments which, whether autocratic or parliamentary, took little stock of public opinion? Or is it only human nature? How many Frenchmen remember that the Chamber, by a huge majority, endorsed Pétain's armistice; how many Englishmen that they averted their ears from Churchill to applaud the imbecilities of Baldwin and Chamberlain?

Having made two unjust wars, the Italians call for a just peace. One sympathizes, but things don't work like that; and, in any case, no peace can be just to everyone. That is no excuse, however, for making it needlessly unjust to the Italians.

What the Italians resent, and justly, is the way we forget the help they gave us. Forget? The British public does not forget, for it has never known. It may be that some Italians like to remember more than actually happened. But the truth is impressive enough, apart from all exaggeration, for nearly 130,000 Italians were killed in the struggle against the Germans. The courage displayed in the north was superb; and to hide the facts from us is ignoble.

A friend of mine who escaped from an Italian prison camp, and was entertained by peasants for a year with supreme courage and kindness, tells me that the War Office still will not let him publish his story. He is profoundly grateful to the Italians and loud in praise of their virtues. I believe that nearly fifty thousand British who escaped owe a similar debt to the Italian people. (A group of officers moved freely for months in good Roman society, frequenting the same restaurants and night-clubs as the Germans. One of them at the opera with Italian friends found Keitel in the next box, and got him to autograph his programme.) Much of the anti-Italian feeling in England is spread by the prisoners who did not escape, and a good many of these did not want to. Mussolini's attack on France was an unsurpassably squalid little attempt to get something for nothing. And, for that matter, Italian foreign policy, even before Fascism, was peculiarly cynical. But common sense suggests that we should never again allow the Italians to alienate themselves from the Western Europe to which they belong, which indeed they have done as much as any other people to create. In a world where there is so much carefully fostered hatred, let us do everything conceivable to make friends again with a people that is prepared to like us.

Turin. The finest square is half burnt out, but Turin is much pleasanter than I remembered. (Yes, it invites one to loaf.) At the same time it is notably un-Italian, nearer to Lyons than to Milan, and centuries distant from Naples. A number of people here, as everywhere in Italy, have been charming to me: I only hope that none of them was equally charming to the Germans. This business of meeting those who may have been 'collaborators' is in every country very tiresome. The blacker a man's record, the more gracious, as a rule, his welcome to the English visitor. When first I went back to Paris, I felt obscurely once or twice that old acquaintances were using me as Persil or Lux.

Visiting the Church of the Consolazione, which I remembered for its singular baroque, I have found a cloister hung with votive pictures recording escapes owed to the miraculous Madonna. There must be a school of Sunday painters who provide these ingenuous tributes for a few *lire*. After looking at the usual men, women and children falling out of windows, pinned under trams, cutting their wrists instead of the sausage, I came on a large group of pictures, relics of air-raids upon Turin: the sky a swarm of Lancasters, bombs falling, flames rising, corpses everywhere, and the grateful donors wonderfully preserved. Some of these touching works showed a tenement building (with a bomb just missing it), and had been given jointly by all the tenants.

I have still to be convinced that what was called the 'psychological' bombing, that is to say, the indiscriminate bombing, of Milan and Turin was not a miscalculation as well as a wickedness. It wounded or killed miserable people who were already longing for peace, and, indeed, demonstrating against the war. It made them not only less well-disposed to the Allies but less able to oppose their Government and the Germans.

Milan again. Castiglione Olona, an hour or so from here, is one of the few places that I have seen for the first time on this journey. A delicious village, climbing up a narrow ridge above a river, with the earliest Renaissance church in Lombardy, and a Gothic church with enchanting frescoes by Masolino. Nearby, I called with a letter of introduction upon the Italian owner of a noble villa. He was, alas, ill and I was taken round the garden by an elderly Lancashire woman, who had come here some thirty years ago as nurse to the owner's granddaughter. During the war she was hidden from the Germans in a convent: 'I hated it. I am a Protestant, you know. Those nuns! They come up behind you without your hearing them, so quiet, and all in black, too!' She heard sometimes, she told me, from her sister in Blackpool, but she didn't think of going to England. Too expensive. Obviously her employers were devoted to her, but I think she spoke only indifferent Italian. Thirty years! Again I wish I knew how to write short stories.

The *Cimitero monumentale* here in Milan deserves three stars from Baedeker. The richest burgesses compete in the ostentation of their family tombs, edifices some of them two or even three storeys high, and shouldering one another in an extravagant disparity of styles. Egyptian, for some reason (perhaps the Egyptian cult of the dead) is the most popular, so that you wander apparently among stage settings for *Aida*. Often the interior is embellished with frescoes. Then there are Roman, Gothic, Romanesque, Renaissance, and even modernistic structures—the last looking like pavilions in an international exhibition. And the sculpture! One titanic figure with a foot a yard long sprawls over elaborately irregular rocks to look down on a full-size yoke of oxen. A twenty-year-old girl lies supine with a crucifix between her naked breasts. (The vagaries of Italian religion are apt to discountenance English Catholics.) The expense and exuberance of the whole affair are fabulous. The acme of parvenu ostentation? Yet these monstrosities differ from the magnificent monuments of the fifteenth, sixteenth, and seventeenth centuries only in design: the purpose is identical. Several large bombs have exacerbated the surrealism of the cemetery. (Milan is by far the most damaged of the cities I have visited.) Pyramids have been split asunder, columns with lotus capitals thrown down, and the masterpieces of the 19th Century Milanese sculptors stand headless and armless, premature antiques.

Domodossola. This frontier brims with memories. Breakfast between Lausanne and Brigue; the tunnel; and Italy, at first in the Alpine gorges reluctant to unveil, then in an instant exposing proudly, overwhelmingly, its most voluptuous *appâts*, the Beautiful Island in the Major Lake. How this repeated excitement, these acts of possession, have stamped themselves on my heart! Of the journey in the opposite direction I have no memories, although I know that I have made it just as frequently. It is the life-enhancing hours that one, how wisely, selects to remember; and today, after passing Baveno on my way north, I felt that I was being gently disanimated.   ? de - not dis

Though the half-hour I spent at the railway station at Milan, which has claims to be the ugliest building in Italy, marked the end of my six weeks' escape into Elysium, it brought me a deep happiness. My luggage was in the train, and I strolled up and down the platform, without impatience, without anxiety, knowing exactly when I should leave, far from the *Picture Posts* of 1945 that furnish the waiting-rooms of airfields; and I saw for the first time in seven years railway coaches labelled *Roma Milano Parigi*, *Venise Lausanne Calais*. The Yugoslavs refuse to let the Orient Express pass their savage frontier, but through the arteries of historic Europe, *deis gratias*, the blood is running once again.

The Spell of Venice

He was extremely earnest, dogmatic and German. After a whole week in England, he explained how feeble our architecture had always been. Next, he treated me to a second lecture—upon Gropius—and asked: 'In your opinion what is the best building put up in this century?' I answered, 'The Campanile of St. Mark's'; and, as I had hoped, he now saw that I wasn't worth talking to. The Campanile, completed in 1912, is a replica of the one that had collapsed, a twelfth-century tower with a sixteenth-century top. I cannot bear to think that a fake, however skilful, is the most beautiful building of our time. If I like it the best, it must be as a symbol of the city I love above all others.

Love does not blind me. (I have sometimes wished it could: no faults are more exasperating than those of the best-loved.) The nastiest thing about Venice is that it has so many admirers beside oneself. In summer the crowd of tourists would be intolerable, except that most of them mercifully don't wander far from the shops and cafés in the Piazza. I must admit moreover that Venetian architecture is not comparable with Tuscan or Roman. The interior of St. Mark's and the Gothic exterior of the Ducal Palace are wonders of the world; and later two great architects worked here—Sansovino, a Florentine trained in Rome, and Palladio from Vicenza. The general run of Venetian building, however, was finicky when Early Renaissance and coarse when Baroque. Even the superb Salute is poor in the façades below the domes.

Why then is Venice the city I most enjoy looking at? First, I think, because no city approaching it in size is so little spoiled. There are some hideous nineteenth-century buildings, and a few further atrocities have been committed since the last war. (Recent-

224

ly there was talk of embellishing the focal point of the Canal with a Frank Lloyd Wright façade in a comically 1920 style.) In the main, however, we see the same city as Canaletto and Guardi: compare Venice with London, Rome, or even Florence, and it shines like a good deed in a naughty world. Secondly, its light is unparalleled. This lends enchantment to buildings that elsewhere would look ill-proportioned or even vulgar, and adds a shimmer to timeworn brick and flaking paint. (Does a deposit of Adriatic salt further enhance this special quality of colour?) Thirdly, this most iridescent of cities is also the pleasantest for strolling—the only one I know, except Fez, where there is no risk of being run over.

I have walked here hour after hour, week after week, with eyes perpetually ravished. There are well over a hundred churches and fine paintings to be peered at in most of them. You saunter from one to another, sometimes losing yourself in the labyrinth or needing guidance to a ferry, always discovering new details—a marble relief set in a shabby wall, an oleander rising from a secret garden, or bright shirts on a laundry-line strung across a sleeping canal.

When you are fagged out, your gondola is waiting at a place you have appointed. Or rather, it was—for now the most delicious of vehicles has become, alas, the most expensive. In the old days a gondola could be hired by the week or month at no great cost, and this doubled the delightfulness of Venice. Two Octobers I have spent there, sharing a diminutive house—and a gondola—with friends. This is the season I recommend: the crowds diminish; barges heavy with fruit move across the waters; and every evening unfurls a sunset sumptuous as a Veronese, which then fades into the opalescence of a Tiepolo.

Most important, the façade of Palladio's Redentore, the noblest of frozen music; and next, the interior of S. Maria Formosa, a gentle adagio of round arches and circular vaults. Then let me recommend a variety of less important sights that the visitor may easily miss, special favourites of mine, though some of them are merely curious.

The island of Burano; the apses of S. Giacomo dell'Orio; S. Francesco della Vigna—Palladian façade (unhappily elbowed by a gasometer), cloister, and charming altarpiece by Negroponte; the façade of S. Giovanni in Bragora and the Cima inside the church; the interior of the Spanish synagogue designed by Longhena;

the archaic Greek lions in front of the Arsenal, with runes carved by the Byzantine Emperors' Varangian Guard; the Longhi frescoes on the staircase of the Palazzo Grassi; the stained glass (rare in Venice) in S. Zanipolo; the bronze relief (Francesco di Giorgio?) in the Carmine; the plasterwork in the nearby Armenian College; the *trompe-l'oeil* columns in S. Geremia; the Persian carpet imitated in marble around the high altar in the Gesuiti; the extravagant ceiling of S. Pantalon; the Guardi paintings on the organ-loft of the Angelo Raffaele; the Tiepolos in the Gesuati (*sic*), in S. Maria della Pietà, in S. Alvise and . . . but once started on the pictures in Venetian churches and museums one might go on indefinitely. Let me just mention the Carpaccio in S. Stefano, because you may be vainly trying, unless your guide-book is recent, to find it in S. Vitale.

One more recommendation: try to get hold of two old books, Howells's *Life on the Lagoons* and Augustus Hare's *Walks in Venice*; they abound in picturesque details about the history and habits of the Venetians. But be warned! When you decide light-heartedly that you must take a look at the place, you are exposing yourself to an enchantress, a Circe. One of our best-known novel-ists was drawn back to Venice year after year so inexorably that Rome and Florence remained unknown to him. You too may succumb to a lifelong infatuation.

In my dreams a gondola sometimes wafts me to quarters of Venice that I do not recognise, non-existent quays ennobled by palaces I must have remembered from Claude Lorrain, islets in the lagoon with resonant gardens from Watteau or Fragonard. The reality is hardly less dreamlike—the Zattere with great ships towering above the roof-tops; the church and monastery of S. Giorgio floating (it seems) so precariously with gunwales awash; the towers, cupolas and volutes of the Salute curving behind the blanched Dogana; the Ducal Palace nacreous in the twilight; the Piazza invaded by a spring-tide, a flooded ballroom with arcades and pinnacles reflected in its floor; and, dominating all else, peremptory in its assault upon the night sky, the majestic Campanile.

The Gabfest

In 1928 I went to New York for a couple of months just before Christmas. I did not go for any particular purpose, but to look at the place and meet the people. But I had two experiences which caught my imagination more than anything else. One was New York at night seen from an aeroplane, my first flight after dark, the other was the Gabfest. I had no idea before what a Gabfest was. It turned out to be a contest for the title of Champion Talker of the World.

It began at 2 p.m. on Christmas Day, in the Armoury of the 71st Infantry Regiment in New York. Thirty-seven men and women went in for it. The one who kept his or her lips moving, with the shortest time off for rest between that time and 11.45 p.m. on the succeeding Saturday—Christmas was on a Tuesday—was to receive the title of Champion and a prize of one thousand dollars. For half an hour three times a day they retired together for meals. Apart from this, every minute they spent off their platforms, night or day, counted against them. There were a doctor and a nurse present to keep an eye on their health.

A couple of hours after the beginning of the contest I went to the Armoury. Outside it looked like a castle made of gingerbread; inside it is a large drill hall. Even in the daytime it is lighted artificially. The competitors were a neatly-dressed lot. Most of them were persons who liked talking, public speakers, actors, journalists, charlatans. I am sure some had been persuaded to enter by their long-suffering friends. There was a French girl, a Hungarian, a German, a Red Indian, and an Italian who was being encouraged by a black shirted gentleman to win the coveted title for Fascism. Several of the competitors were clearly eccentric, 'cuckoo' as they say in America. Some brought musical instruments on which to accompany themselves, almost all had books or magazines. One man was going to devote all his talk to arguments in favour of abolishing capital punishment, an elderly woman announced her intention of reading the Bible straight through from beginning to end. Each had a small platform, some seven feet by five, with a table and chair on it. Behind this was a small tent containing a camp bed for rest.

On the first day all the competitors were in the highest spirits; at last they could talk as much as they liked. The public could talk to them, and though they were allowed to pause for an instant to hear what was being said to them, they could hardly bear to do so. Men and women behaving as if they were in the parrot house at a Zoo—it was rather a shocking spectacle. One even felt a little shy of looking at them, as one does at midgets or bearded ladies at a fair.

However, I returned the same evening, and again the next after that. Half the contestants had given up the struggle. Their voices had tired, or their legs. For not only did they have to keep talking, but they were made to stand up most of the time. It was to be a test of sheer endurance. Four of the competitors had taken no rest at all. Others had slept an hour or so and were congratulating themselves on their wisdom in keeping up their strength. The next day, Thursday, the Health Authorities insisted on everyone's taking an hour's rest. But that night they all looked exhausted. They had been talking or reading for sixty hours, and had been on their feet for forty-eight. From being comic the spectacle was becoming tragic.

Four of the contestants had aroused my particular interest from the first. There was a middle-aged woman with spectacles, a school-teacher from a small town. She would hardly leave off her reading or reciting for a moment to answer a question. She was painfully respectable, and it was odd that she had the courage to face the gaping crowds. But Emily (I remember only the Christian name) obviously had not the stamina to win. Then there was a middle-aged married woman, Madam Wilson. Fat, dressed in a shoddy, white evening dress, she stood surrounded by paintings by her husband, and at least twenty large volumes of a history of civilisation. She had also brought as an ornament the most elaborately ugly lampshade I have ever seen. She looked bad-tempered and blowsy, as she recited poems of her own composition, but there was something very pathetic about her. When she won ('when', she said, not 'if'), she was going to spend the money taking her invalid husband to the country. Then there was Betty, a handsome girl, smartly dressed, who had already been successful as a long distance swimmer. She had once swum, she told me, for thirty-six hours. Physically she appeared the fittest of the contestants, and her mother had come half across America to look after her.

But from the beginning the competitor who captured my imagination was Howard Williams. A rather fragile looking man of about twenty-nine, with a sensitive and intelligent face, he had been a professional dare-devil. He had caught a bullet in his leg at the age of twelve in a Mexican raid; he had sailed all over the world as third mate; he had been a hobo (this is the American for a tramp); he had travelled with a circus, showing the 'cats', as he called them, a leopard and three panthers. He had been a professional high diver, diving with burning petrol flaming from his back, and diving for films from almost incredible heights. He had broken at different times almost every bone in his body. He had written short stories. He had performed steeplejack stunts, hanging by his knees from the top of a twenty storey building. Naturally intelligent, he had a theory that all morality depends upon our desire for the esteem of our neighbours. It was by nervous, rather than merely physical, energy that he hoped to win the prize. He was going to set up an 'airplane circus' with the proceeds, for he had both a passionate belief in aviation and some experience as a parachutist and wing-walker.

When I reached the Armoury on the Friday night, the strain was becoming almost intolerable. Three of the contestants had still taken no time off. Two others had only had ten or fifteen minutes. There were still a dozen or so left in. Their legs had swollen with long hours of standing, their throats were hoarse, their eyes dazed and haggard. One or two were obviously out of their senses. And then suddenly, at midnight, the site of the Gabfest was changed. From the high-roofed spacious Armoury, the competitors were moved to a dance-hall, low-ceilinged, ill-ventilated, noisy with jazz, frequented by prostitutes and their customers. Soon the air became thick with the smell of menthol and liniment, added to that of cheap scent. The dancing continued on the floor, while the contestants were crammed close to one another in a corner of the hall. Their mutual jealousy and hatred broke out and several had to be moved from one platform to another to prevent violence. The little school-teacher, though she had taken some rest, still continued. But her character was giving way under the strain. The atmosphere of the dance-hall at once affected her. As she mounted her platform, she attempted a few steps of a 'Black Bottom'. She forgot the respectability which she had made the foundation of her life. She even began to say very odd things to the men present. In other ways, too, her language became surprising. A sort of poetry welled up from her sub-conscious mind. 'What do you think we are like, standing on our platforms?' she said to me. 'Magpies, that's what we are, magpies, but magpies have wings.' And again 'When I read something religious, the crowd goes away; when I start something about painted lips, they return. They are a tide that comes and goes, and I am the Heavens that move it.' When I last saw her, she was reading 'The Ancient Mariner' and a cheap tart who was looking up at her said to a friend, 'Funny the ways some folk have of earning their living'. Soon afterwards Emily's strength failed.

There were only two competitors who had taken no time off at all, Betty and Howard, the swimmer and the dare-devil. An odd thing was that six or seven others persisted, though they must have known that they had no chance whatsoever of winning. They had set themselves a test, and they were going through with it. A girl with fair hair had begun the contest looking as coarse as the women in the dance hall. But fatigue had beautified her mirac-ulously. Her face had recovered its innocence. Betty now looked ghastly. Her eyelids were swollen and she seemed not to know what she was saying. 'I am flying, I am flying' she would whisper hoarsely, waving her arms. Howard was in agony. His ankles had become twice their natural size, and the massage he was receiving tortured him. His wife, a dark little Spanish woman, had had little sleep herself. She worked in a factory all day, and looked after him all night, encouraged him, prayed for him tirelessly. And as she massaged his legs, kneeling at his feet, with her head pressed against his thighs, she showed a completeness of devotion that was savage and very beautiful.

The last few hours of the contest on the Saturday night seemed interminable. Every sort of story was running round about dope and foul play. It was rumoured that the judges had huge bets on one of the contestants. Certainly some of the competitors seemed to have been treated with unfair indulgence, while others were hustled out of the contest very brusquely. Cheers were now being raised by their friends for the two who were still neck and neck; songs were sung in which they joined. 'What do you think of the Briand-Kellogg Pact?' Howard was asked by a woman—she must have been very callous. 'I don't know, lady', he answered, 'Can't you see I have something big on?' He was at the very edge of his endurance. At last when they could do little but whisper weakly 'one, two three, four . . .' the hour struck. The contest was declared a tie. And the prize was divided between Betty and Howard. They had both talked for a hundred and five hours, for four and a half days, with only one hour off for rest.

The Gabfest was a financial failure. The public attendance was too small to pay the expenses. And most people, no doubt, feel that such a contest should not be permitted. People may be ready to earn money by suffering, but there is something disgusting about a showman trying to profit from this. It is true that the competitors were not obliged to enter, and, if the contest proved more exacting than they expected, they were free at any moment to drop out. The fact that so many went on to the end suggests that they were deriving some deep satisfaction from being in the limelight: for the first time in their lives, perhaps, they were centres of interest for the curiosity of the public. And this more than compensated for their ghastly physical exhaustion and anguish. I felt then, and I still feel, that the whole business was monstrous and a nightmare, but that it also uncovered something in mankind that is ineradicably noble.

The Look of India

In 1952 I had a sudden hunch. I fancied I should like India. (One reason, by the way, was re-reading *Kim*.) I had never wanted to go there. Now I began to want to go desperately. I liked India far more than I ever expected. In fact I fell in love with it. It is a tragic country. Most of the inhabitants are undernourished and there is every sort of frightful disease. In Calcutta, for instance, the newspaper every morning tells you how many people were taken to hospital the previous day suffering from (a) smallpox, (b) the plague, (c) cholera. Millions die of malaria; leprosy abounds; and one sort of mosquito gives you elephantiasis. The Indian Government has already done a great deal and enormous schemes are in hand. The poverty is hideous, the over-population seems incurable. India is in many ways terrible to think about. But it is glorious to look at, a country for those who live a great deal through their eyes. As a rule the English living in India have not been of this type. Many of them have written admirably about the daily life, the agriculture, the religions, the castes; very few about the look of India. And no good painter, as far as I know, has gone there during the past hundred years.

From the day I arrived my eyes were continually entranced. Take the clothes. In the north the women, ordinary poor women, go in for the most brilliant colours, scarlet, emerald, blazing yellow. In the south the skins are darker, and so are the clothes; puce, deep crimson, olive green, indigo, even black. The north is made for Matisse, the south for the young Bonnard or for Sickert. You never see an Indian woman in European clothes, unless she is playing golf or lawn tennis. Men in the educated class, on the other hand, usually dress like ourselves; and the others are apt to wear the most horrible get-up, shirts like ours with the tails hanging outside their trousers. In the south the labouring men are almost naked, and look very fine—like statues, almost Greek, but the marble is black—working in the fields, or twenty of them together hauling and pushing a great waggon in the streets of Madras. Down there you see no horses.

The street life is prodigiously picturesque: countless little stalls cooking all sorts of food, clouds of flies, shops (with no windows) full of pots or silver or silks, also the cheapest European shoes; family parties of a dozen or more in horse-shays; rickshaws, water-carriers, vagrant holy men, almost naked, with long snaky hair; everything that one sees in old illustrated books. Gradually you get to know the different races, the Punjabis, many of them bearded Sikhs, with their long delicate noses; Rajputs with the features we call classical; Dravidians from the south with skin that looks black until you see the real black of an umbrella close to it. Children everywhere, swarming. And then cows, humped, sacred, half-starved, strolling nonchalantly among the motors, trying to snatch fruit from the greengrocer's stall, licking any brown paper they find in the street.

Architecture? I confess I did not think very much of the famous Mogul buildings in Delhi and Agra and Fatehpur Sikri. They seem to me a decadent, provincial version of the great Islamic style that one sees at its best in Egypt and Persia. The most famous of the Mogul buildings, the Taj Mahal, has been gushed about by thousands. Aldous Huxley has dismissed it as merely an expensive mass of marble. I cannot swallow either of these views. The Taj is finely situated in a large, enclosed, formal garden, thanks to Lord Curzon, and the white marble inlaid with black gives it the charm of an elaborate ivory casket. The effect is deliciously picturesque. But the minarets are ugly, like ill-proportioned lighthouses; and the building itself struck me as pleasant rather than sublime—shall I say Mendelssohn rather than Mozart? Everyone says 'You must see it by moonlight'; and I did not. But the greatest architecture does not need moonlight. Nobody says 'You must see the Parthenon by moonlight', or Durham or Beauvais or Santa Maria Maggiore or St. Paul's. I think that this demand for moonlight gives the show away, proves in fact that the Taj is what I may snobbishly call second-rate.

Hindu architecture I found far more interesting. It is very various in quality; it can hardly be judged apart from the sculpture with which it is encrusted; and it is designed in forms so unfamiliar to us that any judgment is difficult. I was, however, profoundly impressed by the temple at Ellora, carved entirely from the living rock, by the great temples of Conjeeveram near Madras and Tanjore in the deep south, by the carvings in Elephanta and Belur, by one temple at Bhubanisvar, and, above all, by the Black Pagoda in the province of Orissa. This is in ruins, and so I was able to clamber all over it. It is covered with the most intricate and exquisite carving, much of it erotic. The effect is stupefying, hallucinating.

The great Indian cities have one most inconvenient feature; they straggle over enormous spaces. In the middle of Madras there are vast waste lands, in the middle of Calcutta a racecourse; my hotel in Delhi was fifteen miles from the Prime Minister's house. I found that I spent more on taxis than upon board and lodging. The older European buildings are noble in scale and often in design. There are churches in the eighteenth century style with porticoes and spires, rather like St. Martin-in-the-Fields, but white. Calcutta has the most beautiful cemetery I have ever seen, with colossal eighteenth-century tombs in the shape of classical temples and obelisks. Bombay has the most extravagant Victorian buildings imaginable, Venetian Gothic and Wagnerian Romanesque, beside which even St. Pancras Station would look austere. Here, and also in Calcutta, there are nineteenth-century houses that I found full of charm, bedizened with elaborate wooden balconies. One word about New Delhi. The trees everywhere are delightfully refreshing; the Viceroy's house (now the President's) has a glorious garden; but the Lutyens scheme for the approach to it was turned down. There is too much of Baker. The recent architecture in other places is almost always beneath contempt. In Bombay, for instance, land has been reclaimed from the sea and the waterfront is covered with hideous modern concrete flats. It is like a comfortable-looking, middle-aged woman getting a very ugly new face.

The smaller cities are often enchanting. Bunji, a Rajput principality, is marvellously unspoilt, a medieval Indian city with no modern building within its walls. I was warned by E. M. Forster not to go to Jaipur, 'a rose-pink wash-out'. I went all the same, and was bowled over. It is an eighteenth-century walled city, laid out on a gridiron plan rather like New York. Every building is painted pink, with the ornament sometimes picked out in white. Jaipur entranced me. I strolled along the dimly lit streets one night after dinner and came upon a wedding procession: musicians, dancers, men carrying flares, fireworks crackling in front, guests in their finery behind, and on a white horse the young bridegroom magnificent in brocade. I had wandered into a Hindu version of the Arabian Nights.

Two of the other places I specially enjoyed are Goa and Pondicherry. These are still respectively Portuguese and French. Panjim, or New Goa, is a happy little town on a delicious estuary with palms leaning over the water, and a few miles away are the remains of Old Goa, six elaborate baroque churches standing in the forest, and otherwise only a few ruins left of a flourishing city. Huge churches stand white upon every surrounding hill. Pondicherry is even smaller than Goa. The town is pure Louis-Philippe, very little affected in appearance or even in ideas, I fancy, by the past 100 years. I stayed with the French Governor whose residence is surrounded with verandahs. He most kindly took me about in a car without a chauffeur or a flag, and was everywhere warmly welcomed.

Now for the landscapes. Most of India during the first quarter of the year, when I was there, is parched: tawny beige or oyster-coloured. It rains only in summer and autumn. The absence of what we expect from spring seems a symbol of the tragedy of India. Through most of the day, moreover, the light is greyish, and drains colour from landscape and buildings. Even the sea is sand-brown: at any rate I spent five days in a tiny coasting steamer and never saw a gleam of Mediterranean blue. Railway journeys are apt to be very lowering; the seats are rather hard, it is too hot to shut the windows, and grit pours in over everything. Hour after hour one dawdles across sun-baked plains, stopping for a quarter of an hour in almost every station. But then the stations almost make up for the trains, they are so lively with people who seem to have settled on the platform for a long stay, cooking their meals there and even washing their clothes.

Where there are gardens, they display in January the brilliance of an English midsummer, petunias, phloxes, salvias, snap-dragons, and riotous roses, as well as dazzling creepers that we do not have here. April comes, and dust-storms: then everything collapses. The countryside is adorned with fabulous flowering trees growing wild; some have no leaves and look as if they had been designed by Fabergé or Bakst. In the south the tropical vegetation can be splendidly luxuriant. Cochin, for instance, is a port on a lagoon some 100 miles long, with an archipelago densely covered with palms, very like my notion of the South Sea Islands. Gleaming nets, the size of sails, hang from the masts of fishing boats, and smaller craft are paddled by men with huge, round, mushroom hats. In South India I saw also superb dancing in the courtyard of a temple. It goes on all night gathering impetus.

It is in the extreme north that the Indian landscapes are most beautiful, attaining in the foothills of the Himalayas a majesty I have found nowhere else. From Darjeeling one looks across valleys 7,000 feet deep to the long range glorious with snow, Kangchenjunga shouldering above the other peaks. Up here you find yourself as it were in a different continent: the people are Nepalese, the women and tiny children smoke, the jewellery is out-size, earrings as big as saucers and pendants the size of soup-plates. In Kalimpong, a few hours from Darjeeling, I met hundreds of caravaneers from Tibet, arriving with bales of wool on their mules, furred, gaitered, their faces red from their icy, native winds. Here, too, there is a Tibetan monastery, with prayer-wheels and prayers inscribed on cotton, fluttering like flags from high poles.

Loveliest of all, the Vale of Kashmir. I flew up there over the snows at the beginning of April—earlier it is too cold—and found a broad valley with lakes and a river, apple blossom everywhere, willows breaking into leaf, wild irises, the trunks of the poplars blanched as if to match the cumulus clouds and the circle of snow-topped mountains. The final charm is that here one can live in a house-boat. There are hundreds of these, just like those I remember in my childhood at Henley, but not painted. I took one on the lake; it cost no more than staying at an hotel. Moored just behind was a smaller one with the servants and kitchen. I can think of no more entrancing place in which to spend a summer. The only thing against Kashmir is that the people are poverty-stricken, even by Indian standards. The shapeless, brown, sack-like stuff they wear is as sad as their lives; and they are not so handsome as the other Indian peoples.

One last word, about the birds and beasts, which do so much for the look of India. You see a cluster of green leaves suddenly rush screaming from a branch: it is a flight of parakeets. Every-where the birds are dazzling, and much less shy than here, but usually they have hideous voices. In Rajputana there are wild peacocks, busy, like our sparrows, on the cottage roofs; wherever I went I saw egrets, mynahs, drongos, birds as small as butterflies and butterflies as large as birds. Snakes? I never saw one except in a zoo; but tiny striped squirrels dart like lizards over trees and buildings. And then there are the monkeys. They swarm all over the place, by the roadside, on the housetops and temple roofs, on railway platforms, ready to invade the compartments. They are said to eat enough food for 100,000,000 men. Pests, of course; but I found their liveliness irresistible.

Angkor (1958)

The pleasure we get from ruins is curious, varied and intense: a long, brilliant book on the subject has been written by Miss Rose Macaulay. She would go anywhere to see a first-rate ruin; and I too am a ruin-collector, not to say a ruin-snob. I have never reached the Great Wall of China; but I have had the luck to see Karnak, Persepolis, Palmyra, Baalbek, Leptis, Ellora, Pagan in Burma and many pre-Columbian temples in Mexico and Guatemala. Angkor is incomparably more spectacular than any of these. Nowhere else is there such a quantity of ruins in so fantastic a setting.

These include gateways, terraces, towers, bridges and bathing-pools, but the largest monuments are the temples. These symbolise the dwelling-place of the gods, Mount Meru (the Indian equivalent of Olympus); and the kings, who were worshipped as gods already in their lifetime, built them as their own mausoleums. In shape, as in purpose, they resemble the Pyramids, but they have towers sprouting from them and courtyards at their summits; and everywhere a luxuriance of carving.

There are some twenty of these temples, and the largest is called Angkor Vat, (a name often wrongly applied to the whole huge group). Indeed this is the largest place of worship in the world: it is not so high as St. Peter's in Rome but covers a larger space and contains far more masonry. Enclosed by a moat over 200 yards wide and a wall nearly 5,000 yards long, the temple rises to five towers by way of three terraces, the lowest of which has a frieze of bas-reliefs extending for over 800 yards. The upper staircases are so steep that I had to crawl down them: the more venerable priests must have had themselves carried to and from the crowning sanctuary.

Angkor Vat is stupendous not only in its size and the richness of its decoration but in the grandeur of its composition, which is symmetrical and intricate. This temple, moreover, is wonderfully well-preserved. Yet there are several monuments in the neighbourhood I found even more impressive. A mile or two away there is, for instance, the Bayon, built a century later as the centre of a new city called Angkor Thom. Hitherto the Khmer kings had been devotees of Hinduism: the older temples, including Angkor Vat, abound in images of Siva and Vishnu. The builder of Angkor Thom was a passionate Buddhist. From a distance the Bayon looks like some extraordinary rock-formation with steep, eroded crags. The stone used at Angkor is a darkish grey, and at first sight seems rather grim, except when coloured by the setting sun. As one approaches, it becomes almost phosphorescent; and then one sees that it is coated with lichens, white, silver, verdigris-green, and rose-pink, mingling into a delicate varicoloured mosaic. The crags of the Bayon now turn out to be colossal Buddhist heads. In the courts below them, dominated by their huge, stone-cut lips and brooding eyelids, you feel caught in a De Quincey opium-dream, a serene hallucination. This is the most imaginative architecture I have ever encountered.

The king who built the Bayon placed colossal heads also above the huge gateways to his new city of Angkor Thom, and one passes beneath these as one moves about the surrounding forest. How violent a forest! The Angkor monuments are scattered on its floor, sunk in the depths of dark greenery. When discovered by the French, they could hardly be seen, they were so densely overgrown, so ferociously torn apart. It was a herculean task to clear away the trees, and then to fit the stones back into their original places. Some of the gateways and two of the largest temples have only been partly disengaged; and these carry picturesqueness to an unparalleled intensity.

The trees belong for the most part, I think, to the fig family, and their pale bark is delicately figured so that it suggests the drawing of Paul Klee. To support their enormous height—150 or 200 feet— they throw out buttresses shaped like sails. They have seeded themselves on the roofs and towers of the temples and gateways, embracing them voraciously, erotically, splaying out into the shape of waterfalls down the walls or thrusting huge python roots between the stones and then horizontally for thirty yards or more. The heavy leafage allows only a mottling of sunlight to penetrate:

one is lost in dusky, sweating labyrinths of masonry hardly distinguishable from the enveloping tree-trunks. Creeping through courtyards and sanctuaries that have thus been overwhelmed, I discovered for the first time the full fierceness and gluttony of the vegetable realm. At any moment, it seemed, the forest might stretch out one of these massive tentacles, and I should be crushed, swallowed, digested. The great butterflies fluttering around my head were furry and almost black; the steamy air was loud with the hootings as of owls, but of far greater volume: gibbons. And through the leaves I could just see these swinging their longarmed way across the roof of the forest, using each bough they touched as a trapeze.

No, I must throw in my hand. Angkor is far beyond my power to describe. One should remain for at least a week (Somerset Maugham, he told me, stayed for a happy fortnight) but I was able to manage only four nights and to work hard at my sightseeing. Cambodia is extremely hot; and my visit was in May, when it is even hotter than usual. I used to get up at 6.30, soon after dawn, dash out to the ruins, retreat to the hotel for the noonday blaze, and then make another sortie as the sun became less fierce.

Little can be said about the builders of Angkor. Known as the Khmers, they were the ancestors of the modern Cambodians, and racially akin to both the Chinese and some Pacific islanders. Their religion and their arts, however, were profoundly influenced by India. Hindu traders came there at least two thousand years ago, and the civilisation that developed in the sixth century derived from India rather as ours did from Rome, though Cambodia, unlike Britain, was not conquered and colonised. The modern Cambodians are a gentle, charming people with a gift for dancing: the Khmers were formidable warriors, and the buildings at Angkor were piled up by slaves, most of them prisoners of war. The country around was scientifically irrigated, and provided food for the multitudes busy adorning the capital with these mountains of stone.

The Khmers had been evolving their characteristic architecture and sculpture in other parts of the kingdom since the sixth century A.D., but the Angkor monuments belong to the years 950–1220, roughly the same period as Romanesque architecture in Europe. In the thirteenth century the Khmer kingdom fell into a slow decline: Siamese invaders ruined the country, and in the fifteenth century Angkor was abandoned. Nobody in Europe knew even that such a city had existed until less than a hundred years ago, when a French officer named Mouhot arrived here by pure chance. At first he saw only hillocks covered with trees, and he could hardly believe his eyes, finding himself among the stupendous ruins of a vast forgotten capital.

BOOKS REVIEWED

The Fine Art of Reading	David Cecil	Constable	1957
Fowler's Modern English Usage	Sir Ernest Gowers (rev.)	Oxford University Press	1965
'Modern Judgements' Series (Literature made Difficult)	A. E. Dyson (edit.)	Macmillan	1968
Directions in the Teaching of English (Eng. Lit.)	Denys Thompson (edit.)	Cambridge University Press	1967
The Rise of English Studies (The Tympany of English Studies)	D. J. Palmer	University of Hull	1965
The Common Pursuit (Dr. Leavis)	F. R. Leavis	Chatto & Windus	1952
Poems of Tennyson	Christopher Ricks (edit.)	Longman	1969
Tennyson	Christopher Ricks	Macmillan	1972
James Anthony Froude (2 vols.)	W. H. Dunn	Oxford University Press	1961
Bagehot	St.-John Stevas	British Council	1959
Newman and Bloxam: an Oxford Friendship	R. D. Middleton	Oxford University Press	1950
The Young Mr. Newman	Maisie Ward	Sheed & Ward	1948
Jowett	Geoffrey Faber	Faber & Faber	1958
Oxford Common Room (Mark Pattison)	V. H. H. Green	Edward Arnold	1957
The Collected Letters of Thomas and Jane Welsh Carlyle (4 vols.)	Charles Sanders, General Editor	Duke University Press	1970

The Carlyles at Home	Thea Holme	Oxford University Press	1965
Anabasis (Two Fine Poets in Tandem) poem by transl.	(3rd edition) St. John Perse T. S. Eliot	Faber & Faber	1959
Colette: Oeuvres Complètes	Maurice Goudeket (edit.)	Flammarion	1950
Marcel Proust 1871–1922: A Centenary Volume	Peter Quennell (edit.)	Weidenfeld & Nicolson	1971
Marcel Proust	George Painter	Chatto & Windus	1932
Historical Memoirs of the Duc-de Saint-Simon	Lucy Norton (edit. & transl.)	Hamish Hamilton	1967
Coco Chanel: Her Life, Her Secrets	Marcel Haedrich	Robert Hale	1972
Autobiography	Leonard Woolf	Hogarth Press	1967
Virginia Woolf	Quentin Bell	Hogarth Press	1972
Letters, Virginia Woolf & Lytton Strachey		Hogarth Press	1956
Letters of Roger Fry	Denys Sutton (edit.)	Chatto & Windus	1972
Ramakrishna & His Disciples (Krishnapher's Phenomenon)	Christopher Isherwood	Methuen	1965
Ronald Firbank	Miriam J. Benkovitz	Weidenfeld & Nicolson	1970
G. M.: Memories of George Moore	Nancy Cunard	Hart-Davis	1956
Emerald and Nancy (Mother & Daughter)	Daphne Fielding	Eyre & Spottiswoode	1968
The Unquiet Grave	'Palinurus' (Cyril Connolly)	Hamish Hamilton	1945
Life and Work of Picasso	Roland Penrose	Gollancz	1958